Fighting for Napoleon

Fighting for Napoleon

*French Soldiers' Letters
1799–1815*

Bernard Wilkin
and René Wilkin

Pen & Sword
MILITARY

First published in Great Britain by
PEN AND SWORD MILITARY
an imprint of
Pen and Sword Books Ltd
47 Church Street
Barnsley
South Yorkshire S70 2AS

ISBN 978 1 47383 373 9

Printed and bound in England by
CPI Group (UK) Ltd, Croydon, CR0 4YY

Typeset in Times by CHIC GRAPHICS

Pen & Sword Books Ltd incorporates the imprints of
Pen & Sword Books Ltd incorporates the imprints of Pen & Sword
Archaeology, Atlas, Aviation, Battleground, Discovery,
Family History, History, Maritime, Military, Naval, Politics,
Railways, Select, Social History, Transport, True Crime,
Claymore Press, Frontline Books, Leo Cooper, Praetorian Press,
Remember When, Seaforth Publishing and Wharncliffe.

For a complete list of Pen and Sword titles please contact
Pen and Sword Books Limited
47 Church Street, Barnsley, South Yorkshire, S70 2AS, England
E-mail: enquiries@pen-and-sword.co.uk
Website: www.pen-and-sword.co.uk

Contents

List of Illustrations

Acknowledgements

The authors would like to express their thanks to a number of individuals and organisations who have assisted in the preparation of the book. We are particularly grateful to Brunot Dumont, Sébastien Dubois and the employees of the *Archives Générales du Royaume* of Belgium. We would also like to thank Cédric Istasse, Timothy Baycroft and Hannah Probert. Let us not forget Sabine Grimm and Alexis Wilkin, who have advised us. Finally, we would like to express our gratitude to Rupert Harding, from Pen & Sword Books, who believed in our project and gave constant feedback.

Introduction

Military Correspondence

Fighting for Napoleon is an attempt to let ordinary French soldiers describe their military experience in their own words. The Napoleonic Wars brought millions of men on the roads, mainly in Europe, but also in Africa, Asia and America. For the first time in European history, soldiers of all ranks left a substantial body of letters describing not only extraordinary events but also their daily lives. The rise of mass communication was a significant break with the past. Officers had described their military experiences since antiquity but the lower ranks had usually been voiceless. More educated than previous armies, the citizen-soldiers of the French Republic, later the Imperial army, changed the relationship between the military and the civilian world.

The conscripts did not write for posterity or for glory but for pragmatic reasons. Draftees leaving their homes for the depot of their regiment had little or no idea of where they were headed. In fact, they did not even know for how long they would serve. French laws were supposed to protect them; conscription was limited to four years, later increased to eight, but the constant need for men meant that there were only three ways to escape the army: death, invalidity or an exceptional favour. For example, the class of year VII of the Republic (1797–8) fought until at least 1814. Having a son, brother or father serving in the French army was a difficult experience. The relatives of soldiers had no way of knowing where their beloved ones were and no one to turn to for information. The army bureaucracy partially registered casualties but rarely gave lists of losses to the civilian authorities. Mutilations, wounds and captivity were often ignored in the registers. Even the depots where the regiments were stationed had difficulty keeping track of their troops. In these circumstances, correspondence was the only way for a soldier to maintain a tenuous link with his family.

Conscripts had many things to tell their families. The first act of a draftee who had just arrived to the regiment was to write to his relatives to say where he was and in which regiment he served. The following letters often described military life, battles or unfamiliar encounters in foreign countries.

Most soldiers wrote to their parents or relatives but also reserved a paragraph to address the wider community. They might give news of a friend serving in the same regiment or just send their regards to a neighbour. As a result, families sometimes learnt of the death of their son from the correspondence of another soldier from the same area. The conscript also wrote to ask for money. Seeking financial assistance from his parents or a brother was almost a ritual. More rarely, soldiers wrote to their relatives to reassure them about their religious faith, their morale or their behaviour. Many more letters were sent from the depot or when serving in France than on campaign. Physical and mental tiredness, danger and the lack of time, were probably to blame.

The Napoleonic armies relied on the efficient postal system of the French Empire to deliver their mail. Soldiers and civilians either put a stamp on the letter or expected the addressee to pay for the delivery. Even prisoners of war in Britain had the opportunity to correspond with their families. The lack of literacy made the task of the postal system harder. In many cases, the addresses were so poorly spelled that the correspondence went through various departments before being delivered to the right place. There are several examples of conscripts complaining about their letters being lost during the journey. Soldiers often expected their correspondence to include money as it was possible to fill and send a postal order from the post office. This payment method was guaranteed in case of theft or loss and was therefore far safer than the practice of putting coins in the envelope.

The considerable number of letters written during this time raises the question of literacy. The Napoleonic Wars preceded the advent of mass education, beginning in the middle of the nineteenth century. It is almost impossible to determine the precise number of illiterate soldiers in the French army at the beginning of the nineteenth century. However, a study of the replacement contracts[1] drafted in the Ourthe department shows that only 38 per cent of the peasants, labourers and artisans, the poorest and most common professions, knew how to write. On the other hand, almost all the men from wealthier families had some literary skills. Most soldiers, even the illiterate, kept in touch with their relatives. Educated friends or non-commissioned officers usually helped those who could not write. In a few cases, these transcribers even identified themselves at the bottom of the letters.

The historical interest of these letters has little in common with the

---

1. The concept of replacement is explained in Chapter 1. See R. Wilkin, 'Le remplacement militaire dans le département de l'Ourthe', *Bulletin de l'Institut archéologique liégeois*, CXII (2001–2002), p. 275.

autobiographies written by soldiers after the fall of the French Empire. In the English-speaking world, the memoirs of Sergeant Bourgogne, Captain Coignet and General Marbot are widely available.[2] Many more can be found in French. These accounts, as fascinating as they can be, were written long after the fall of the Empire. Mainly penned by officers from the most privileged strata of society, they glorified a period of French domination over Europe. These autobiographical accounts fulfilled an agenda of self-justification and self-promotion. To take only one example, Marbot painted a flattering portrait of his own actions during the most prestigious battles of the French Empire. However, he wrote less than a page about his role during the campaign of 1815.[3] By contrast, the letters found in this book were written by humble men. Their authors did not contact their families to talk about strategy and politics or to polish their image for the generations to come. The letter was an intimate object aimed at their relatives, their friends and their community. This correspondence offers unusual details about daily life in the Imperial army and even in some cases contradicts our vision of the French military. These men gave valuable insights about their occasional unwillingness to serve France, their revolt at having to pay for their uniform and equipment, or even their surprise at the good treatment they received while being held captive in Britain.

Despite their interest, historians must not always take these letters at face value. Soldiers exaggerated or even lied for various reasons. They might have been bragging to impress someone or they might have been afraid of censorship. The men kept silent about a range of topics, like rape or theft, to avoid shocking deeply Catholic communities. Soldiers had trouble remembering the names of battles, made up confrontations with the enemy and always exaggerated the number of casualties inflicted by the French army. They had no sense of chronology and sometimes wrote a single letter over a period of six months. However lies, omissions and imprecision tell us as much about the psychology of the French soldier as the truth. In addition the letters offer a counter-point to the idealised vision of the *Bulletin de la Grande Armée*, a work of official propaganda widely distributed in the army and in France.

The Survival of a Collection
In total millions of letters were written during the Napoleonic Wars. Most of them disappeared during the nineteenth century but a small proportion

---

2. Adrien Bourgogne, *The Retreat from Moscow: the Memoirs of Sergeant Bourgogne 1812-1813*, London, 1985; Jean-Roch Coignet, *The Note-books of Captain Coignet: Soldier of the Empire, 1776-1850*, Tyne and Wear, 1996; Jean-Baptiste Marbot, *The Memoirs of Baron de Marbot: late Lieutenant-General in the French Army*, London, 1988.
3. Marcellin de Marbot, *Mémoire du général baron de Marbot*, Paris, 1891, p. 404.

survived in the archives or in private hands. This book is built around the collection of the *Archives de l'Etat à Liège* (the State Archives in Liège: AEL), which is the largest of its kind. The prefecture of Liège kept more than 1,500 letters from Napoleonic conscripts, all of them written by soldiers from the Ourthe department. This territory, now the Province of Liège in Belgium and the western part of the Rhineland and Westphalia in Germany, had belonged to the Prince-Bishopric of Liège, the Austrian Netherlands and to the Holy Roman Empire until its annexation by the French Republic in 1794. Its people served in the French armies until the first fall of Napoleon in 1814, after which the Ourthe department was absorbed by the Netherlands and Prussia.

The bulk of the collection held in the Liège Archives was built by chance from the letters of families who had kept them as insurance against a number of situations:

1. The most common reason to give the authorities the letter of a relative was to avoid the accusation of desertion. The family of a missing soldier risked a fine of 1,500 francs, a considerable amount of money. Soldiers needed to provide a regimental certificate of presence, dated after the alleged date of desertion, to avert the charge. A conscript's letter was a sign of good faith while waiting for the certificate.

2. The parents of draft-dodgers (also called refractory soldiers) also used letters to avoid paying hefty fines. They had often been caught in neighbouring departments and sent to a regiment without the knowledge of their relatives or the local authorities to which draft-dodgers answered. Their correspondence was supposed to prove their presence in the army.

3. The third reason to provide a letter was to avoid military duty altogether. Until October 1813, the brother of a soldier currently in the army, or who had died or been mutilated while serving France, qualified for military exemption. This rule was only valid for one brother out of two.

4. The last reason to provide a letter was to prove a soldier's death, as many men disappeared without a trace. As stated before, the army rarely identified the dead on the battlefield and the hospitals often misidentified their patients. The registers of the regiments, kept at

the French military archives in Vincennes, are full of comments such as 'disappeared', 'removed for long absence at the hospital' or 'presumed captured'. Proving the death of a relative was nonetheless essential to discharge a brother, as explained above, or to settle questions of inheritance. In a few cases, a letter might also be used for the opposite reason, to show that a conscript was still alive.

Almost all the letters in the Liège Archives were written by conscripts between 1799 and 1813. Only a few were penned by volunteers and even fewer by officers. There are also two letters from recipients of the Legion of Honour in the archives, both of which are reproduced in this book. On 22 January 1814, the Allies took the city of Liège and put conscription to a halt while deciding the fate of the defunct Ourthe department. Belgian soldiers[4] serving in the French army were demobilised as foreign citizens. The Allies eventually agreed to give the left bank of the Meuse River to the Netherlands and the right bank to Prussia. When Napoleon returned in March 1815, conscription was reactivated in the area of Liège. This time, Belgian veterans of the Napoleonic army fought against the French. This book reproduces a few letters, also kept in the Liège Archives, from a handful of soldiers who served in the Dutch army against Napoleon at that time. We have also included a few texts from other archives or private collections.

Many of the letters reproduced in this study are being published for the first time. Only a few of those contained in the following pages were previously transcribed in the 1936 book *Lettres de Grognards*, edited by Emile Fairon and Henry Heuse.[5] None, with the exception of a few extracts in Alan Forrest's *Napoleon's Men*,[6] were translated into English. The transcription and translation of these letters was not without its difficulties. The men of the Ourthe department used French, German or Flemish in their correspondence, but in fact spoke regional dialects such as Walloon. Most lacked the necessary skills to express themselves with ease or to build a coherent narrative. In many cases, the text was poorly written. This book has stayed as close as possible to the original structure and content. In rare cases, there was no other choice but to modify the text, without altering the meaning, for the sake of clarity.

---

4. Modern Belgium was created in 1830 but the name 'Belgium' has been used since Antiquity. Even Napoleon and his Generals made a distinction between French and Belgian soldiers. Gaspard Gourgaud, *La Campagne de 1815*, Paris, 1818, p. 85.
5. Emile Fairon and Henry Heuse, *Lettres de Grognards*, Liège, 1936.
6. Alan Forrest, *Napoleon's Men*, London, 2006, p. 88.

All letters followed this format:

(Place and date)
Dear parents (or brother, sister, friend)
I write to tell you that I am well and I hope that your health is fine.
Send me a letter.
Life is expensive. I am hungry and I have to pay for my equipment.
Please send money.
Many greetings to my friends, my uncles and aunts, my godfather,
etc . . .

Except for a few specific letters, this way of writing is monotonous and unnecessary to understand the psychology of the soldier. We have decided to shorten the texts in order to highlight the most interesting parts. In all cases, we identified the author of the correspondence and have provided a short biography, including his place and date of birth, his regiment and, where possible, his fate after having been drafted. The dates are also problematic. The Gregorian system was replaced by the Republican calendar on 22 September 1793. Despite its unpopularity, the soldiers and the administration used it in their correspondence, until Napoleon reverted to the Gregorian calendar on 1 January 1806. For the sake of clarity, we have systematically used the Gregorian equivalent.

All the chapters follow a specific theme and place the letters within the wider narrative of the wars. In the first chapter, we look at conscription, the ways to avoid military duty, but also at the journey of the soldier to the regiment. The next chapter investigates various aspects of the life as a soldier in the French army such as material conditions or the duties in the barracks. In chapter three, we turn to the wars against the Third, Fourth and Fifth Coalitions. Chapter 4 is entirely dedicated to the Peninsula War. Several volumes would be needed to do justice to the history of the First Empire and to the many topics approached in this book. We invite the reader to look at the bibliography for further reading.

Bernard and René Wilkin
2014

Chapter 1

Serving France

Conscription, Desertion and Denunciation

The first steps towards mass conscription in France were taken by the National Convention in the summer of 1792 while the Prussian army was marching toward Paris. The *levée en masse* of the next year strengthened the idea that the state had the right to requisition citizens to defend the nation. These measures were revolutionary but had no definitive legal justification as the law was to change on several occasions. Mass conscription was truly introduced in France with the so-called Jourdan law of 19 *fructidor* year VI (5 September 1798). Having been at war for the previous six years, the Republic desperately needed new soldiers to reinforce the strength of its armies. Under the Jourdan law, all men aged 20 to 25 were now liable for military duty and divided between five different classes corresponding to their age. The youngest class would systematically be called first but a potential conscript who had not served would only be dismissed definitely once aged 25. Although the overall number of conscripts to be drafted was set by the government, local authorities had much to say in the selection process.

This system evolved during the Consulate and the Empire to become more standardised and efficient as Napoleon Bonaparte constantly needed more men to satisfy his ambitions. During the Empire, the number of conscripts was as shown on the diagram on page 8.

Conscripts of the same class were selected in each canton by lottery – the lowest numbers drawn automatically meant active duty. Once selected, conscripts underwent medical checks; those assessed unfit for military duty were discharged or included in the next levy. The law was fundamentally unfair for poor people, as wealthy conscripts were able to find their way out of military service by paying someone who had been free from military obligations to take their place. If the replacement deserted within the first

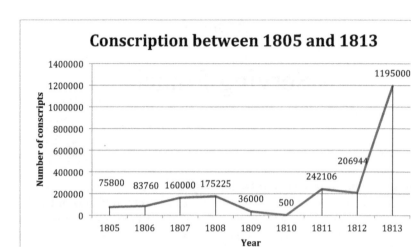

Figure 1.1: Number of men conscripted in 1805–1813.
Source: Alain Pigeard, *L'armée de Napoléon, Paris, 2000, pp. 345–8.*

two years of service, however, the original conscript was required to serve. Finding a replacement became more difficult as years went by: in the Ourthe department, prices jumped from 300 francs in 1798 to an enormous 6,000 francs in 1813.[1] In addition, even if a person was able to hire a conscript who survived and remained in the army it was still possible that he himself would be called up. For example, Philippe-Auguste Doucet[2] paid for a replacement, a man named Jean-Joseph Mohimont, in 1811. The fact that his replacement stayed in the army meant that Doucet was legally exempt from military duty. However, the young man was called up to the 2nd Regiment of the *Gardes d'Honneur* (Honour Guard) in 1813. As the prefect explained in a letter, this regiment was a way to guarantee the loyalty of wealthy families to the regime by holding their sons hostage.[3] Doucet wrote to the prefect to try to get out of this uncomfortable situation:

Baron de Micoud prefect of the Ourthe department

I am honoured that you selected me for his majesty's Guard. I would gladly take this opportunity to show my gratitude to the state if my family situation did not require my presence at home.
My invalid father is deaf and has a nervous disease. My brother

1. Wilkin, 'Le remplacement militaire dans le département de l'Ourthe'.
2. Philippe-August Doucet was born on 11 August 1791. He was the son of Pierre-Henri Doucet and Scholastique Noël.
3. The *Gardes d'Honneur* had to pay for their horse and equipment. On the subject, see Georges Housset, *La Garde d'Honneur, 1813-1814*, Paris, 2009.

has been hit by an axe and will probably be permanently disabled. This leaves me alone to run the property that helps us survive. I say that I am alone because my two other brothers are still children. The one who is wounded is not physically or morally fit to run a farm.

Far from my family, I would be very worried about my relatives and our possessions and would be sad and discouraged. This is why, sir, I want to introduce you to Henri Joseph Simon, my cousin. This young man is filled with zeal and good spirit. He is the nephew of the police superintendent Simon, who is also a member of the electoral board of the 1st district.

[. . .] Lastly, I would like to attract your attention to the fact that I already paid 6,000 francs for a replacement to stay with my family in 1811 [. . .].[4]

Despite offering to pay for a second replacement, Doucet was drafted in the *Gardes d'Honneur* on 5 July 1813. He did not serve long in the French army as he deserted on 5 April 1814.

A potential conscript was also authorised to join the reserve if he met one of the following criteria: being an orphan with younger siblings or the son of a widow, being the oldest son of a man aged seventy or more, having a wife before being drafted, studying to become a priest, or having a brother on active duty or who had died while serving France. As mentioned in the introduction, this last condition was difficult to meet as there was usually little evidence. Jean Pire[5] sent the following letter to the prefect in 1808:

To the Prefect

Jean Pire [. . .] is the third child of the house to be exposed to conscription. The first brother, named Gérard Pire, was killed while serving for Dumourier [Dumouriez] at the battle of Fleurû [Fleurus].[6] The second brother, named Nicolas Pire,[7] was conscripted in year 15 [1806] and is currently serving in the 4th battalion of the 93rd regiment. The following letter shows that he will ask for a certificate to the army corps. [. . .]

The following message was inserted at the bottom of the same letter:

We certify that we witnessed the death of Gerard Pire, shot and killed by the enemy, in year II of the Republic. He was a fusilier of

---

4. AEL: FFP 1220. Philippe-August Doucet to the Ourthe prefect, April 1813.
5. Jean Pire was born in Liège at an unknown date. He was drafted in 1808 but put into the reserve, probably as a result of the letter reproduced in this book. He was called to serve in 1813 but fled.
6. This is not accurate as General Dumouriez had already fled France. The battle of Fleurus, on 26 June 1794, was won by General Jean-Baptiste Jourdan.
7. Jean-Nicolas Pire, born in February 1785 in Liège, was conscripted into the 93rd Regiment of the Line in year XIV (1805).

the first battalion of the *Tirailleurs Liégeois* and died in a village named Fleru [Fleurus], near Lille. [. . .].[8]

To prove that a draftee had a brother in the army was just as difficult. It was the task of the family to provide a certificate issued by the regiment. Even if the document arrived in time, it was sometimes incorrectly filled in, and therefore useless. Madeleine Welter wrote to her son Jean-Jacques-Joseph Jansen,[9] who was serving in the 18th Regiment of the Line, to tell him that his brother was having problems with the certificate provided:

Membach [Belgium], 17 February 1812

My dear son
I received your last letter and the certificate attached to it. I am glad to know that you are well and hope to see you soon. The certificate arrived just on time but is filled with mistakes.[10] It arrived on the day conscripts were examined. Your brother Jean Pierre was among them. He could not use the certificate because problems with the identity were noticed.
   Here are the problems

The place of birth says Membach instead of Baelen
It says the canton of Lembourg instead of Limbourg
Your family name, Jeansin instead of Jansen
Your first names, Jean Baptiste instead of Jean Jacques Joseph
My first and last names, Marguerite Vallere instead of Madelene Welter

Your brother is held in the reserve for the time being and has received a certificate from the mayor of our borough. He will stay there until the prefect receives the confirmation from your army corps of your presence in the military. To stay in the reserve, all the mistakes in the certificate must be rectified. Give this letter to the administration unit of your army corps and send a new certificate to me as soon as possible with the correct place of birth, name and first names, as mentioned above. Rectifying the mistakes is more than necessary. If the prefect receives the same certificate that you sent, your brother will lose his right to the reserve and will not be considered to be your brother [. . .].[11]

---

8. AEL: FFP 1042. Jean Pire to the prefect of the Ourthe department, 1808.
9. Jean-Jacques-Joseph Jansen was born in Baelen on 20 June 1790. He was conscripted into the 18th Regiment of the Line on 16 March 1809 and captured by the Russians on 5 November 1812.
10. The registers of the regiment held correct information, meaning that the mistakes were made by the author of the certificate. Service Historique de la Défense (SHD): GR 21YC 161, register of the 18th Regiment of the Line, p. 345.
11. AEL: FFP 1061. Madeleine Walter to Jean-Jacques-Joseph Jansen, 17 February 1812.

The certificate was supposed to be free but corruption was common. Joseph Fraiteur[12] wrote the following letter to his family:

Metz [France] 17 September 1811

My dear father,
Here is the certificate for my brother. I hope it will help him as it is done as it should.
     [. . .] I am currently at the hospital in Metz. I have been there for two months and a half but I am better, thanks God. [. . .] I have to tell you that when I arrived in Metz, I still had money. The certificate was very hard to get and I had to flatter many people and pay six francs, given by a friend. My dear father, I ask you to send money because I am in need. Send it as soon as you can because they say that we will soon leave [. . .].[13]

Relatives sometimes did not know which unit their son was serving in. Moreover, the time allowed to provide the necessary document was very short and even the regiment could not always tell if the soldier was still serving, especially in Spain. To be discharged, or at least transferred to the reserve, draftees sometimes wrote to the prefect of the department or to the council of recruitment. Prosper Brixhe[14] sent the following letter:

To the president and members of the recruitment council of Liège

Sirs!
Prosper Brixhe, living in the north of Liège, conscript of 1813, states [he uses the third person] that he has two brothers serving in the *Grande Armée*. One is a knight of the legion of honour and a captain in the hussar regiment of Jérome Napoléon.[15] The other is a military surgeon and was made director of the war administration before being conscripted. When he was drafted, he was placed in the reserve, because his brother was a captain. This reason is even more valid now that he has a second [brother] serving in the army.

---

12. Joseph Fraiteur was born in Latinne on 8 December 1786. He was conscripted into the 8th Regiment of *train d'artillerie* on 23 December 1808.
13. AEL: FFP 1044. Joseph Fraiteur to his father, 17 September 1811.
14. Prosper Brixhe was born in Spa on 16 June 1793. He was transferred to the reserve in 1813.
15. Louis-Guillaume-Martin Brixhe, born in Spa on 11 November 1787, served in the 13th Dragoons. He fought in Prussia and Poland in 1806 and 1807 and in Spain and Portugal from 1809 to 1810. Brixhe was shot in the left arm in Siles (Spain) on 13 November 1810. He went back to Spain in 1811–12 but was once again wounded, this time in the right leg. He was promoted to the rank of lieutenant on 1 April 1811 and to the rank of captain on 17 August 1813. After the first fall of the Empire in 1814, he joined the Belgian hussars in the army of the Netherlands and fought against the French in 1815. He became the first colonel commanding the Belgian gendarmerie in 1830 and died in Liège on 4 December 1876.

Moreover, he [Prosper Brixhe] is the son of a widow, who has three other children, and he is the only one working to help her. The oldest son is married and has his own family and the two other brothers are doing their duty. For these reasons and because he has faith in your equity, he begs you, sirs, to keep him in the reserve.[16]

In other cases, families gave letters, sent by their relatives serving in the army, to obtain a delay. This is, incidentally, one of the reasons for which so many letters survived.[17]

Many Frenchmen felt that the draft was a burden imposed to serve a cause that they only vaguely understood. This sentiment was particularly common in rural areas, where people were afraid of being removed from their communities, and in the newly annexed territories like Belgium.[18] Potential conscripts would often try to evade military duty. Some bought replacements while others wrote to the prefect in the hope of being discharged, or at least to stall the process. A few even tried to denounce other young men, saying that they were faking disabilities, to convince the prefect that they were more useful at home than in the military. Jean-François Pirard[19] wrote such letters[20] to the prefect, denouncing so-called shirkers in an attempt to escape military duty:

Hodeige [Belgium], 22 April 1811

To Mr Micoud Baron of Empire, prefect of the Ourthe department
Monsieur le Baron

Jean Pirard [he used the third-person], conscript of year 1811, of Hodeige, reminds you that he drew the number 54 at his canton's lottery. Noticing different attempts to escape conscription, he has already denounced: 1) a conscript from the borough of Oreye, who claimed to be insane. I proved that he was sane. 2) a conscript from the borough of Hollogne sur Geer, who claimed to have eye problem. I managed to demonstrate that the problem was faked. 3) Someone named Orÿ, from Grenville, who tried to avoid his duty under false pretences. He was discovered by the recruitment committee, thanks to the tip I gave. I would like to highlight that the

---

16. AEL: FFP 1049. Prosper Brixhe to the recruitment council of Liège, 1813.
17. Harold Blanton, 'Conscription in France during the era of Napoleon', in D. Stoker, F. Schneid and H. Blanton (eds), *Conscription in the Napoleonic Era: a Revolution in Military Affairs?*, New York, 2006, pp. 6–23.
18. Alan Forrest, *Conscripts and Deserters: the Army and French Society during the Revolution and Empire* Oxford, 1988, pp. 4–5.
19. Jean-François Pirard was born on 1 January 1791 in Hodeige. His attempt to escape military service was unsuccessful; he was sent to the 8th *bataillon bis du train d'artillerie*.
20. The archives saved four different letters written by Pirard. They were written on 13 February, 22 April, 31 July and 5 August 1811.

tips provided so far have all been good. I hope that you will let me give more information as I would like to be as useful as I can be and would like to deserve your goodness and your justice. I hope that you can transfer me to the reserve and would even dare to hope that you can give me a job matching my skills, such as rural policeman [*garde champêtre*].[21]

The prefect received hundreds of letters of men claiming to be unfit for duty. Pierre-François Humblet,[22] conscripted in 1813, wrote the following in an attempt to be given permission to remain at home:

To the president and members of the recruitment council of the Ourthe department

Pierre François Humblet, conscript of 1813 of Selles, district of Waremme, would like to argue that his seemingly good shape does not mean that he is fit for duty. He is begging you to believe that despite being in the spring of his life, there is a hidden hereditary vice inside him. Soon, this vice will prevent him from doing any hard labour, like his father who has asthma.

His duty is to help his family. He managed to help his old father, aged seventy, and his mother, who is in her sixties, as well as his young brothers and sisters.

His older brother[23] was conscripted in 1807. As soon as he started serving in the army, he had to be hospitalised, where he is still now. The certificate of his regiment, the 9th Hussars, certifies this [. . .].[24]

The authorities launched various investigations to discover faked disabilities. The notary of Housse, Henri Fafchamps, wrote a report concerning this matter:

Secret note about the conscripts of Dalhem 1807

[. . .] Many valid conscripts bragged about being reformed or being pushed back to the conscription of 1808, paying crooks to help them. These crooks tell the conscripts how to look like mentally retarded, to look pale, to look like someone incapable of enduring

---

21. AEL: FFP 909. Jean-François Pirard to the Ourthe prefect, 22 April 1811.
22. Pierre-François Humblet was born in Celles on 23 November 1793. He was conscripted in 1813, the reason for which he wrote the letter reproduced above. His request denied, Humblet fled to avoid serving in the French army.
23. Nicolas Humblet, born in Celles on 19 February 1787, was conscripted into the 5th Battalion of the *train d'artillerie* in 1807 but was immediately sent home. He was drafted again into the 9th Hussars on 20 November 1808 but was sent home in 1811.
24. AEL: FFP 1057. Pierre-François Humblet to the authorities, 1813.

the tiredness of war, or to fool anybody who is not trained to detect these tricks. They also give them other ways but I do not have the time to describe them here [. . .].[25]

A significant number of conscripts took the matter into their own hands by deserting. The case of François-Joseph Warrand[26] was quite common. Conscripted in the year XIV (1805), he was arrested in 1808 following an attempt to hide. The authorities sent him to the refractory depot of Charlemont (Givet, France) but Warrand managed to escape. He turned himself in on 18 January 1809 and was attached to the 4th Regiment of the Line on 15 April 1809. Deserting soon after, he wrote the following letter to the sub-prefect after the 1810 amnesty:

Theux [Belgium] 9 May 1810

To Pérignÿ sub-prefect for the Malmedy district [Belgium]
Sir, I heard about the decree of his majesty the Emperor, who grants an amnesty to the refractory conscripts who come forward and ask to join a regiment of their choice. I am concerned by this decree and declare that I would like to join the 66th Regiment of the Line.
      I had a child about seven months ago with Marie Joseph Vincent, a spinner living in Theux. Before leaving for the army, I would like to marry and legitimise the child [. . .].[27]

Warrand changed his story when he finally met the mayor and the sub-prefect. Claiming that he had not served in the army, he managed to get a permanent discharge. The 1810 amnesty did little to convince unwilling soldiers to leave their hiding places and risk their lives in these faraway wars.[28] In fact, desertion became an even greater problem after 1810. The campaigns of Spain, and later the retreat from Russia, had a serious impact on the men and their morale. Thomas-Joseph Braipson[29] wrote from a military prison, where he explained to his mother why he had deserted:

Comblence [Koblenz] 4 June 1813
My very dear mother, brother and sister
This letter to let you know that I left [deserted] the regiment on 25

---

25. AEL: FFP 898. Henri Fafchamps to the Ourthe Prefect, 1807.
26. François-Joseph Warrand was born in Theux on 16 January 1785. He worked as a labourer before being drafted.
27. AEL: FFP 1192. François-Joseph Warrand to the sub-prefect of Malmedy, 9 May 1810.
28. Isser Woloch, 'Napoleonic conscription: state power and civil society', *Past and Present*, 111 (1986), pp. 101–29.
29. Thomas-Joseph Braipson was born in Hermalle-sous-Huy on 14 November 1790. He was conscripted into the 8th *Voltigeurs* of the Imperial Guard on 14 May 1813. Braipson was last seen in the hospital during the battle of Leipzig, on 18 October 1813. He was probably wounded during the battle and died soon afterwards.

May at ten in the evening. I was arrested and brought to the mayor of Luszradhe on 30 May. From there, they brought us to the gendarmerie and there to the military prison of Maanse [Mainz]. I was with my friend Lambert Scaclin[30] of Nandrin [near Liège]. We deserted together. I know, my dear mother, that I would not have done it if I had listened to you. You forbad me to do it before I left. It was a stupid thing that I did. I can assure you that I will not do it again and I can see that I have to stay. But we would have met once more. It would have made me feel better. I did it because I was badly advised on the road. But now I will not listen to anybody [. . .].[31]

Soldiers commonly talked about desertion with their relatives. Jean-Léonard Hastier[32] discussed his friend's attempt to flee the army:

From La Motte a Chard [La Mothe-Achard, west of France] 12 August 1807

My dear mother and father
[. . .]. I am in the same company as Sandron.[33] He deserted as soon as we arrived but was arrested after having walked for seven days. The gendarmes brought him to a prison and he is well. He sends his regards to his mother and to his family [. . .].[34]

Napoleon, facing increasing pressure on all fronts, turned to harsher measures to find the draft-dodgers. The authorities sent military units to pursue deserters in their home towns. These soldiers lived in the home of the missing men not only to prevent them from coming home but also to put financial pressure on their families. Jean-Jacques Morisseau[35] searched for deserters in the countryside around his native Liège:

To the Baron de Micoud, prefect of the Ourthe department, knight of the Legion of Honour

We were sent in 1811 in various cantons of the department to find missing refractory conscripts. We stayed with their families to force

---

30. Hubert-Joseph Chatelin was born in Nandrin on 16 March 1792. He was conscripted into the 8th *Voltigeurs* of the Imperial Guard on 14 May 1813 but deserted the following day.
31. AEL: FFP 1042. Thomas-Joseph Braipson to his mother, 4 June 1813.
32. Jean-Léonard Hastier was born in Modave on 9 January 1788. He was conscripted into the 26th Regiment of the Line on 28 July 1807 and died at the hospital of Niort (France) on 25 October 1807.
33. Henri-Joseph Sandron, born in Modave on 9 May 1788, was conscripted into the 26th Regiment of the Line in 1807. His desertion was not recorded in the archives, probably because of its short duration.
34. AEL: FFP 1042. Jean-Léonard Hastier to his parents, 12 August 1807.
35. Jean-Jacques Morisseau was born in Liège on 18 February 1789. He worked as a locksmith before being drafted as sergeant in a reserve company of the Ourthe department. He was later sent to an unknown regiment and died in Russia after 1811.

them to cooperate. We visited their homes and their retreats days and nights and have managed to arrest many of them. You can have a look at our reports to be sure that we did not neglect any lead. We thank you for your trust [. . .].[36]

The men who left for the army sometimes held a grudge against those who had managed to escape military service. It was not uncommon for them to express their anger or even take more radical measures. For example, a group of soldiers on their way to the 3rd Cuirassiers wrote this anonymous letter to the prefect of the Ourthe department soon after having left their hometown:

Daix [Aachen, Germany] 21 February 1813

To the prefect. We want to let you know that Simon Collée,[37] a year 1811 conscript from the borough of Vivegnis [Belgium], canton of Glons, Ourthe department, is faking a head disability. It is not fair and we could have pretended to have the same thing. Three weeks after being discharged, he will be healed. He is a refractory conscript who wants to cheat the Emperor and his friends. We took the initiative, sir, to write on our way [to the army] to tell you that we are not happy to see him being discharged. You are pleasing one man but you are upsetting all the conscripts from Glons. We should all serve.

One cannot be favoured more than another. Once we are in Mâance [Mainz], I will write to my father to know if he [Simon Collée] has left for the army. Since you do more for him than for the others, we are determined to get the hell out [*foutre le camp,* an expletive] and join the Russians once we are in Russia.

Beware, sir. All of us salute you, prefect baron etc. . . etc. . . etc . . . [here, the conscripts are making fun of his titles]. We have not signed this letter as we have too much to do.[38]

In theory, military service was limited to eight years (war years counted double) but soldiers knew that this rule was never respected and that the only ways to leave the regiment were either to suffer a disabling wound or die. Indeed, those who survived the first wave of conscription of year VII (1798) would not return home until 1814. This lengthy service did not mean

---

36. AEL: FFP 1167. Jean-Jacques Morisseau to the Ourthe prefect, June 1811.

37. Simon-Joseph Colleye, born on 13 February 1791, was from the canton of Glons. He was indeed discharged for medical reasons.

38. Although anonymous, it was possible to identify the authors of the letter. The archives showed that a group of conscripts from Glons left for the 3rd Cuirassiers in Mainz on 19 February. These soldiers were supposed to arrive in Aachen on 21 February, precisely where and when the letter was written. The authors were therefore probably Thomas Hoven from Lixhe, Louis Jobbé from Oupeye, Michel Pâque from Lixhe, Jean Rossoux from Vivegnis and Hubert Seronvaux from Glons. AEL: FFP 1029.

that soldiers would never see home. Leaves lasting up to six months were granted on rare occasions. If the regiment was close to the hometown of a soldier, the man was also sometimes authorised to leave for a few days. These permissions were only granted when the military situation was favourable. Henri-Joseph Fraigneux,[39] who served in the 8th Regiment of the Line, came home for a few days in 1809. Having been away for the previous six years, he wrote to the prefect to prolong his stay and even tried to be discharged:

To the prefect of the Ourthe department

Henri Joseph Fraigneux [he uses the third person], from Liège, conscripted in year X, is a corporal serving in the 8th Regiment of the Line, 1st battalion, 4th company, based in Venloo. He is at the present in Liège, having been granted a fifteen day furlough. He asks you to prolong this furlough.

Here are the reasons: when he was conscripted, he was forced to leave behind a wife and two children. His wife was pregnant when he departed and gave birth five months after. Six years later, he was delighted to be reunited with his family and notice that everybody was well. Are fifteen days enough to compensate for such pain and such a long separation?

You are a father, sir, and your heart tells you to grant this request, either through military channels in Liège, or by directly asking the commander of the 8th Regiment of the Line in Venloo. H. J. Fraigneux adds to this letter the necessary information to grant the request.

The author of this letter asks for an even bigger favour. This bigger favour is a fair one and might not even be hard to grant. You can already guess that Henri Joseph Fraigneux does not want to leave again his beloved family and would like to be discharged as he deserves to be.

Here is why:

He has served for six years in the same corps and has fought against the Austrians, the Prussians and the Russians.[40] War years have always counted double. He has therefore done much more than eight years of service, the period required to be discharged.

---

39. Henri-Joseph Fraigneux was born on 28 November 1780 in Liège. Conscripted on 4 *fructidor* year XI (22 August 1803), he was sent to the 8th Regiment of the Line. The request reproduced here was not granted but Fraigneux deserted on 19 March 1813.
40. Fraigneux must have served in the wars of the Third, Fourth and Fifth Coalitions.

There is no other proof needed for his good conduct than the rank of corporal.

The author of this letter would willingly continue to serve with the same zeal if the sight of his dear family, which he can cherish at the present, was not forcing him to ask for freedom.

Such reasons and rights do not need to be developed further to a man like you. Be the noble protector of your soldier and citizen [. . .]. You can present this as a way to encourage the citizens who are called for duty. They will go happily, knowing the acts of justice done to the one who salutes you respectfully.[41]

The prefect was sometimes confronted by extraordinary stories. Gérard Frisson[42] tried to be discharged on the grounds that he had been a slave and had served in the British army:

Gerard Frisson, *chasseur* in the fourth foreign regiment serving for France fifth battalion fourth company is begging for your protection.

He was sold [as a slave] in the Dutch islands [the Dutch Antilles] fourteen years ago and stayed there for four years. The English captured the island[43] and took him as a prisoner of war. After a while, he joined their army, hoping that he could desert and go back to his fatherland. He managed to reach France but was arrested as a foreigner, having no passport. He wrote three different letters to his mother asking for his birth certificate but these letters either did not arrive or the mother did not reply. He was forced to serve in a regiment but deserted to go home. According to all laws, he should not be forced to serve. Knowing your kindness for the people of Liège, discharge a man who has been away from his country for eighteen years.

When he was away, his mother and father were cruel enough to sell all his valuable belongings. If he could be discharged, he would use the protection of the law to get back what he owned [. . .].[44]

Each departmental centre had a council of recruitment in charge of examining potential complaints. Made up of the prefect, the commanding officer of the gendarmerie, the recruiting captain and the mayors of the cantons,

41. AEL: FFP 895. Henri-Joseph Fraigneux to the Ourthe prefect, 1809.
42. Nothing further is known of this man.
43. The British captured the Dutch Antilles in 1795.
44. AEL: FFP 1176. Gérard Frisson to the prefect, between 1811 to 1813.

this council had the power to grant both exemptions and discharges and was even allowed to postpone the recruiting process to collect evidence. The council's work was the last step before finalising the lists of conscripts. Local administrations were responsible for the selection, based on the lottery numbers, and for sending the tallest men to the cavalry and the Imperial Guard.

The Journey to the Regiment
Future soldiers would receive a letter from the local mayor telling them where to assemble for departure. Conscripts did not know which would be their new regiment or where they were going. Jean-Jacques-Joseph Crutzen[45] described the journey to the 86th Regiment of the Line to his family:

Saint-Malo [France] 9 June 1808

Greetings father, mother, family and friends,
I hope that you are all in good health. I write this second letter because I have not received an answer to the first one. I will be here long enough so please answer this one. I might leave Saint-Malo. The rumour says that we will embark on a boat. I asked for money in the other letter but I did not receive anything. I have only half the money that I received when I left home. I could not walk with my comrades because my foot was painful. Travelling alone for more or less 200 leagues seemed very long. I did not receive money or bread until I arrived in Paris. There, I received two crowns [coins] and that was all. Now, we receive a *sou* [coin][46] every day, a pound and a half of bread, half a pound of meat and a little piece of white bread in a vegetable soup. We received one pair of white trousers and a blue uniform with red lapels. With the *sous*, we have to buy clay to whiten our trousers.

   Gilles-Joseph Collin[47] of Henri-Chapelle is also with me in Saint-Malo. He is in good health but has also written a letter without receiving any answer [. . .].[48]

Lambert-Joseph Renard[49] also walked for a long time to reach his

---

45. Jean-Jacques-Joseph Crutzen was born on 11 September 1789 in Henri-Chapelle. A servant, he was conscripted on 3 June 1808 and sent to the 86th Regiment of the Line. He disappeared in Spain on 18 June 1809.
46. The *sou* had disappeared with the French Revolution but most people used the name to talk about a twentieth of a franc.
47. Gilles-Joseph Collin, born in Henry-Chapelle on 14 December 1789, was drafted in the 86th Regiment of the Line on 28 May 1808 but was discharged on 16 December 1808.
48. AEL: FFP 1042. Jean-Jacques-Joseph Crutzen to his family, 9 June 1808.
49. Lambert-Joseph Renard was born on 22 March 1788 in Jupille. He worked as a nailer before being drafted on 2 August 1807. He first served in the 57th Regiment of the Line before being moved to the 115th. He was demobilised on 15 May 1814.

regiment. His letter seems to suggest that conscripts found interesting ways to keep themselves busy on the road:

Strasbourg [France] 4 August 1807

Dear father and mother
I arrived on the second of this month and the next day I was dressed as illustrated here [the letter was written on paper with a picture of an infantry soldier]. I have nothing interesting to tell about my way in except that I suffered a lot. It was a long journey and the weather was very hot. All the places were very ugly if we exclude Lorraine, which look a lot like Liège. There, the wine is abundant and you can buy a bottle for three *sous*. This means that I found a bit of joy with my comrades of misfortune. We emptied quite a few bottles. Everything here is expensive and they tell us that we will receive nothing from the corps until we have served for two years [. . .].[50]

Travelling was far from common at the beginning of the nineteenth century. In fact, most people would stay in their home town or village for their entire life and die without seeing the sea or a mountain. Being on the road for the first time was therefore a source of excitement. French conscripts wanted to share this unique experience with their relatives but lacked literary skills. Jean Stoff[51] tried to describe his route to Brittany, where the 86th Regiment of the Line was stationed at the time. Writing in German, his letter looked more like a succession of raw emotions than a coherent story:

Saint-Malo 1st November 1809

Me in a foreign country and you in my fatherland![52] I am, thanks to God, in good health. I do not need anything and I still have the money I had when I left Liège. I left Liège on 26 September. That day, we travelled on water. Then I met a soldier going the same way. After that I travelled alone. I arrived in Rouen on 11 October. There is a big bridge over the river there. I sailed for four hours and, on 24 October, arrived in Saint-Malo. The city is surrounded by the sea. You can walk in the city for six hours but there is so much water during the six other hours that boats can sail in the city. I slept in Paris on 5 October and then walked for 28 hours. I have now some German friends. The weather is nice. This city is 250 leagues from

---

50. AEL: FFP 1045. Lambert-Joseph Renard to his parents, 4 August 1807.
51. Jean Stoff was a worker born in Schleiden (now in Germany) on 11 June 1789. He was conscripted into the 86th Regiment of the Line on 21 October 1809. He died of fever in Rio Seco (Spain) on 10 May 1810.
52. It should be highlighted here that Jean Stoff did not see himself as French.

home. It is as warm in this place as it is in our country. I have no news except that the French made peace with the German Emperor.[53] The rumour says that they [the French] will use all their military might against the English. I am at the English border. This city was controlled in the past by the English. We train twice a day: from 7 to 9 in the morning and from 2 to 4 in the afternoon [. . .].[54]

Jean-Louis Collienne[55] travelled through Belgium and France to find his regiment before being redirected to Spain. His letter seems to suggest that he was proud of having seen so many places:

Tour [Tours, France] 8 September 1810

My very dear sister
[. . .] I need to tell you that our orders changed when we were in Len çon [perhaps Alençon, Normandy] and that we are now headed for Spain. We are leaving today. A lot of men are going because the peasants are not good there. In the country where we are at the present, there are not many men; it is even worse than back home. We went to mass and there were only girls. They have conscripted the last four classes. I thank God for giving me everything I need so far and I still have what you gave me before leaving. Here are the cities I have been through so far: Liege Saintrond Tirlemon Louvain, Bruxlette, Braine le Cont, Mons, Valancienne, Cambrai, Peronne, Rocroÿ, Mondie, Beauvais, Gisord, Vernon, Evreux, Conches, Verneuil, Mortagne, Alançon, Beaumon, Lonche, Focas, Maon Chateau-du-Loir[56] [. . .].[57]

François-Joseph Lemaire,[58], on his way to the 85th Regiment of the Line, also described his route day by day:

25 February 1813

My very dear father and mother [. . .] We arrived in Coblance

---

53. The Treaty of Schönbrunn, signed on 14 October 1809, brought the war between the French and the Austrians to an end.
54. AEL: FFP 1043. Jean Stoff to his parents, 1 November 1809.
55. Jean-Louis Collienne was born in Waimes on 17 August 1790. He was drafted into the 32nd Regiment of the Line on 25 November 1809 but deserted on 5 January 1810 while in Paris. He was caught, pardoned and sent to the 45th Regiment of the Line on 16 May 1810. He was removed from the regiment's registers on 2 May 1812, after a stay in the hospital.
56. Lège, Saint-Trond, Tirlemont, Louvain, Bruxelles, Braine-le-Comte, Mons, [here Collienne entered modern France] Valenciennes, Cambrai, Péronne, Rocroi, ?, Beauvais, Gisors, Vernon, Evreux, Conches-en-Ouche, Verneuil, Mortagne, Alençon, Beaumont, ?, Focast, Laon, Château-du-Loir.
57. AEL: FFP 1042. Jean-Louis Collienne to his sister, 8 September 1810.
58. François-Joseph Lemaire, born on 15 July 1791, was drafted on 24 February 1813. He was removed from the regiment's book following a long stay in the hospital.

[Koblenz] on 24 February and we will receive a uniform today. We hope that we will all be equipped in a few days. We received two *sous* a day and a pound and a half of bread but I think that we will only receive one *sou* and bread from now. We will start exercising on 26 February. Life is very expensive in this city. My bed comrade is from Bra.[59] [. . .]. Here is my road:

City of Liège, city of Haive, city of Aise, village of Citrot, city of Cologne where we had a break, city of Bone, village of Sansey, city of Endernach.[60]

Detachments of new conscripts were usually escorted by two non-commissioned officers who were also responsible for preventing desertion, a common occurrence by 1813. They also carried the pay and in theory had to find a place to stay for the night. In practice, soldiers spent a lot of money to improve their living conditions. Jean-Léonard Mafatz[61] described the road to Metz (France):

Metse [Metz] 16 July year 1807

[. . .] My very dear father and mother, I spent a lot of money while on the way. I spent at least three *couronnes* before arriving to the barracks and had to give another half *couronne* to the kitchen. We had no choice because, during the journey, they only paid for the nights. They were usually miserable because we had to sleep on straw. During the nine days that it took to reach Metz, we only slept once in a bed [. . .].[62]

Joining the regiment on foot was an excellent introduction for the life to come. For years, infantrymen marched relentlessly across Europe. Soon after the fall of the French Empire, Jean-Joseph Henry[63] wrote in his diary:

[. . .] We crossed the Rhine in Strasbourg and stayed in Cherbug [Cherbourg], Normandy. From there, we left for Brest in Brittany. We stayed there for six weeks. From there, we left for [word missing]. We stayed there 15 days before leaving for Nantes and then to Bordeau [Bordeaux], Bayonne, and from Bayonne to

---

59. Here, François-Joseph Lemaire talks about the *camarade de lit* or bedfellow. See next chapter and B. Martin, *Napoleonic Friendship: Military Intimacy and Sexuality in Nineteenth-Century France*, New Hampshire, 2011, p. 76.
60. Herve (Belgium), Aachen [Germany], ?, Cologne, Bonn, Sinzig, Andernach. AEL: FFP 1043. François-Joseph Lemaire to his parents, 25 February 1813.
61. For a biography and other letters of Jean-Léonard Mafatz, see chapter II.
62. AEL FFP: 1045. Jean-Léonard Mafatz to his parents, 16 July 1807.
63. Jean-Joseph Henry was a farmer born in Liège. He was drafted on 17 March 1807 in the 105th Regiment of the Line and promoted to the rank of corporal on 20 February 1814. He came back alive.

Burgos, a Spanish city, then Madrid, Saragossa, Pamplona, Valencia, Tudelle, Vitoria, Tolosa, Bilbao, Cadix, Cartagena, Malaga, Monesteryol, Beberscal, Logrono, where I thought I would die of smallpox, Arol, Esléals, Astafeast, Poinlest, Laa Rinne, Hurins, a French town, Orisse, Pau, Hocche (Auch), capital city of Gascony, Toulouse, Montpellier, Lyon, Nimes, where there is a very pretty fountain, Valence, Vienne in the Dauphiné [. . .].

We used a pair of shoes each month. From 1807 to 1814, I raced from Liège to Brisach, Berlin, Tilsit, Danzig, Silesia and Frankfurt. From Frankfurt, we met with our regiment in Danzig and then went to Vienna and went back to Cherbourg, Normandy. I travelled three times through Prussia and two times through Germany, Poland, Bavaria, Saxony, Wurttemberg, Bade, Darmstadt, and a part of Bohemia. As for France, I went through it four times and explored all its corners: from Liège to Alsace, from Strasbourg to Cherbourg, from Cherbourg to Bayonne. I also travelled through Spain. I have seen the whole of Navarre, Aragon, Castile and parts of Catalonia [. . .].[64]

In this chapter, we have highlighted the impact that modern conscription had on individuals and local communities alike. With the exception of a few soldiers, men of the Ourthe department perceived compulsory service as a burden. Military duty upset their traditional way of life and family structure. In many cases, years of service in the army also deprived households of their main providers. There were a few specific circumstances in which the law offered a way out of the military. Unsurprisingly, many of those who did not qualify for exemption either tried to dodge the draft or to desert. In rarer cases, men even faked disabilities or denounced other conscripts in an attempt to save themselves.

This unwillingness to serve was not entirely due to the question of national identity. The Ourthe department had belonged to the Holy Roman Empire before the French Revolution. The fact that the French forcefully invaded this region did not mean that its people felt like an occupied population. In *Napoleon's Men*, Alan Forrest came to the conclusion that 'conscripts recruited in Belgium, in Holland and in Italy were not immune to the appeal of *la Grande Nation*'.[65] To support this, Forrest reproduced the letter of an enthusiastic conscript from Liège who claimed to fight for the motherland. However, this man was an exception. The vast majority of the soldiers did not fight for France or for any abstract reason. Like other

---

64. This extract was reproduced in Fairon and Heuse, *Lettres de Grognards*, pp. 368–9.
65. Forrest, *Napoleon's Men*, p. 88.

provincial soldiers, the men from Liège strongly identified with their region and were largely indifferent to France. In fact, the personal prestige of the Emperor probably did more to guarantee their fidelity then an attachment to the abstract French nation. The men of the Ourthe department, like many soldiers from other French regions, also fought because they had no other choice. The alarming rate of desertion, especially after 1812, is a sober reminder that the charisma of Napoleon had its limits.

Chapter 2

Life in the Army

Citizen to Soldier

Life in the Napoleonic army was far from what volunteers had experienced during the Bourbon monarchy. No longer subjected to abusive aristocratic commanders, the men relied instead on experienced non-commissioned officers and officers whom they usually trusted. New conscripts were generally sent to a garrison where they joined the ranks of existing units. There, they followed a rigorous training programme during which they learned combat manoeuvres and fighting techniques. Although the relations between officers, non-commissioned officers and soldiers were better than in the Royal army, life in a Napoleonic regiment was not enviable. Soldiers were exposed to exhaustion, deplorable material conditions, hunger and disease.[1] Most of these unpleasant elements of army life were not obvious in the first weeks. In fact most new conscripts would promptly write reassuring letters to their families. Drafted on 8 February 1807, Jourdan Lambert[2] gave encouraging news about his health before presenting himself as a model soldier. He died in Portugal only five months after writing the following words:

Coutances [Normandy, France] 26 July 1807

My dear father, mother and brothers
I was very happy to receive your letter and to know that you are all in good health. I received the two crowns that you sent. You did not need to tell me to use them wisely as it is my most important duty after obeying my superiors. I want them to think highly of me. Militarily speaking, I am disciplined and keep myself clean. You tell me that if, by any chance, we were forty or fifty hours from our country, you would come and see me [. . .].[3]

---

1. Martin, *Napoleonic Friendship*, pp. 36–7.
2. Jourdan Lambert was born in Romsée on 2 November 1786. He was drafted into the 58th Regiment of the Line on 8 February 1807 but died in December of the same year in Portugal.
3. AEL: FFP 1042. Jourdan Lambert to his parents, 26 July 1807.

Lambert-Joseph Drapier[4] had been with the 26th Regiment of the Line for a few days when he wrote home:

Périgueux [Aquitaine, France] 24 vandemiaire [*vendémiaire*] year 13 [16 October 1804]

Dear father and mother
I write these few words to reassure you. I am really well and I can tell you that I made sure of having a good time during the journey. I will try to do my time with patience and behave like an honest man. If you can do the same, we will be happy. It was very warm on the road and we are in a very nasty country, 250 leagues from home. Wine is very cheap but I heard that we might not stay long [. . .].[5]

Drapier wrote another letter to his parents a month and a half later. He was already looking forward to the prospect of demobilisation:

Périgueux 18 *frimaire* [year 13, 9 December 1804]

Dear parents
I received your letter with great pleasure. The money made me happy but I was even more delighted to hear that you are in good health. I am still well and still have courage. I hope that it will never change as long as I am in the army. I hope that I will be demobilised in four years so I can kiss you all after having served the Emperor with honour [. . .].[6]

Most young men had always lived with their parents. Separated for the first time from their family, they often had a hard time coping with their new life. Hubert Renard[7] wrote the following letter to his mother:

Chapelle Hermiée [La Chapelle-Hermier, western France] 19 July 1807

My good and sweet mother
I have to tell you that I reached the regiment on the seventeenth. I suffered a lot but the biggest pain is, without a doubt, this cruel

---

4. Lambert-Joseph Drapier was born in Mons-lez-Liège on 6 January 1784. He was conscripted in year XIV (1805) and sent to the 26th Regiment of the Line. He disappeared in Spain on 14 November 1809.
5. AEL: FFP 1042. Lambert-Joseph Drapier to his parents, 16 October 1804.
6. AEL: FFP 1042. Lambert-Joseph Drapier to his parents, 9 December 1804.
7. Hubert Renard was born in Landenne on 9 April 1788. He was conscripted into the 26th Regiment of the Line on 17 July 1807.

separation. It is always in my mind and my heart is burdened by this bitter pain. O sweet mother, it is so difficult to be separated from you [. . .].[8]

Antoine Ernst[9] gave a detailed account of the first days at the barracks:

Nancy [Lorraine, France] 12 November 1808

My father and mother
[. . .] As for my travel, we walked for twelve days and we stopped twice. The travel was quite good. We arrived on Saturday in Nancy, our destination. They immediately sent us with the 4th line regiment, based in Nancy, and the 4th battalion, as we have to fill their ranks. We were examined by a surgeon on Sunday and he found me fit for duty. You do not need to be sad about my fate because I have come to accept it. The law wants us to serve so we have to obey. The fact that this is a beautiful regiment gives me hope. The barracks are nice and the city of Nancy is very entertaining. They dressed us on Monday and on Tuesday we began to exercise. We train for four hours a day, split in two sessions [. . .].[10]

The case of Eustache Boveroux[11] was more unusual. He volunteered for a dragoon regiment without informing his parents and only broke the news months later in the following letter:

Bois-le-Duc [now 's-Hertogenbosch, Netherlands] 3 October 1806

My very dear father, brother, and sisters
These words to let you know that I am still in perfect health, thank God. I hope that you are all well. I beg you not to be sad or mad at me for not writing earlier. It was pure madness but I did not dare writing to you. God did not make me a wealthy man. I had to do something as it was not possible to buy both butter and bread. I decided to volunteer with the army. I joined for four years. I was a dragoon but I am now with the third hussars of the King of Holland. Our regiment left to fight against the Prussians and we will have to go soon [. . .].[12]

---

8. AEL: FFP 1042. Hubert Renard to his mother, 19 July 1807.
9. Antoine Ernst was born in Thimister on 28 February 1788. He was called up in 1808 and initially rejected as an invalid but was later conscripted into the 4th Regiment of the Line on 5 November 1808. He was captured in Russia on 18 November 1812.
10. AEL: FFP 1042. Antoine Ernst to his parents, 12 November 1808.
11. Eustache Boveroux was born on 27 November 1783. Nothing else is known of him.
12. AEL: FFP 1044. Eustache Boveroux to his parents, 3 October 1806.

Friendship was an excellent way to ease integration into the military. Men usually stayed with other comrades from the same region to speak familiar dialects and talk about people from back home. Having familiar faces around was also a way of retaining some degree of normality in such a different life. In fact those who came back alive looked back at their companionship as one of the most pleasurable aspects of an otherwise difficult life.[13] Mathieu Courtois[14] wrote a letter to his brother in which he highlighted the importance of social relations and regionalism:

> Perigeux [Aquitaine, France], 26 *messidor* year XIII of the republic [15 July 1805]
>
> My very dear brother,
> [. . .] I am very well here and there are four hundred Liégeois [people from the city of Liège]. I know almost all of them [. . .].[15]

Jean-Noël Watelet[16] became friends with other men from his region. Together, they enjoyed good wine:

> St Martin [probably Saint-Martin-en-Ré] 8 March 1806
>
> My very dear father and mother
> [. . .] Despite being unwell during an exercise, my health is still fine. In the country where we are at the present, all the fruit trees have been blossoming since the beginning of February. At home, they would only do the same in May. We drink very good wine for two *sous* a bottle. There is no wood in this country and we heat with vine wood. It is not very cold because we are closer to the sun. I promised not to be sad and have found good friends from the country. I will follow your advice and salute you dear mother, brothers and sisters and all my friends. I wish you a perfect health and finish this letter by giving my holy benediction.[17]

The reception of the uniform was usually reported to the family. This significant moment marked the point where the conscript truly realised that

---

13. Forrest, *Napoleon's Men*, p. 134.
14. Mathieu Courtois was born in Cerexhe-Heuseux in December 1784. He was conscripted in year XIII (1804) but became a refractory. He was eventually arrested and sent to the 26th Regiment of the Line.
15. AEL: FFP 1042. Mathieu Courtois to his brother, 15 July 1805.
16. Jean-Noël Watelet was born in Neuville-sous-Huy on 9 April 1785. He was drafted into the 93rd Regiment of the Line on 8 January 1806 and killed in Spain on 26 November 1808.
17. AEL: FFP 1043. Jean-Nöel Watelet to his parents, 8 March 1806.

he had left his previous life behind. Jean Léonard Mafatz[18] described to his parents the equipment received on the first day. He also mentioned the routine in the barracks during the following weeks:

Metz 28 June year 1807

[. . .] My very dear father and mother, there is no need to be sad. We hope to stay in our barracks for at least a year. My very dear father and mother, I need to tell you that they measured me for my white uniform. We received our *fusique* [musket – this word is written in Walloon and not in French] on the twenty-seventh. I would like to be made corporal but you need to know the drill. We sleep in good beds and we have the right to fit out our space. Otherwise, when I drink I feel like a rooster singing and jumping on its hen. I do not spend my money but have many comrades asking me to teach them how to write [he received free drinks for his lessons]. Every day we train for four hours. Since I arrived in Metz, I have grown by at least an inch [. . .].[19]

Mafatz soon wrote another letter to his family to announce that he had been promoted to the rank of corporal:

Metse [Metz] 16 July year 1807

My very dear father and mother
I am still very well, thank God, and hope that you are as well as me. I received your first letter on 3 July and the second one on the tenth. I was so happy when I received your letters; it was like receiving a *Louis* [a gold coin]. I went to drink a bottle of wine and it made me very happy [in this case, he implies that he was drunk]. My very dear father and mother, they gathered all of those who could write to promote them to the ranks of corporal or sergeant. They gave me the rank of corporal.
    [. . .] My very dear father and mother, you do not need be afraid about my faith. I pray every evening and morning and I go to mass when I can. I only miss the mass when I do not have any choice. I ask for your blessing [. . .].[20]

---

18. Jean Léonard Mafatz was born in Malmedy on 29 December 1808. He was from the 1808 class but was conscripted in 1807. Mafatz fought in the 2nd *Légion de Réserve de l'Intérieur*, but died of disease in Spain in 1808.
19. AEL: FFP 1045. Jean-Léonard Mafatz to his parents, 28 June 1807.
20. AEL: FFP 1045. Jean-Léonard Mafatz to his parents, 16 July 1807.

Jean Paque[21] also described the moment he received his first uniform:

Strasbourg, 9 March 1813

My very dear mother
I am happy to let you know that we have arrived and that we are in perfect health. [. . .]. We received our clothes on the same day we arrived, including a shirt, three handkerchiefs from Brest and other things that make me very happy [. . .]. I will write again when we receive our full dress uniform.[22]

Material conditions varied greatly between units. New conscripts were sometimes welcomed with brand-new equipment but might also receive rags. Jean-François Godin[23] left his native Amay for the Imperial Guard in December 1812. He displayed enthusiasm for his new life:

Paris, 11 December 1812

Sir,
[. . .] I arrived on the second [of December 1812], after having walked for fifteen days. I had fun except that it was really cold. Thanks God, I enjoy serving. I exercise from morning to evening. I am very well dressed and all my wishes are fulfilled. I am happy to be in the grenadiers of the Imperial Guard and hope to leave for Fontenbleaux [Fontainebleau] in a few days. There I will learn to manoeuvre with a cannon and join a Regiment of the Line as a non-commissioned officer [. . .].[24]

On the other hand, Joseph-Martin Launoy[25] did not receive any equipment when he was transferred from the dragoons to the *chevaux-légers* (light cavalry):

Chateaudun [Châteaudun, Eure-et-Loir, France] 27 October 1811

---

21. Jean Paque was a labourer born on 4 December 1791 in Heure-le-Romain. He was drafted in the 3rd Regiment of horse artillery in 1813 and died of fever on 16 March 1814 in Choisy.
22. AEL: FFP 1045. Jean Paque to his mother, 9 March 1813.
23. Jean-François Godin was born on 11 April 1793 in Amay. He joined the Imperial Guard as a replacement and disappeared in 1813. See also Chapter 6 for another letter by Godin.
24. Letter found in Camille Moreau, 'Le remplacement d'un conscrit amaytois de 1813', *Annales du Cercle Hutois des Sciences et Beaux-Arts*, LII (1998). Jean-François Godin to the Rome family, 11 December 1812.
25. Joseph-Martin Launoy was born in Huy on 23 May 1788. He was discharged for health reasons in 1808 but conscripted later the same year. He served in the 9th Dragoons and was captured in Russia.

My very dear father and mother
[. . .] I heard that the son of Mahi[26] of Viercet and the son of Jaman[27] both died in Spain. I am still with my friend Philippe Jerard and we are waiting for the new batman of the regiment. We have been transferred from the dragoon regiment to the fourth regiment of light horse. They took away all our equipment to give us a new uniform but we did not receive it. We are very poorly dressed and we have to face winter almost naked [. . .].[28]

Jean-Noël Hardy[29] also complained about his uniform not being warm enough:

St Malo 10 October 1808

My very dear mother
[. . .] I am very happy to read that my sister is always with you. My dear mother, I am very happy that my brother and my sister assist you as I always did before leaving. I am very happy to see that they are faithful and that they relieve you as much as they can. I am back in St Malo and I am very happy at the present because we do not exercise. We are expecting one thousand conscripts in fifteen days and we will teach them. For fifteen days, we must learn how to command.

My very dear mother, you said that I must fear God. Since I came back to St Malo, I have not missed mass once because in this country, unlike at home, there are many young priests.

Many greetings to Ernotte. I am very grateful for your kindness, my dear friend Ernotte. I am based near the sea and it is very cold. We only have small canvas pants for winter. If you could send me something, it would be the greatest happiness in the world. But if you cannot, do not worry [. . .].[30]

In the following letter to his parents, Dominique Rutten[31] bitterly complained about the quality of the clothes received:

---

26. Jean Mahy, born in Fraiture on 15 November 1787, was conscripted into the 9th Dragoons on 24 February 1807.
27. Jean-Hubert Jamagne, born in Huy on 22 September 1787, was conscripted into the 9th Dragoons on 24 February 1807. He died in Ciudad Rodrigo (Spain) on 11 April 1811.
28. AEL: FFP 1044. Joseph-Martin Launoy to his parents, 27 October 1811.
29. Jean-Noël Hardy was born in 1789 in Agenteau-Sarolay. He was drafted into the 86th Regiment of the Line on 21 May 1808 and died of fever in Leon (Spain) on 21 February 1809.
30. AEL: FFP 1043. Jean-Nöel Hardy to his mother, 10 October 1808.
31. Dominique Rutten was born in Aubel on 30 March 1790. He was conscripted into the 18th Regiment of the Line in 1809 but was removed from the registers the same year after a stay at the hospital.

Strasbourg 23 March 1809

My very dear mother and father
[. . .] I send you a picture of how I am dressed.[32] But it is in fact pure
misery. You should see the uniform they gave us. If I went home
dressed like this, everybody would mistake me for a beggar. I really
need to feel better about this but at least everybody is dressed like
me [. . .].[33]

Conscripts were expected to look after their equipment. Pierre-François
Dessouroux[34] lost his bag and belongings while travelling. He was thrown
in a cell until he could afford a new set:

Harbourg [Harburg, a borough of Hamburg] 26 June 1813

I wrote this letter to enquire about your health. I am very well,
thanks to God. I took the stage-coach to Bremen but unfortunately
lost my bag and my belongings. I ask you, dear friend, to send me
money so I can replace the items I lost. Send three *Louis* now as I
will stay in the cell as long as I do not have money to replace my
belongings [. . .].[35]

The actual training exercises were rarely described. In fact, most soldiers
complained about them being tiring but then quickly switched to another
subject. Jean-Joseph Danthinne[36] was one of the few to explain their nature:

Brescia [Lombardy, Italy] 3 August 1807

Our salary is already not significant but they also use it to buy our
clothes. We have almost nothing. Every day we learn to use the
sabre. On Sunday, there is an inspection by three different people:
the sergeant is the first, then the commander and then the colonel.
You need to be impeccable from head to toe. We need to polish our
shoes every day or they put you in a cell. [. . .] We trained as if we
were in a real fight. They ordered us to run with the musket and the
backpack and load the musket while running.[37]

---

32. The heading of the letter shows a pre-printed illustration of a soldier in uniform. It was a
common practice to colour in these pictures with the colours of the regiment.
33. AEL: FFP 1045. Dominique Rutten to his parents, 23 March 1809.
34. Pierre-François Dessouroux was born in Herve on 26 November 1793. He replaced Jean-Pierre
Hubau on 8 April 1813 and left for the 21st Regiment of the Line. He was captured by the Russians
on 13 November 1813.
35. AEL: FFP 1045. Pierre-François Dessouroux to a friend, 26 June 1813.
36. Jean-Joseph Danthinne was born in Vielsalm on 29 November 1786. He was conscripted into
the 53rd Regiment of the Line in 1806.
37. This letter, originally in the AEL: 1042 collection, was also stolen. Luckily, a reproduction is
available in Fairon and Heuse, *Lettres de Grognards*, pp. 137–8.

The initial period of training in a military camp was usually quite acceptable. As this section showed, soldiers were pleasantly surprised by the level of material comfort and the joy of an intense social life. Conscripts had no idea that these living conditions were only temporary and that they would soon face hardship. Following his draft in the 39th Regiment of the Line, Jean-Marie Duchesne[38] wrote an enthusiastic letter to his father in which he said that he loved military life so much that he regretted not having joined earlier. This eager young man was removed from the regiment's records just a year later, probably because he had died of disease in a Spanish hospital:

Landau [Pfalz, Germany] 26 December [1808]

My very dear father I write to enquire about your health. I am very well here and I made a lot of friends [. . .]. You must know that we will leave soon for Spain. Give me news as soon as you can. I do not need money at the present as I still have three crowns. Life is expensive here but I do not spend a lot. Let my friends know that if they are drafted, they should not try to flee as it is a very unfortunate fate to be a deserter. We saw one who was dragging a ball and chain. There is nothing sadder than this [. . .]. Give my regards to the family and to my friends. For those who want to know about me, tell them that I will be a soldier for life. If I had known that serving in the army was such a good life, I would have joined four years ago. If they offered me a leave, I would not take it. I kiss you with all my heart.[39]

Depending where they were based, soldiers faced varying conditions. The sanitary situation was sometimes poor and the men had to sleep in revolting places. André Deflandres[40] stayed in a pigsty and then on a boat. As with many other soldiers, alcohol became a way to make life more bearable:

Saint Martain lil de rés [Ile of Ré, near La Rochelle, France] 29 January 1807

My very dear mother, brother and sister
[. . .] We are entering a new year and I pray the lord that he will make you happy and healthy. I hope that this year will be better than

---

38. Jean-Marie Duchesne was born in Fraipont on 18 December 1789. Conscripted on 4 December 1808, he fell ill on 29 September 1812 and probably died in hospital.
39. AEL: FFP 1042. Jean-Marie Duchesne to his father, 26 December 1808.
40. André Deflandres was born in Jupille on 2 November 1786. He left for the 26th Regiment of the Line on 15 October 1806 and was captured by the British in Spain. He survived and came home safely.

the last one. When we arrived at Lil daix [Ile-d'Aix], they made us
sleep on straw filled with vermin in a pigsty. We are a bit better now.
We embarked from Lil Daix [Ile-d'Aix] for the Lil des Rés [Ile de
Ré] on 28 December and we do not sleep on straw anymore. We
sleep in a bed and everything is better than before. We buy bottles
of wine for two *sous* but those who do not have money from home
cannot drink. It is not with one *sou* a day that you can drink wine or
smoke. Thanks to God, I had enough money so far to buy those little
things but now I have nothing left. You would make me happy, my
very dear mother, if you could send me a bit of money [. . .].[41]

To save money, the French army expected its soldiers to share a bed.
This unexpected intimacy with another man was a practical way to keep
warm but could seem initially unpleasant. General Marbot famously
described the shock of his first night as a soldier. A smelly veteran jumped
on the bed, stole most of the space, and immediately began to snore.[42]
However, Marbot was from a wealthy background and was used to luxury.
Most men did not seem to mind and even sometimes developed strong
friendships with their bedfellows. Dominique Rutten, already encountered
in this chapter, described this relationship:

[. . .] Really, father, I have already seen a lot of countries. I stay
mainly with Louis Joseph Longuehaÿe[43] and Cloes Wecquemans
[Nicolas Weckmans].[44] He is my friend and I go out with him. I still
sleep with him and we always get along as two brothers [. . .].[45]

Relations were not always as warm. Joseph-Clément Hamoir's[46] bedfellow
stole his money before deserting:

Amiens [northern France], 11 March 1805

My very dear mother,
[. . .] A great misfortune happened to me. My bedfellow deserted.
The one who sleeps in my bed. He took most of my money with
him. I need you to send three or four crowns if you can. I am in a
difficult position. They keep my pay until I can give some money

---

41. AEL: FFP 1042. André Deflandres to his mother, 29 January 1807.
42. Quoted in Martin, *Napoleonic Friendship*, p. 76.
43. Mathieu-Joseph Longuehaye, born in Charneux on 28 August 1790, was conscripted into the
18th Regiment of the Line on 8 March 1809. He was discharged for having been disabled while
serving on 1 October 1809.
44. Nicolas Weckmans was born in Aubel on 9 November 1788. He was conscripted into the 18th
Regiment of the Line on 16 March 1809 but deserted on 11 April of the same year.
45. AEL: FFP 1045. Dominique Rutten to his parents, 23 March 1809.
46. Joseph-Clément Hamoir was born in Esneux on 23 November 1780. He was called to serve in
year XI (1802–3) but tried to flee. He was arrested and sent to the 11th Dragoons. Hamoir was later
discharged after having sustained severe injuries.

and my chief forced me to write this letter [. . .] I think we will not stay long in Amiens because we will go fight the Russians [. . .].[47]

Food was a real obsession for many soldiers. It was one of the few pleasures of life still accessible when things were quiet and an essential component of survival when the situation was bad. As Alan Forrest highlighted, 'nothing was more likely to cause unrest or mutiny than the fear of starvation, especially since in their daily manoeuvres they were being forced to expend so much energy'.[48] The failure of logistics meant that soldiers were often forced to skip a meal or even fast for days. Charles-François Mathieu[49] complained bitterly to his parents:

From the island of Daix [Aix, off the west coast of France] 22 August 1808.

My very dear father and mother,
I write these words to let you know that I received your letter. [. . .]. We are truly miserable and more than often without bread or money. We sleep on the ground and we all fall ill because we are so miserable [. . .].[50]

The situation was worse in foreign countries, especially when there was unrest, than in France. Henri-Joseph Ravet[51] had just arrived in Spain when he described the food to his parents:

Gironne [Girona, Catalonia, Spain] 28 January 1812

My very dear father and mother
This letter to let you know that I left Marsin [Marcin, France, near the border] for Spain on 15 December. My very dear father and mother, I am in good health, thanks be to God, and hope that this letter will find you equally well. We are in a country where everything is broken or in ruins. I have never seen such misery. We only receive four pounds of bread [the law of 7 April 1795 stated that a French pound was 489.5 grams] and no meat or wine. There is only cabbage and a bit of rice for soup [. . .].[52]

---

47. AEL: FFP 1044. Joseph-Clément Hamoir to his mother, 11 March 1805.
48. Forrest, *Napoleon's Men*, p. 151.
49. Charles-François Mathieu was born in Ferrières on 13 May 1788. He was conscripted into the 26th Regiment of the Line on 8 August 1807. He was later captured in Germany and brought to England.
50. AEL: FFP 1042. Charles-François Mathieu to his parents, 22 August 1808.
51. Henri-Joseph Ravet was born in Liège in March 1791. He was drafted into the 5th Regiment of the Line on 1 June 1811.
52. AEL: FFP 1042. Henri-Joseph Ravet to his parents, 28 January 1812.

Martin-Albert Parent[53] also faced terrible food while in Holland and Germany. Working as a baker in the city of Liège prior to being a soldier, he was particularly interested in the bread:

Wuiselle [Wesel] 14 May 1813

To my very dear father
[. . .] Everything was so expensive on the road from Holland. We crossed the Rhine on 14 May and saw hundreds of builders working on the stronghold of Woiselle [Wesel, North Rine-Westphalia, Germany]. The army promised to give us thirty francs a month but they only gave sixteen and a half *sous* per day. We have no bread and no meat. A small white bread is so expensive. It costs three *sous* but would be only worth one *sou* at home. Bad beer is five *sous* for a litre. We thought we would stay here but we will leave soon to join the *Grande Armée* in Magdeburg [Saxony-Anhalt, Germany]. We need to be frugal to live with such a small pay. [. . .] Please do not forget me in your prayers. I ask for your forgiveness for everything I did when I was young.[54]

Food was not only scarce but also unsafe. Many soldiers died as a result of diseases contracted while drinking or eating unhygienic ingredients. For example, Jean-Joseph Piraprez[55] complained about rotten meat:

Cologne 16 July 1813

My very dear father
[. . .]. We see many soldiers going to Mainz and I think we will not stay there very long. My very dear father, I have not received any money since I left.
    The food is really not good. The smelly meat that they give us is infested with worms. They should give us four or five French *sous* but instead give us nothing [. . .].[56]

The fact that the army failed to provide decent food or reasonable pay, insufficient and rarely given, encouraged the men to find other ways to survive. Almost all soldiers relied on their family to send small sums. Some

---

53. Martin-Albert Parent was born in Liège in November 1790. He was initially reformed for being too short in 1810 but was conscripted as a military baker in 1813.
54. AEL: FFP 1045. Martin-Albert Parent to his father, 14 May 1813.
55. Jean-Joseph Piraprez was born in Meeffe on 9 August 1794. He was conscripted into the 76th Regiment of the Line in February 1813 and captured by the British at the battle of Nivelle (in the south of France) on 11 November 1813.
56. AEL: FFP 1045. Jean-Joseph Piraprez to his father, 16 July 1813.

parents were keen to help but others had to be convinced. Men detailed their misery as a form of emotional blackmail while other mentioned Christian charity or promised to pay back later. As for the availability of food, prices were not the same in every country. France, as Jean-François Claude[57] explained, was so expensive that soldiers hoped to be stationed elsewhere:

Renne [Rennes, Britanny] 28 August [1808]

My very dear mother
[. . .] We left Saint-Malo for Renne [Rennes] but I do not think that we will stay for long because many left and we will go to Portugal. I am happy to leave because everything here is expensive and we hope that where we go things are cheaper. It will be good for us if everything is not so expensive [. . .].[58]

Hubert-Joseph Dantinne[59] was conscripted into the 57th Regiment of the Line on 24 July 1807. By December, he had not received any pay at all and was forced to rely on his parents:

Strasbourg 3 September 1807

My very dear father and mother
I write to know about your health and the one of my brother and sister and to let you know that I am fine. I hope the same for the whole family. I am still in Strasbourg where everything is good except that since I arrived I have not been paid once and do not know if I will be in the future. You would make me happy if you could send me money. I have not spent everything you gave me but since everybody is saying that we might go away, you might find it difficult to send me money then. The party of our village is close and you must get entertained as you have always done. You must not be sad for me. I end this letter by kissing you and will wait for news. If you need a certificate for my brother, tell me. I end this line by giving you my regards and kissing you. You are my father, mother, brother, sister, family and friends for life.[60]

---

57. Jean-François Claude was born in Malmedy on 23 October 1789. He was drafted into the 86th Regiment of the Line on 12 May 1808 and died of fever in Jarez (Spain) on 2 August 1811.
58. AEL: FFP 1042. Jean-François Claude to his mother, 28 October 1808.
59. Hubert-Joseph Dantinne was born in Ville-en-Hesbaye on 20 May 1788. He was conscripted into the 57th Regiment of the Line on 24 July 1807 and transferred to the 115th Regiment of the Line on 1 July 1808. He was removed from the regiment's book on 31 December 1808 for long absence at the hospital.
60. AEL: FFP 1042. Hubert-Joseph Dantinne to his parents, 3 September 1807.

Jean-Guillaume Cordier[61] relied on his brother to buy new clothes:

Venlo [in the south-east of the Netherlands] 11 August 1811

My dear brother
[. . .] Tell me how you are and how my sister and my poor mother
are. Her unfortunate fate is more haunting than mine. Try to do
everything you can to help her as I cannot do anything. To go back
to the matter of the previous letter, we are really poorly dressed. I
need you to send one of your old jumpers, one or two ties,
preferably black as we only have black wool ties that hurt our neck
like the devil. One thing that would be even more useful is a pair of
shoes and a pair of stocks. The heat and these big boots are the
cause of many wounds on my feet. Since your old coat is of no use
to you, you would help me very much by turning it into a pair of
pants. We only have grey canvas pants at the present. Do not forget
to send me interesting books. It is all I need and it is well enough as
you would say. But you cannot refuse this to your brother. It is the
biggest thing you can do because our pay is only of five *sous* every
five days. Half of it goes for soap, to clean our trousers, and to buy
all these little things to keep our weapons in a good state. About
food, I cannot complain. At the military kitchen, you eat enough.
Anyway, if you can do a little package, you can give it to a boatman
that we know [. . .].[62]

Soldiers also lent money to their colleagues. As Jean-Henri-Joseph
Moÿse[63] explained, lending to others sometimes led to difficult situations:

Chambery [Savoie, France] 18 May 1812

My very dear brother
As for Degueldre.[64] He is really not worth talking about because he
is a wicked person, my friend. He always borrows money in the
cabarets or asks for money from everybody and he never gives
anything back. Once, he asked me for money while walking from
Liège to Grenoble. I lent him fifteen francs. He promised to give it
back once in Grenoble. In Grenoble, he did not give anything back.

---

61. Jean-Guillaume Cordier was born in Liège in January 1793. He volunteered for the 3rd Hussars
before being conscripted.
62. AEL: FFP 1044. Jean-Guillaume Cordier to his brother, 11 August 1811.
63. Jean-Henri-Joseph Moÿse was born in Ougrée on 20 October 1791. He was conscripted into
the 5th Regiment of the Line on 1 June 1811. He survived the Napoleonic Wars and came home in
1814.
64. A letter written by Degueldre can be found in Chapter 6.

I had to be cunning to recover my money. In Marseille, I heard that he had received a postal order. I came straight to the sergeant-major and asked him if it was true. He told me that it was and I asked him to keep my fifteen francs on his postal order. This is how I recovered my money. In Marseille, he was acting as the domestic for our surgeon. One day, our surgeon gave him a shirt to clean and he [Degueldre] sold it. He even asked the captain for money and did many other things. He still owes nine francs to Lallemand[65] of Sclessin and to many other people [. . .].[66]

As a result of poverty, even eager soldiers changed their mind about the army. Jean-Léonard Mafat, whose two enthusiastic letters were reproduced at the beginning of this chapter, warned his parents:

Bayonne [in France, near the Spanish border] 16 December 1807

[. . .] Here is my advice: do whatever you can to prevent my brothers from serving in the army. It is such a misery to be a soldier. It is not even that I dislike serving but soldiers are too poor and too unwell [. . .].[67]

Léonard Colsoul[68] wrongly assumed that he was leaving for Russia and prepared for the event of his death:

Versailles 22 *frimaire* year XIV [13 December 1805]

Dear father,
I hope your health is better than mine. Since I arrived in this country, I had a fever and lost half of my weight. I am without money and lost half of my belongings. I had to sell my watch to improve this pathetic situation. I hope that you can relieve me, dear father, and send me three Louis. They will be useful as I am about to leave for Russia. If I am killed by the Russians, I leave everything to Catherine Evrard [. . .].[69]

A few soldiers were interested by a career in the army and wanted to climb the promotion ladder. Men who could read and write quickly reached

---

65. Nicolas Lallemand, born in Ougrée on 4 September 1791, was conscripted into the 5th Regiment of the Line on 1 June 1811. He was discharged on 17 June 1814.
66. AEL: FFP 1042. Jean-Henri-Joseph Moÿse to his brother, 18 May 1812.
67. The original letter has disappeared but the text was reproduced in Anon., *La Vie Wallonne*, Liège, 1930–1, p. 146.
68. Léonard Colsoul was born in Landen on 9 September 1785. He tried to flee conscription but was arrested and sent to the 5th Dragoons. He was later discharged at an unknown date.
69. AEL: FFP 1044. Léonard Colsoul to his father, 13 December 1805.

the rank of corporal or even sergeant. Others used their relations to progress in the military. Etienne Bailleux[70] was one of the very few soldiers who were awarded the coveted Legion of Honour. The following letter strongly suggests that he flattered his superiors to gain personal advantages:

Lebrÿa [perhaps Lebrija, Spain] 1 April 1812

Dear father and mother

[. . .] Mister Henault said to me in Seville that my brother Noel is an officer and that you forbade him to tell me. Mister Henault is not in the regiment anymore. He left for France. Our colonel has been captured with other men of our regiment at Arroio Malino [Arroyomolinos, near Madrid].

I would give you more details but I am afraid that this letter, important to know how you are, might be intercepted. My horse died two months ago and as a result I am at the depot. The regiment is out of Extremadura and is in front of Cadiz. I am seven leagues from there. I had to walk for sixty leagues to reach the depot and my belongings, being on the wagons of the regiment, have been pillaged. A surgeon gave me some of your letters. He told me that he found them in the room where they left the supplies of the regiment. I only have one shirt left. I have not received anything for a year and they will not give me new clothes. See how well I am.

Mister Servais[71] is also at the depot. He was very ill for three or four months but he is now better. I am very happy that he is here because he does everything he can to introduce me to non-commissioned officers and he talks to the officers about me. He is very well regarded and he is doing that to prove that I should not be with the *chasseurs*. He also found a room in the city for me while all the other *chasseurs* sleep at the depot. I would like to show my gratitude [. . .].[72]

Becoming a non-commissioned officer or an officer had obvious advantages, as Nicolas-Joseph Counen[73] explained to his family:

Requana [Requena, near Valencia] 11 September 1812

---

70. Etienne Bailleux was born in Liège on 3 June 1788. He volunteered for the Belgian light horse regiment in 1807. He received the Legion of Honour on 25 February 1814 and the Order of the Lys on 4 August 1814. Bailleux was reformed as a foreign citizen on 21 August 1814.
71. There were three people named Servais and serving in the regiment: Antoine-Joseph Servais, Henri Servais and Henri-Joseph Servais.
72. AEL: FFP 1043. Etienne Bailleux to his parents, 1 April 1812.
73. Nicolas-Joseph Counen was born in Jalhay on 15 June 1778. He was conscripted into the 20th *Demi-Brigade* during the year VII (1798–9). By 1813, he was a *sous-lieutenant*.

[. . .]. I have to tell you that I was made a non-commissioned officer on 16 June. This is a great advantage. I do not have to carry my backpack or my musket anymore and my pay is doubled. It is also easier to become an officer now than it was when I was sergeant [. . .].[74]

Soldiers commonly wrote about living conditions or food but were much more reserved about their love lives. They would break this silence on exceptional occasions. In a letter to his parents, Martin-Joseph Detif[75] hinted that he had a girlfriend in Switzerland:

Geneva 20 November 1811

My very dear father, mother and sister
[. . .] The girls in Geneva are really prettier than the women back home. I go for walks with one of them. It is really cold in Geneva and the winter is strong. There is snow all year round on the mountains and there is at least twenty feet of snow. In Geneva, at least three quarter of the city is protestant but there is one Christian [he means Catholic] church. [. . .] I was thinking about joining the cavalry but the cavalry left. I am happy and we are quite pretty. I would not like to be back home and I prefer to be a soldier than to break my arms in the woods [. . .].[76]

A year later, a romance had developed and Detif told his mother that he wanted to marry a Swiss woman. He also described the rather complex love triangle, involving another Swiss girl and his cousin serving with him in the French army:

Geneva 22 December 1812

[. . .] My very dear mother, I am very happy to say that I have a pretty friend [the complexity of the French language is lost in the translation. He means girlfriend]. My friend, corporal Godinas[77] of Louvegnée, has also a very nice girlfriend, the daughter of a *broqualle* [Walloon word meaning match] merchant. My friend and I are very unfortunate because the priest refused to marry us.[78] [. . .] Could you tell me if the girls back home behave like the women of

---

74. The original letter, in the AEL collection, was stolen. This is an extract from Fairon and Heuse, *Lettres de Grognards*, p. 293.
75. Martin-Joseph Detif was born in Soiron on 5 February 1791. He was conscripted into the 60th Regiment of the Line on 24 October 1811 but was transferred to the 10th Regiment on 10 February 1813.
76. AEL: FFP 1043. Martin-Joseph Detif to his parents, 20 November 1811.
77. Hubert Godinas was a bricklayer from Louveigné. He was conscripted into the 60th Regiment of the Line in 1811.
78. A Calvinist priest would indeed refuse to marry Catholic soldiers to Protestant girls.

the *rue de la Boulle*?[79] Please tell me the truth on that matter. [. . .] Cousin Janette, I need to tell you that Hubert Godinas, my corporal, still loves you. If it was not for the merchant's daughter, I think he would become mad. He says to me every day that you are so nice and have so much talent and even more spirit.[80]

Napoleonic soldiers were away for so long that women occasionally got tired of waiting. Nicolas Joseph Evrard[81] heard from the person he had replaced as a conscript that his fiancée had married another man:

10 October [1808]

[. . .] I have to ask you to send my regards to Jean Hanri Gerion and Martin Pirre Pirot[82] and all my friends and have to say that I am very happy that my mistress [he means fiancée] married. I wish her happiness and end this letter by kissing you with all my heart.[83]

Others tried to keep the flame of romance alive. Augustin Moyaerts[84] wrote a long love letter to a woman named Marianne. A Flemish-speaking farmer, Moyaerts probably asked someone else to write the following letter for him:

On board the *Trajan*[85] 27 August 1812

My dear Marianne, this travel causes me displeasure because I am far from you. It seems to me that I have no interest in anything since I left you. Nothing interests me except if it relates to you. There is not even one thought that is about something else than you. I am not afraid because being away will not stop you from loving me, you said so yourself. I have such esteem for you that I cannot doubt the sincerity of your virtue. I feel perfectly safe about your fidelity but I am sad to be away. The reasons for which I love you are tormenting me. Miss, these days without you are lost. You must

---

79. This is rather obscure. *Rue de la Boulle* (or Bowl Street) was probably a place where prostitutes worked. Detif, who was obviously sexually active in Switzerland, presumably realised that the women at home might behave like him.
80. AEL: FFP 1042. Martin-Joseph Detif to his mother, 22 December 1812. The content seems to suggest that Hubert Godinas, and not Martin-Joseph Detif, wrote the letter.
81. Nicolas-Joseph Evrard was born in Andrimont on 29 November 1781. He volunteered to replace Jean-Baptiste Géréon. The rest of the letter, in which he describe the massacre of civilians in Spain, is reproduced in Chapter 4.
82. Jean-Henri Géryon from Malmedy and Martin Pierre Pirotte from Stavelot, both friends of Evrard.
83. AEL: FFP 1042. Nicolas Joseph Evrard to the person he replaced, 10 October 1808.
84. Augustin Moyaerts was born in Laer on 20 August 1789. He was conscripted in 1809 but tried to escape military duty. He was arrested and sent to the 4th *Régiment d'Artillerie de Marine*.
85. There was a ship named *Trajan* in the French Navy but she was broken up in 1805. It is perhaps a homonym or was misidentified by Moyaerts.

know how impatient I am to finish travelling. Your letters comfort me in my exile. I am your most faithful and tender servant. I received your letter on the fourth of this month. I was very pleased to know that you are in perfect health. I am well and we left for Antwerp. As soon as we arrived, we embarked again. I hoped to come home before embarking but I also hope to see you during winter. I end this letter by kissing you. With all my heart, I am for life your faithful friend. Greetings to your father, mother, brother and sister.[86]

Sex was even more taboo. For most soldiers, it was unthinkable to admit using the services of the prostitutes who accompanied each unit, having temporary adventures with foreign women or raping innocent victims.[87] François Paquay[88] was unusual in that respect. He defied social conventions of the times when he openly expressed his sexual frustration to his parents:

Mendenne [Minden, North Rhine-Westphalia, Germany] 12 November 1811

My very dear father and mother
[. . .] You know that I was libertine before leaving for the army. I am still the same but I am really unhappy because I cannot understand what the girls say in this country [. . .].[89]

Conscripts found it easier to admit sexual relations when writing to someone other than their parents. Dieudonné-Lambert Wéry[90] described to his sister what he and another friend had done on the road after leaving home for the regiment:

Frankfurt [Frankfurt am Main] 28 May 1812

Dear sister
I am happy to say that I am in a very good health and hope that you are well. My regiment left for Mainz the twenty-first at four in the morning and arrived at eight. I wanted to cross the Rhine but they did not let me [he was going home, having been granted a leave] [. . .]. I finally reached Verviers [Belgium]. The day after leaving you, I

---

86. AEL: FFP 1044. Augustin Moyaerts to Marianne, 27 August 1812.
87. Forrest, *Napoleon's Men*, pp. 140–1.
88. François Paquay was born in Seraing on 3 March 1791. A farmer, he was conscripted into the 8th *bataillon bis du train d'artillerie* on 23 August 1811.
89. AEL: FFP 1044. François Paquay to his parents, 12 November 1811.
90. Dieudonné-Lambert Wéry was born in Huy on 23 January 1788. He served in the 4th *Tirailleurs* of the of the Imperial Guard.

caught up my friend around Malmedy [Belgium, near the border with Germany]. He was on the road with two ladies from Verviers. No man could have been happier than him. When I caught up with him, he introduced me to one of the ladies. Apparently, they had worked hard and he was obviously very tired. I must say that travelling to Mainz was very entertaining.[91]

The same observation can be made of Alexandre Picard,[92] who wrote in a diary about his life in the Napoleonic armies. In 1812, he listed the most promiscuous women of Europe:

Here [in Russia], women are pretty and courteous but very dirty. They wear a short canvas dress and a cloak made of lamb skin but they are filled with fleas. On their feet, they have sandals held with rope and on their head a cloth made of marmot skin. These girls let you touch them easily, but not as much as Prussian women. If you cannot find a girlfriend in Prussia within a day, you are really worth nothing. Prussia is the brothel of Europe. Wurttemberg, Germany, Poland, Russia, this is the order. At the top, the Prussian girls: they are full of love.[93]

The parents of the conscripts occasionally mentioned sex, recommending their sons to live according to the principles of the Catholic Church. Soldiers, like Jean-François Couvet,[94] did their best to reassure them:

Strasbourg 18 April 1812

My dear parents
[. . .] You tell me that it is hard to live without me. I can tell you that it is the same for me. But you say that we need to accept and have faith in divine providence. Be assured that I will use the principles of religion to guide me my whole life. I know that it is impossible to be happy without them. Despite being a soldier, I will flee with horror the libertines, who could drag me in their crimes, and will only do my duty [. . .].[95]

---

91. AEL: FFP 1044. Dieudonné-Lambert Wéry to his sister, 28 May 1812.
92. Alexandre Picard was born in Villeneuve-le-Roi on 21 October 1791. He was conscripted into the 12th Regiment of the Line on 19 April 1811 but was captured by the Russians. He came home in 1814 and died on 13 August 1853.
93. A. Picard, *Le journal de route d'un soldat de la Grande Armée*, Gilly, 1946, p. 49.
94. Jean-François Couvet was born in Theux on 11 January 1792. He was conscripted into the 7th *Chasseurs à Cheval* on 27 March 1812 and later captured by the Allies. Couvet died in captivity in Russia or Hungary on 13 January 1814.
95. AEL: FFP 1042. Jean-François Couvet to his parents, 18 April 1812.

Duties and Events

If life in the army was sometimes monotonous, there were also opportunities to witness extraordinary events. In 1804, Bonaparte mobilised representatives of the states and the army to support the transition to the Empire. This propaganda campaign played a significant part in convincing the French people to abandon executive powers to Napoleon Bonaparte and his heirs. There were quite a few republican and former Jacobin officers in the army but they were too disorganised and had too many pro-Bonaparte soldiers under their command to oppose the proclamation of the Empire.[96] The senate invested the republican government with an Emperor on 18 May 1804 and the coronation of Napoleon as Emperor of the French took place on 2 December 1804. Lambert Stellingwerf,[97] a soldier of the Imperial Guard, was on duty during the coronation and in the following days:

Fontainebleau [France], *nivôse* year 13 [22 December 1804 to 20 January 1805]

Dear father,
[. . .] Two days before the coronation, I slipped on a patch of ice and hurt the thumb of my left hand. It is very unfortunate because another injured finger was just starting to heal. The New Year is coming and I want to thank such a nice and generous father, without forgetting mother and the family. As long as I live, you will be dear to me.

I cannot explain in details the celebration because there would not be enough paper in Fontainebleau. I just have enough paper to describe the Emperor's stay in Fontainebleau. It reminded people of the old regime and there was nothing more spectacular than the court. We were so close that we could see everything.

In the evening, we saw the maids of honour going through the corridors to salute the Empress. These ladies were dressed with such luxury. Only another woman could criticise them.

In the morning, we saw the Emperor walking and hunting with only a few of his generals. I told myself that it would only take one individual to deprive France of her dearest.

In the evening, there was a concert. That day after the ball, I was on guard duty at the door and it made me think of the redoubts in Liège. I still hope to see them again, not as a soldier, but with a rank that would reward my determination [. . .].[98]

---

96. Philip Dwyer, 'Napoleon and the Foundation of the Empire', *The Historical Journal*, 53 (2010), pp. 339–58.
97. Lambert Stellingwerf was born around February 1786 in Liège. He volunteered for the *grenadiers-vélites* of the Imperial Guard on 30 August 1804. Stellingwerf disappeared in Poland during the War of the Fourth Coalition.
98. AEL: FFP 1044. Lambert Stellingwerf to his father, January 1805.

Jean-François Godin[99] was in the French capital when he saw the Empress and the son of Napoleon:

> Nothing new in Paris, except that I saw the Empress and the King of Rome. There are no more talk of a revolution[100] but we patrol every night. I have done so twice already. I went to the museum and saw [the painting of] Goffin[101] receiving the cross [Knight of the Legion of Honour]. During this short stay in Paris, I have seen the main attractions. J. F. Godin[102]

Other soldiers were on guard duty in less glamorous places. Toussaint Walthéry[103] was waiting to invade the United Kingdom with the *Grande Armée* in Boulogne when he wrote the following letter to his brother in 1805:

> From the barracks of St Pierre Calais [France] 21 *thermidor* year 13 [9 August 1805]
>
> My dear brother
> This is the second letter and I do not understand why you are not answering me. If I have displeased you, please be friendly enough to say so in a letter. The lack of news is making me anxious. Answer me as soon as you can because we are about to invade England. I am poor my brother. At the camp, we do not have enough supplies. Bread costs nine *sous* for a pound. Everything else is unavailable and a beer costs ten *sous* a bottle.
> My dear brother, I am in such misery and I suffer a lot. It is perhaps my last letter because I can see my grave in front of my eyes. We are at the camp, sleeping on the floor and being cold. We are carrying our weapons from morning to evening and we often fight. All of that is very hard my dear brother. I kiss you ten thousand times and I am your brother for life.

From May 1806, the British used their naval power to blockade France and her allies. Napoleon answered by implementing a large-scale embargo

---

99. Jean-François Godin was born in Amay on 11 April 1793. He was a surgeon when he was conscripted into the Imperial Guard on 2 December 1812. He disappeared in 1813. See also Chapters 5 and 6 for other letters by Godin.

100. Here, Godin talks about an attempt to seize power by General Claude-François de Malet (1754–1812). Malet was executed for this on 19 October 1812.

101. Hubert Goffin was a miner from the region of Liège. He became a hero when he tried to save fellow miners in an accident on 28 February 1812, an act for which he received the Legion of Honour. Godin probably saw a painting by Bordier du Bignon.

102. Moreau, 'Le remplacement d'un conscrit amaytois de 1813', p. 115.

103. Another letter and a biography of Toussaint Walthéry can be found in the next chapter.

on British trade across the Continent in November of the same year.[104] Many soldiers were stationed on the Atlantic coast of France to protect the ports from English incursions. Conscripts were so excited by the sight of an English ship that they made sure to tell their families. Jean-Baptiste Joseph Lonnay[105] was one of them:

Saint-Malo 28 September 1808

My very dear father, mother, brother and sisters
[. . .]. While we were in Renne [Rennes], the English tried and failed to take Saint-Malo. Since there are not many soldiers in the city, we came back to guard the city. We can see them [the English] every day on the sea and they sometimes come to greet us with their cannons [. . .].[106]

François Joseph Bourguignon[107] bragged even more:

Laguillon [L'Aiguillon-sur-mer, Vendée, France] 27 April 1807

My very dear father and mother
[. . .] We left the Île de Ré a long time ago but I do not think that we will stay a long time where we are. I think that we will join the *Grande Armée*. We are very happy to be back on the great land [mainland France]. Where we are, we are always ready to fight the English. They come near the coast to debark but they do not dare to do so because we would knock them down. [. . .][108]

Staying on the coast was not always comfortable, as Simon Pip[109] explained:

Lilse Daiz [Ile-d'Aix], 10 October 1806

My dear parents,
Here is the certificate that you asked for.[110] I feel happy that my brother can avoid military duty. Despite being miserable, I find

---

104. François Crouzet, 'Wars, blockade, and economic change in Europe, 1792-1815', *The Journal of Economic History*, 24 (1964), pp. 567–88.

105. Jean-Baptiste Joseph Lonnay was born in Amay on 24 June 1789. Drafted into the 86th Regiment of the Line on 6 May 1808, he disappeared in Spain on 31 January 1809.

106. AEL: FFP 986. Jean-Baptiste Lonnay to his parents, 28 September 1809.

107. François Joseph Bourguignon was born in Landenne on 1 September 1786. A conscript of 1806 in the 26th Regiment of the Line, he was wrongly accused of desertion in 1811 but had in fact died of fever in Spain on 31 August 1811.

108. AEL: FFP 1042. François Joseph Bourguignon to his parents, 27 April 1807.

109. Simon Pip was born in Saint-Vith on 3 September 1784. A wigmaker, he was conscripted in year XIII (1804–5) and sent to the 26th Regiment of the Line. He was discharged in 1814. Pip, a German speaker, probably asked a friend to write this letter in French.

110. The certificate stating that Simon Pip was serving in the French Army and used to exempt his brother Michel Pip, a shoemaker born on 29 May 1787, from military duty.

satisfaction in making my brothers happy. My dear parents, can you imagine that, due to the lack of straw, we have been sleeping for five months in the sand? We had some straw but we had to throw it to the sea as it had turned into manure. Everybody was sick or dead; wounds and sickness were everywhere. On 25 September, six hundred men of our battalion left on four frigates and brigs[111] to join the regiment in America.[112] Tell the parents of Matias Berque of Crombach that their son left for Martinique. He says farewell. Everybody embarked except for our company. We almost went on three different occasions but each time we were lucky. Our battalion has now only two hundred strong men but we are waiting for the conscripts of year 15 to arrive. We really want to leave our tents and go back to France to stay under a good roof. These, my dear parents, are the recent events. Thanks God for not falling ill since I became a soldier. Despite having been on a boat for six weeks without setting foot on the ground, I have always been well. I kiss you with all my heart. Give my regards to all the family and to my friends, brothers, and sisters. I am forever your respectful son Simon Pip.[113]

Simon Pip was extremely lucky. The convoy mentioned in his letter was spotted on 25 September 1806, soon after having left the port of Rochefort, and intercepted by Commodore Sir Samuel Hood. All the French ships were captured and the soldiers on board were either killed or taken as prisoners to Great Britain, where they stayed until the fall of the French Empire.[114] As this chapter showed, the life of a soldier stationed in France was not easy. However, it was nothing compared to the conditions endured during a campaign.

This chapter has described everyday life in the armies. There is no doubt that this intense experience was far removed from the romantic vision born during the middle of the nineteenth century. Soldiers were often poorly dressed, dirty and exhausted. They sometimes wore civilian clothes and had to pay for their own equipment. Memoirs published during Louis Philippe's reign and the Second Empire generally concentrate on battles. These vivid explosions of violence were far more spectacular and memorable than years of duty in a military camp. With time, veterans

---

111. The registers of the 26th Regiment of the Line mentioned the following frigates and brigs: the *Armide*, the *Hermione*, the *Glorieux* and the *Lynx*. The register also said that they left on 15 September 1806 but were captured by the British Navy. This information was not entirely accurate. The squadron was composed of five frigates (*Gloire, Minerve, Armide, Infatigable* and *Thétis*) and two corvettes (*Lynx* and *Sylphe*. Simon Pip called them brigs). William James, *The Naval History of Great Britain, Volume 4: 1805-1807* (London, 2002), p. 262.

112. It was in fact an expedition, led by Commodore Eleonore-Jean-Nicolas Soleil, to bring supplies and reinforcements to the French West Indies. James, *Naval History Vol. 4*, p. 148.

113. AEL: FFP 1042. Simon Pip to his parents, 10 October 1806.

114. James, *Naval History Vol 4*, p. 262.

usually forgot about the hardship and the boredom. However, these letters remind us that the men spent most of their time training or guarding coastal cities rather than fighting the enemy. In fact, combat was not a common occurrence.

Everyday life in the army was not an entirely negative experience. There is no doubt that hardship, military discipline and homesickness were difficult to endure, but it was also a time of discovery and friendship. As demonstrated in the previous chapter, many conscripts enjoyed travelling and exploring new countries. They were the first generation to experience foreign cultures on such scale. This new life allowed them to enjoy greater sexual freedom, far from the moral boundaries of the church and the family. Many formed tight bonds with their comrades, strong friendship only met in times of danger and duress. Together, the men escaped reality with the help of food and, more importantly, alcohol.

Chapter 3

War against the Austrians, the Russians and the Prussians

Marengo and the Occupation of Italy

When Bonaparte seized power on 18 *brumaire* year VIII (9 November 1799) France had already been at war for years. Even the collapse of the First Coalition in 1797 had not prevented Britain from continuing the conflict against the Republic. France was also threatened by Austria, unsatisfied by the treaties of Leoben and Campo Formio. Together with the British and the Russians, the Austrians formed a second coalition at the end of 1798 aimed at bringing down the French Republic.[1] Their plan was simple: multiple offensives from different fronts to overwhelm the French armies. This strategy initially worked, putting the French in a difficult position during the first half of 1799. Yet the coalition lost the advantage when André Massena defeated the Austrian and Russian armies at the second battle of Zurich (25–26 September 1799). This decisive victory led the Russians to abandon the coalition, leaving the British and Austrians in an uncomfortable situation. By 1800, the Austrians had been defeated by Bonaparte in Italy and were on the defensive in Germany. The war would go on until 1802, but the French had survived the worst.[2]

Only a handful of letters survive from this early period. The most interesting of these was written by a labourer named Simon-Joseph Lepersonne,[3] who fought at the battle of Marengo on 14 June 1800. He wrote to his mother soon afterwards:

> From Lemon [probably Limone, Lombardy] 12 *thermidore* year 8
> [31 July 1800]

1. Karl Roider, 'The Habsburg foreign ministry and political reform, 1801-1805', *Central European History*, 22 (1989), pp. 160–82.
2. Edward Ingram, 'The geopolitics of the first British expedition to Egypt – I: the cabinet crisis of September 1800', *Middle Eastern Studies*, 30 (1994), pp. 435–60.
3. Simon-Joseph Lepersonne was born in Theux on 1 March 1778.

My very dear mother

[. . .] During the month of jerminal [*germinal*], we left for Dijons [Dijon] and then, as soon as we arrived, we were asked to go to Switzerland where there was a lot of snow. We passed by a mountain named Mount St Bernard, where there was more than twenty feet of snow. After entering in Italy, we fought every day. We were at the forefront of the army of Italy; general Bonpard [Bonaparte] always walked at the front of the army and encouraged us by saying: 'Courage my brothers, we fight for glory and for Gaul's peace. We will have victory'. My very dear mother, despite all the rivers and forts, we conquered in two months what [word missing] took one year to take.

We began with the fort of Bort [Bard, Aosta Valley][4] which we defeated in fifteen days. The enemy destroyed the bridges on four different rivers but we crossed them nonetheless. We took Milan[5] in one day. We fought days and night for two days in a city named Laudit [Lodi, Lombardy].[6] There, we crossed a river that was at least two hundred feet wide. We crossed it on board of small boats equipped with small pieces [of artillery]. We left for Plaisance [Piacenza, Emilia-Romagna][7] at two in the morning. We arrived after having marched for at least seven hours. We were really tired but we fought from noon until eleven in the evening without eating or drinking. We were brought back until the next day. At seven in the morning, we attacked the enemy until the evening. We left and we crossed a river named Paut [Po], three leagues from the city. We attacked them from behind. Then we besieged the fort of Tourton [perhaps Tortona, Piedmont] and we marched to Alexandrie [Alessandria, Piedmont].[8] When we arrived in the field, we attacked the enemy who had forty thousand men.[9] We were driven back three times but then we returned and pushed them back. We took three thousand prisoners, eight flags and twenty-four cannons.[10] I cannot tell you how many men were lost on both sides. Some say that at least twenty thousand men were out of action, either killed or wounded. My dear mother, you cannot believe how much we suffered but I thank God for preserving my life and sparing me from being wounded. Of my detachment, the son of Franquinais of

---

4. The fort of Bard, near the Great Saint-Bernard pass, was besieged from 19 May to 2 June 1800.
5. Milan was captured on 2 June 1800.
6. Lodi, capital city of the province of Lodi, Lombardy.
7. Piacenza is the capital of the province of Piacenza, in the north of Italy.
8. Allessandria, capital of the province of Allessandria, Piedmont.
9. The battle of Marengo, 14 June 1800.
10. The Austrian army had 29,000 men, of which 963 were killed, 5,518 wounded and 2,921 captured. Thirteen guns were also taken. The French had 28,127 men, of whom 1,100 were killed, 3,600 wounded and 900 captured or missing. Digby Smith, *The Greenhill Napoleonic Data Book*, London, 1998, pp. 186–7.

Doneux was killed as well as the son Inglaibert of Juslanville. All
the others are well. Lebout and Janson and Collettre Pouhaut and
the son of Chavois send their regards to their parents. Waaffe of
Sonson is with us and the son of Widare[11] is in the dragoons. They
too send their regards to their parents. We all hope to come back
with the triumphant laurels of victory. My dear mother, this is all I
can tell you for now. Italy is in the hands of the French with the
exception of Mantoue [Mantua, Lombardy] and Bres [Brescia,
Lombardy] [. . .].[12]

Following the victory of Marengo, Bonaparte ordered the creation of
the second Cisalpine Republic, replaced by the Italian Republic on 26
January 1802 and by the Kingdom of Italy in March 1805. This kingdom
was created out of various former territories of the Austrian Empire, the
Venetian Republic and the Papal States and was administered according to
the French model.[13] Despite the peace of 1802, French armies remained in
Italy. Soldiers, such as Lambert Stellingwerf,[14] tried to describe this distant
country to their families:

Milan 23 *ventôse* year 13 [14 March 1805]

Dear father
I do not know why you are not answering but I guess it is because
I am travelling to Italy. Such a beautiful trip is quite uncommon. Of
all the countries I have seen, the worst was Savoy, where I did not
have a bed for eight days. I hope that *mardi gras* was better for you
than for me as I was at the moment going through Mont Cenis. It
was not as hard as I had anticipated. I do not know why we are
travelling so much. It seems like there is going to be a King of Italy
[. . .].[15]

The War of the Third Coalition
On 25 March 1802, the French and the British signed the Treaty of Amiens,
putting an end to almost ten years of hostilities between the Republic and
the United Kingdom. Both countries had good reasons to seek peace: the
French hoped to strengthen their new regime; the British wanted to

---

11. Jean-Pierre Lebout, Jean-Baptiste Jason and Nicolas Pouhaut all served in the 9th Regiment of
the Line. Pouhaut died of fever on 2 September 1800. Jacques-Joseph Waaffe, of the 20th *Demi-
Brigade*, later deserted. Jean-Joseph Wudar served in the 6th Dragoons. All these men were from
the town of Theux.
12. AEL: FFP 1045. Simon-Joseph Lepersonne to his mother, 31 July 1800.
13. Alexander Grab, 'Army, state, and society: conscription and desertion in Napoleonic Italy (1802-
1814)', *The Journal of Modern History*, 67 (1995), pp. 25–54.
14. See the previous chapter for another letter and the biography of Lambert Stellingwerf.
15. AEL: FFP 1043. Lambert Stellingwerff to his father, 14 March 1805.

consolidate their industry and trade. There is no doubt that both nations were feeling the strain of war, but it is equally clear that the long-standing animosity was hard to overcome. The press in both countries played a significant role in fuelling the climate of suspicion by misrepresenting each other's intentions.[16] After months of uncertainty, Britain finally declared war on France on 18 May 1803. During the next years Britain tried to form a large coalition against Bonaparte, playing on the fact that the French First Consul was becoming increasingly suspicious in the eyes of other European nations. By ordering the execution of Louis Antoine de Bourbon, Duke of Enghien, on 21 March 1804, Napoleon had attracted considerable negative publicity among the aristocracy. The newly-formed Empire only increased fears that Napoleon had unlimited ambitions. By 1805, the British had succeeded in creating a coalition that once again included Austria and Russia.

Up until then, the situation had been quieter for infantry soldiers. Expecting to invade England, many dreamt of going home or being granted leave. It was not an easy task, as Hubert Rome[17] would soon discover:

Paris 26 *pluviose* year 12 [2 February 1804]

My dear father and mother
[. . .] My health is a bit better. I left the hospital on the 7 of this month. [. . .] I am trying to be granted a permission to go home but there is no way to have one at the moment. It is very difficult to obtain, even for those who live 10 or 15 leagues from Paris [. . .]. You can be assured, dear father, that I did everything to have it [a permission]. It was refused because the war is not over yet.

Here, Hubert Rome turned to another subject. He just heard that an attempt had been made by a royalist from England, Georges Cadoudal,[18] to kidnap the First Consul. Generals Moreau[19] and Pichegru[20] were also involved:

---

16. Simon Burrows, 'Culture and misperception: the law and the press in the outbreak of war in 1803', *The International History Review*, 18 (1996), pp. 793–818.
17. Hubert Rome was born in Momalle on 18 July 1778. He was conscripted into the 98th *Demi-Brigade* on 13 February 1799. He was discharged on 17 January 1804 and afterwards lived in Liège.
18. Georges Cadoual (1771–1804) was a *chouan* leader who left for England in 1799. He came back to France in 1803 to organise the kidnapping of Bonaparte but was discovered and arrested on 9 March 1804. He was sentenced to death and executed on 12 June 1804. Jean Tulard, *Dictionnaire Napoléon*, Paris, 1999, pp. 344–5.
19. Jean-Victor Moreau (1763–1813) was a general who had fought with Dumouriez and Pichegru. He was arrested in the aftermath of the Cadoudal plot but the lack of evidence led to a two-year prison sentence. Pardoned, Moreau left for the United States, before returning to Europe in 1813. He became an adviser to the Tsar but was wounded at the battle of Dresden and died of his wounds on 1 September 1813. Tulard, *Dictionnaire Napoléon*, pp. 347–8.
20. Jean-Charles Pichegru (1761–1804) was a general during the revolution. He joined the royalists in 1797 and was arrested after the plot against Bonaparte. He was strangled in his cell on 6 April 1804. Tulard, *Dictionnaire Napoléon*, p. 501.

I will tell you that three persons conspiring to kill the first consul Buonaparte [Bonaparte] were arrested in Paris. They were general Maureau; Dumourier[21] general in chief of the army in England and Pichegrus. We do not know what will happen to them [. . .].[22]

In August 1805, Napoleon turned his armies from the north of France to Germany to fight the new Austro-Russian menace. The War of the Third Coalition began with the Ulm campaign (October 1805), considered as one of Napoleon's finest strategic victories. Indeed, the French Emperor managed to surround and capture General Mack von Liebereich and his entire army. But France was not yet saved; the *Grande Armée* was apparently isolated in Austria, facing the threat of the Austro-Russian forces. The situation became even more dangerous when the Prussians signed the Treaty of Potsdam on 3 November 1805. According to this treaty, unless the French divided the crowns of France and Italy and also evacuated Switzerland, Italy, Naples, Holland and Germany, 180,000 Prussian troops would join the Third Coalition.[23] Napoleon moved swiftly to anticipate the ultimatum. On 2 December 1805, he crushed the Austrians and the Russians at the decisive battle of Austerlitz. Fought in difficult conditions, the battle brought victory and effectively obliterated the Treaty of Potsdam.

The soldiers tried to explain the events leading up to Austerlitz to their families, knowing that they had witnessed important moments. But describing large military operations and battles was not an easy task for these men, who were usually almost illiterate. More than often, their letters were a blur in which personal stories were mixed with rumours and exaggerations. Toussaint Walthéry,[24] a dragoon born in Embourg, fought in numerous battles during the year 1805, including Elchingen, Ulm and Austerlitz. Despite limited literary skills, the young man painted a lively portrait of the danger faced during the battle of Austerlitz:

Brenne 5 *nivosse* year XIV [26 December 1805]

My very dear father
[. . .] Since the last time I wrote to you, I left Calais to join the army of the Rhine. We did not give a moment of rest to the Austrian army,

21. Charles-François du Perrier du Mourier, also known as Dumourier (1739–1823) was a French general during the monarchy and the revolution. He won the battles of Valmy and Jemappes but changed sides soon after. He was living in England in 1804 but had nothing to do with Cadoudal.
22. AEL: FFP 1043. Hubert Rome to his parents, 16 February 1804.
23. Michael Leggiere, 'From Berlin to Leipzig: Napoleon's gamble in north Germany, 1813', *The Journal of Military History*, 67 (2003), pp. 39–84.
24. Toussaint Walthéry, born in Embourg (now Belgium) on 5 October 1780, was the son of Toussaint Walthéry and Marie-Jeanne Delsemme. He was conscripted during the year X of the Republic (1801–2) but, on his way to the military depot, tried to flee to avoid military duty. He was eventually caught and sent on 5 *vendémiaire* year XII (28 September 1803) in the 13th Dragoons. He survived the Napoleonic Wars and was sent home on 7 July 1814.

which we chased from all of its strongholds and even from its capital. We have fought hard since the crossing of the Danud [Danube][25] where twenty thousand people died and at Oumes [Ulm, Baden-Württemberg, Germany] where another thirty to thirty-five thousand soldiers were killed.[26] I will not give you details about the battles of Bath, Bille, Branaux and Passeaux and also Linzes, Lixze,[27] which were all very hard. They did not want to leave their capital and as a result forty-five to fifty thousand men died on both sides. At the battle of Bonne, we lost so many people because of the river. But I want to talk about the battle of Desterlix [Austerlitz], the biggest fight ever heard of. The three Emperors were there: the Emperor of Russia, the Emperor of Vienna [Austria] and the Emperor of the French. We began firing at six in the morning. The Russians and the Austrians answered five minutes after. The fire was so intense that it was impossible to see anything six feet in front of you. We retreated three times but the fourth time we managed to route the Russians and the Austrians. We fought against the Imperial Guard of Russia; they were very strong but we beat them. My horse was killed during the battle of Desterlix [Austerlitz] and I almost died but I fortunately took the horse of another dragoon who had just been cut in two by a cannonball. Forty thousand French, seventy thousand Russian and thirty-five thousand Austrians were killed at Desterlix [Austerlitz]. For Bresse, I do not know the losses. Dead bodies were buried for fifteen days but it is such a glory for me to have fought in so many battles and to have my horse killed without being killed. I have not received the postal order of 12 frans [francs] but I hope to have it soon so we do not worry. I end this letter by kissing you one thousand times with all my heart. I am forever your son Toussain Waltery. My address

To mister Toussain Waltery Dragon 13th rgt [regiment] 8th compe [company] great army of the Rhine in Moravia.

The bloodshed of the battlefield was not the only memorable fact that Walthéry chose to document. He ended his letter by commenting on local women, a source of curiosity and amusement:

---

25. In fact, the Danube. He is writing about the battle of Elchingen, on 14 October 1805, and is exaggerating the casualties. The French lost (dead or wounded) fifty officers and 800 men. The Austrians lost 6,000 men. Smith, *The Greenhill Napoleonic Wars Data Book*, p. 204.

26. Here Toussaint Walthéry is again exaggerating the losses. At the battle of Ulm, on 15 October 1805, the French lost 150 men. Austrian casualties were unknown but the entire army at Ulm totalled 20,000 infantry and 3,200 cavalry. All of them were captured. Smith, *The Greenhill Napoleonic Data Book*, p. 205.

27. All these names are wrongly spelled as Toussaint Walthéry was almost illiterate. The 13th Dragoons fought at the battle of Schöngraben on 16 November 1805.

Many greetings to Hubert Oroge of Angleur [Belgium].[28] Give me news of the country, especially of those who have been conscripted, and of everything in general. I will tell you that I am in a country where they do not speak German or French. Women have the faces of monkeys, the arms of dogs and the feet of camels. They are so beautiful that I want to bring one home. This is it, I am done. I salute you. We are 400 miles from Liege [Liège].[29]

Mass casualties on the battlefield made an impression on most soldiers. Their letters suggest that they were shocked by the scale of the carnage but also pleased by the extent of the French victory. For Henri-Joseph Rousseau,[30] who fought with the 96th Regiment of the Line at Ulm and Austerlitz, the number of casualties was a means of describing the scale of the battles in which he had fought:

The city of Frankfurt [Frankfurt Oder], 21 February 1806

My very dear father,
This letter to let you know that my health is perfect and I hope the same for you and all the family. I want you to know that I wrote from the city of Passau [Lower Bavaria] but I assume that you have not received the letter since I have not received any news, probably because all the postilions' horses were taken by the troops. I also need to tell you that at the battle of Houlme [Ulm], we fought with our bayonets for one full day. The Emperor thought that our division was lost since we were only 6,000 men against 25,000. Despite the important number of enemies, we managed to retreat with honour. But then we received reinforcement from the carabineers and the Consular Guard.[31] We chased them up to Vienna. After Vienna, we fought again at Storlieze [Austerlitz] where many people were lost; 70,000 men died on the battlefield. My very dear father, the reason that I have not written earlier is that we were always on the road. For the moment, we are based in the city of Frankfurt.[32] As I have used all my personal equipment, I would like you to send the usual sum of money [. . .].[33]

28. Angleur, now a suburb of Liège, Belgium.
29. AEL: FFP 1044. Toussaint Walthéry to his father, 9 October 1805.
30. Henri-Joseph Rousseau, a nailer born on 21 September 1782, was the son of Mathieu Rousseau and Marie Isaye. Conscripted in year XII (1803–4) into the 96th Regiment of the Line, he deserted on 1 December 1811.
31. Rousseau was still using the old name. By 1806, he should have referred to the Imperial Guard.
32. As previously stated, Frankfurt an der Oder, not to be mistaken with Frankfurt am Main.
33. Private collection. Henri-Joseph Rousseau to his father, 21 February 1906.

Pierre-Joseph Seronval,[34] of the 92nd Regiment of the Line, also fought at Ulm and Austerlitz. Like the others, he struggled to describe the events but clearly felt proud for having taken part in the defeat of two Emperors:

From Sividal, Venise [Venice] 9 May 1806

My dear father and mother
[. . .] I am sorry for not giving news for such a long time but we were constantly on the move. We left Nimegue [Nijmegen, Netherlands] and embarked on a boat. We stayed a month on the boat when we heard that war had been declared against Austria. We left immediately for the army of the Rhine. When we faced the enemy we fought different important battles. God has always preserved me and I thank him. So, we fought several important battles, as you must have heard. Our first battle was the blockade of houlme [Ulm]. We did good as we captured 25 thousand men and killed another five thousand. The weather was not in our favour because it was raining a lot. We stayed for six days in the field without being able to shelter from the rain. After we had defeated the Austrian armies, we carried our march to Vienna. We fought different battles but it is not useful to write how many men we killed or captured. Let us just say that when we took Vienna, there were one hundred sixty thousand men either killed or taken prisoner. After Vienna, we continued toward Moravia, where we fought the biggest battle of the campaign,[35] and where the war finished. I cannot exactly tell how many men were killed on the battlefield but it looks like we put out of action more than fifty thousand men, killed, wounded, or captured. I cannot tell you how many cannons and how much ammunition we took but there were convoys leaving for France for two months. Believe me when I tell you that the battle was cruel. Three Emperors were commanding; there was the French one, the Austrian one and the one from Russia. The Emperors of Russia and Austria were almost captured but they took opportunity of the night to flee. After these events, we stayed for a month in Stirie [Styria, southeast Austria] where we rested. Then we left for Venisse [Venice] where it was excessively hot. There are mountains and therefore snow in all

---

34. Pierre-Joseph Seronval was born in Liège on 18 March 1781. Drafted during the year X (1801–2), he was sent to the 98th Regiment of the Line in year XI (1802–3). When this regiment was disbanded, he joined the 92nd Regiment and, on 23 June 1813, the 151st Regiment. He survived the Napoleonic Wars and was sent home in 1814.
35. He is referring to the battle of Austerlitz.

weathers. We marched on a mountain where we saw clouds below us and we marched 560 leagues without stopping.

Seronval ended his letter by giving news of a friend, also from Liège, who had deserted for the Austrian army. It is not known how Seronval would have received news from the Austrian lines:

> I have nothing else to tell you for now. Give my regards to Marie Caterine Palatte and to her family. A big kiss to her. Tell the mother of Michot[36] that he is not serving France anymore. He deserted to join the Austrians. He told me that he is well and he gives you his regards [. . .].[37]

Austerlitz decided the outcome of the war and the fate of the dying Holy Roman Empire, which was formally dissolved on 6 August 1806.[38] The Treaty of Pressburg, signed by the Habsburg monarchy on 26 December 1805, redrew the map of central Europe by giving sovereignty to Bavaria, Baden and Württemberg. This treaty was a clear humiliation for Prussia and the rest of the coalition. With sixteen German states now forming the Confederation of the Rhine, Napoleon was stronger than ever in central Europe.[39]

The War of the Fourth Coalition
Ten months after the Treaty of Pressburg, Prussia, Russia, Saxony, Saxe-Weimar, Brunswick and Hanover were at war with France. Relations between France and Prussia had soured over the fate of Hanover and various other issues. Prussia, confident in her military ability, had almost joined the third coalition before its destruction at the battle of Austerlitz and was now feeling ready to face the French Emperor.[40] The war was a problem for Napoleon who wanted peace to consolidate his regime. It was an even bigger concern for French soldiers who were hoping to be demobilised and were looking forward to seeing their loved ones and resuming their former professions. The new conflict, now known as the War of the Fourth Coalition, came as a blow for most of the men. Pierre Bux,[41] a labourer

---

36. Benoit Michaux, a nailer born in Liège on 21 March 1781. He was conscripted in year X (1801–2) into the 98th Regiment of the Line.
37. AEL: FFP 1043. Pierre-Joseph Seronval to his parents, 9 May 1806.
38. Peter Wilson, 'Bolstering the prestige of the Habsburgs: the end of the Holy Roman Empire in 1806', *The International History Review*, 28 (2006), pp. 709–36.
39. Katherine Aaslestad and Karen Hagemann, '1806 and its aftermath: revisiting the period of the Napoleonic wars in German central European historiography', *Central European History*, 39 (2006), pp. 547–79.
40. Karen Hagemann, 'Occupation, mobilization, and politics: the anti-Napoleonic wars in Prussian experience, memory, and historiography', *Central European History*, 39 (2006), pp. 580–610.
41. Pierre Bux was a labourer born in Beho on 22 May 1781. He was drafted into the 98th *Demi-Brigade de Ligne* (later the 92nd Regiment of the Line) on 29 October 1803. Bux died of his wounds in Arad (Hungary) on 27 August 1809.

serving with the 98th Regiment of the Line, was on his way from Italy to Eastern Europe when he wrote a letter to his parents, in which he betrayed his frustration:

Tolmeza [Tolmezzo, north-eastern Italy] 24 September 1806.
[. . .] It is very cold in the mountains, where we walk barefoot and have no money. We are far from France and we are resigned to a new war. We are currently in a miserable country; the mountains are currently covered with snow and you have to believe that we are really miserable . . . We are so miserable that, in our regiment, we have not received money for five months and we are barefoot [. . .]. We were hoping to return to France soon, but we have received other orders. Once more, the war has been declared against all other powers. Each day, we expect to fight the Austrians. I ask you to keep me informed about the country and tell me if the boys have left [for the army]. In this country, they take those from 18 to 25 [years old], despite the fact that the country has been recently conquered. They do not even organise a draft but take everybody.[42]

Pierre Bux was just one of the many soldiers who complained about their lives. Men were unhappy about the food, the tiredness and even the countries in which they were. As seen earlier, leave was hard to get, especially when war was raging. The letter sent from Warsaw by Jean-Matthieu Collignon[43] to his father was poorly written but conveyed both nostalgia and frustration. It was also the last letter he sent home before he died, probably of disease, in Warsaw on 3 April 1807:

Varsauvie [Warsaw, Poland] 26 December 1806

My very dear father
I did not write for a long time because we have been chasing the enemy for three months, days and nights, without stopping. I can only write now that we are in Varsauvie [Warsaw] in Pôlongne [Poland]. There are no more Prussians but there are still many Russians. We do not know when we will be back to France. We are so miserable. Everything is so expensive in this country [. . .].[44]

---

42. Private collection. Pierre Bux to his family, 24 September 1806.
43. Almost nothing is known of Jean-Matthieu Collignon. There is only one report concerning his death in Warsaw on 3 April 1807.
44. AEL: FFP 1043. Jean-Mathieu Collignon to his father, 26 December 1806.

Jacques-Joseph Beaumont[45] was also in an uneasy position. His mother wrote to let him know that she was struggling without his help at home and that his brother might also be drafted. Urged to ask for leave, Beaumont had no other choice but to tell the truth:

Verona [Italy] 3 February 1807

My dear mother
[. . .] You must let me know if my brother is safe from conscription. My dear mother, what you are asking is impossible. I would be very happy to be with you and help you as I know that you need me back home. For the present, you are only discharged when you suffer from severe disabilities [. . .].[46]

Jean-Joseph Levaillant[47] had been arrested as a draft-dodger and sent to the 5th Battalion of the Genie (Engineers) at the beginning of 1807. He wanted peace to be signed as soon as possible so he could see his family:

Mainz 7 January 1807

My very dear father, mother, brother and sister
I was very happy to receive your letter and I am pleased to read that you are all well. I am very fine, thanks to God, and I travelled for twenty days. The journey went well and I have to wish you a very happy new year, filled with much happiness. I will ask God to preserve you so we can meet again. I have been waiting for a long time to see you again and I hope that we can be together again. We beat all the powerful people and I hope that we can be discharged by our lord the Emperor after this war. I would like peace to come.
   This is what I desire the most. I believe that you are the same [. . .].[48]

Morale might not have been high but French soldiers were nonetheless ready to fight. The Prussians, on the contrary, were unprepared and would endure several humiliations in the months to come. The French struck the first blow of the 1806–7 campaign at the battles of Jena-Auerstädt (14 October 1806), where the Emperor and his men crushed Prussian and Saxon armies twice as large as their own. On 24 October, the *Grande Armée*

---

45. Jean-Joseph Beaumont was born in Saint-Georges on 6 January 1785. He was conscripted into the 93rd Regiment of the Line on 3 January 1806 but recognised as invalid on 21 June 1810.
46. AEL: FFP 1042. Jacques-Joseph Baumont to his mother, 3 February 1807.
47. Jean-Joseph Levaillant was born in Angleur on 11 September 1784. He was conscripted in year XIII (1804) but hid. He was finally arrested in 1807 and sent to the 5th Battalion of *genie*. It seems that he was sent home a few months later.
48. AEL: FFP 1044. Jean-Joseph Levaillant to his parents, 7 January 1807.

entered Berlin, forcing the Prussian royal family to flee.[49] The humiliation continued with the capture of the fortresses of Küstrin and Magdeburg, on 1 November and 8 November respectively. Having knocked the Prussians out of the war in a matter of days, Napoleon turned his attention to Russia. The battle of Eylau (7–8 February 1807) ended in a draw but the Russians were then crushed at Friedland (14 June 1807).

Gaspard Leva[50] was in Warsaw when he described the beginning of the campaign and the battles of Jena-Auerstädt to a friend:

From Warsaw 7 December 1806

To Mister Jonquer[51]
My very dear friend,
[. . .] We have marched a long way. We began with the Austrians and we took Vienna, capital city of Austria, without much difficulty. We fought a battle fifty leagues from Vienna, the battle of Dosterlis [Austerlitz]. It was a bloody battle. We went to Bavaria in garrison for six months and we were very well. We did not think that war against the Prussians would happen but we were wrong. We left Bavaria on 26 September to fight the Prussians but we only met them on 14 October.[52] We fought quite a bloody battle but my company was lucky; we did not lose anybody, thanks to God. Our army corps suffered a lot and some of our regiments suffered many casualties. After that, we took the capital city of Prussia, Berlain [Berlin], without firing one shot. We are currently in the capital city of Polongne [Poland], where there is a huge river. The Prussians and the Russians did not have time to destroy the bridge. They were on one side of the bridge and us on the other. We managed to chase them and we are waiting for the bridge to be repaired to continue. We have two army corps taking them from behind. There are about fifty thousand Russians and Prussians soldiers trapped. Prussians soldiers are surrendering each day.[53]

Antoine-François Pirenne[54] fought at the battle of Friedland, where he was wounded and captured by the Russians. Released the next year, he wrote to his parents:

---

49. Hagemann, 'Occupation, mobilization, and politics'.
50. Gaspard Leva was a farmer born on 24 March 1780 in Bettincourt. He fought in the 1st Battalion of the *train d'artillerie*.
51. Probably Jean-Joseph Jogen, born in Liège on 2 June 1787.
52. The battles of Jena-Auerstädt were both fought on 14 October 1806.
53. AEL: FFP 1042. Gaspard Leva to Jonquer, 7 December 1806.
54. Antoine-François Pirenne was born in Herve on 11 March 1784. He was conscripted into the 21st Dragoons in year XIII (1804).

Hanover, 4 February 1808

[. . .] I have to tell you that I was captured at the battle of Konnisber [Königsberg] and stayed in captivity for eight months. This is why I did not write for so long. I returned to the regiment two months ago [. . .]. I was hit in the leg at the battle of Kinisber [Königsberg], my horse was killed, and two bullets entered my bearskin [. . .].[55]

Thomas-Joseph Charlier,[56] of the 65th Regiment of the Line, took part in the whole campaign. He described it in details to his parents:

Warsovit [Warsaw] 26 November 1807

Dear father and mother
[. . .] I have to tell you about the significant distance we covered and the great misery we faced during this war. We were leaving from Nimegue [Nijmegen] to Vessel [Wesel, North Rhine-Westphalia, Germany] when the war against Russia and Prussia was declared. We stayed at the camp of Vessel for a month. From there, we left for Galicia and Honover [Hanover], going through different countries. We marched days and nights and we also went through Hamburg, a big port. From there, we came to Enllam, a Prussian city on the border of Seleci [Silesia]. We crossed the bridge and entered their country. We searched [the enemy] until strasant,[57] which we besieged for two months, despite the snow, the mud and the cold. From there, we received orders to leave to help the *Grande Armée* in Poland. On 28 March, we arrived at Lynsten [in fact Danzig] where we established a camp. We stayed there for two months. [Words missing]. On 28 June, the army, three hundred thousand men, was on the move. We captured some prisoners and were searching for the main force. We were marching days and nights, without drinking or eating and sometimes for 40 hours without a stop, when we arrived at Goodstud [Guttstadt].[58] We were three hundred thousand and the Russians five hundred thousand. We both fought like dogs and we both lost many men. From there, they left for Voot where there was another big battle. It is impossible to tell how many people were

55. AEL: FFP 1043. Antoine-François Pirenne to his parents, 4 February 1808.
56. Thomas-Joseph Charlier was born on 14 March 1784 in Antheit. He was a labourer when he was drafted. Refusing to serve in the French army, he was arrested and sent to the 65th Regiment of the Line on 21 July 1806. He became a corporal in 1812 and a sergeant in 1813. Like most Belgian conscripts, he became a foreign citizen of France in 1814 and was sent home.
57. He is talking about the siege of Stralsund, lasting from 15 January to 20 August 1807. His regiment did not take part in the whole siege.
58. The battles of Guttstadt and Deppen took place on 5 and 6 June 1807, where 17,000 French fought against 63,000 Russians.

killed. From there, they left for Königsberg,[59] an important port belonging to Prussia. We also took this city, still without drinking or eating. The Russian army retreated to Vredland [Friedland][60] where they lost many more people. They were forced to capitulate at Tilzyt [Tilsit] on 16 July.[61] Forty leagues from there, the Emperors of Russia and Prussia reviewed the French troops.

[. . .] Following the review, the Emperors of France and Russia made peace and we entered Tilzyt [Tilsit]. We were altogether with Russian troops named cosack [Cossack]. They were well-dressed. There was another nation named calmock [Kalmyk, currently the republic of Kalmykia, Russia]. It is a nation of total savages who eat no other meat than horse, which they eat raw. After fifteen days in the city, we left for Warsovit [Warsaw], capital of Poland, where we are now. Dear father and mother, it is impossible to tell how thirsty, hungry and tired I was during this war. I stayed for 12 or 13 days without eating bread [. . .].[62]

The treaties of Tilsit, signed on 7 and 9 July 1807, put the War of the Fourth Coalition to an end. The Tsar of Russia would now enforce the Continental System and accept the creation of the Grand Duchy of Warsaw, based on Prussian territories. Frederick William of Prussia saw his kingdom and population halved and was to lose everything west of the Elbe River. Berlin was also supposed to follow the Continental System, a crushing blow for its economy. Another humiliation was imposed on Prussia with the Treaty of Paris, signed in 1808, designed to limit the size of its army.[63] The destruction of the Fourth Coalition was a source of contentment for Napoleonic soldiers. Henri-Joseph Rousseau, already encountered earlier in this chapter, expressed mixed feelings about the outcome of the war. Visibly proud to have defeated the enemy, the young man was also tired, happy to be alive and probably concerned at the prospect of having to fight the Swedes:

Berlin 26 August 1807

My dear father
I write this letter to tell you how I am at the present. I have not heard from you in a long time. In your last letter, you were well and I hope that it is still the case. My health is, as usual, very good despite the

---

59. Königsberg was attacked on 14 and 15 June 1807.
60. The battle of Friedland, on 14 June 1807, saw 66,000 French fighting against 84,000 Russians.
61. The treaties of Tilsit were signed on 7 and 9 July between the French, the Russians and the Prussians.
62. AEL: Ville de Huy Varia (VHV). Thomas-Joseph Charlier to his parents, 26 November 1807.
63. Leggiere, 'From Berlin to Leipzig: Napoleon's gamble in north Germany, 1813'.

assaults, the tiredness and the dangers that I faced during the campaign. My comrades and I are now in a camp to rest. We are all relieved that we won against those who tried to defeat us. Part of the French army stayed in Poland to maintain order but the other is resting on the border of Prussia. We are waiting to see what happens with the Swedish. If there is no agreement in a month or six weeks, we will go back to war. The Russians and the Prussians have unwillingly accepted peace [. . .].[64]

The prospect of peace was an encouraging thought for many soldiers who dreamt of going home. The War of the Fourth Coalition was not even over when Jourdan Lambert[65] was thinking about seeing his loved ones:

They [the officers] promise us peace and I hope that I will be granted a temporary leave so I can have the sweet satisfaction of seeing my respectable family.[66]

Jean-Joseph Danthinne,[67], already encountered in the previous chapter, also hoped that peace would bring changes:

Brescia 3 August 1807

[. . .] There is peace with Prussia and Russia. This happened on 8 July[68] and they say that they might grant leaves for those of year 7 and year 8.[69] But they say so many things that are not true! Some say that we will leave for Boulogne en mer.[70] I really would like to leave Italy because the heat is unbearable and water is so bad and so dangerous.[71] I am not happy. They say that Bonnepart [Napoleon Bonaparte] will be there this month and that he will inspect the regiment. The vice-King[72] is there and we have been inspected [. . .].[73]

The French army also fought on other fronts during the War of the Fourth Coalition. In 1806 and 1807, Marshal Masséna led the conquest of the Kingdom of Naples in an attempt to put Joseph Bonaparte on the throne. The initial operation went well but the French soon encountered fierce guerrilla

---

64. AEL: FFP 1043. Henri-Joseph Rousseau to his father, 26 August 1806.
65. See Chapter 2 for his biography.
66. AEL: FFP 1042. Jourdan Lambert to his parents, 26 July 1807.
67. See Chapter 2 for his biography.
68. In fact, the peace of Tilsit was signed with Russia and Prussia on 7 and 9 July 1807.
69. The conscripts of 1799 and 1800. But this was a rumour as they served until the fall of Napoleon.
70. This is another rumour. His regiment, the 53rd of the Line, stayed in Italy until at least 1811, except for the war with Austria in 1809.
71. Indeed, hundreds of soldiers from the Ourthe department died of fever in Italy.
72. Eugène de Beauharnais, the son of Empress Josephine and Napoleon's stepson.
73. The rest of the letter can be found in Chapter 2.

resistance. The country was eventually pacified, but not without costly battles against insurgents. Pierre Cajot[74] was wounded during the campaign:

Alessandria 30 August 1807

My very dear father and mother
[. . .] I would be grateful if you could send the money that you promised in your last letter. You need to send it as soon as possible. You need to tell me if my brother is safe from conscription and if he is well and if there is anything new at home. You must know that I will be discharged as my finger was mutilated after six hundred galley slaves of Naples revolted. One musket shot went through my hand and I cannot serve anymore. *De sodart min co bon po al caq de ri* ['Not even good to be a soldier.' This sentence is in Walloon.] [. . .].[75]

The War of the Fifth Coalition
The victory over the Fourth Coalition gave Napoleon no respite. Turning his attention to Portugal and Spain, the French Emperor would soon face difficult challenges in the Iberian Peninsula – a subject covered in the next chapter. The Austrians took the opportunity of the Peninsular War to open another front in 1809. Attempting to mobilise pro-Habsburg feelings in the German-speaking territories, Francis I, the Emperor of Austria, previously known as Francis II of the Holy Roman Empire, recruited prominent writers and newspapers. This attempt to rally the 'German nation' failed and once again the French armies marched east.[76] Jean-Lambert-Joseph Saive,[77] a sapper, described the journey from France to Austria to his mother:

Vienna 28 bre [September] 1809

[. . .] When we arrived in transbourg [probably Strasburg], we received cartridges as we feared bandits, but there was nothing. [. . .]. After crossing the Rien [Rhine], we were fed by peasants. But 30 leagues from Vienna, we were rationed because people had abandoned the houses and many were burned. Small towns and villages were all burned. During these days, we were not so well. We were also very tired during the great wave of heat, especially when

---

74. Pierre Cajot was born in Hermée on 2 November 1788. He volunteered for the 93rd Regiment of the Line on an unknown date and was discharged in 1808.
75. AEL: 1043. Pierre Cajot to his parents, 30 August 1807.
76. Michael Rowe, 'France, Prussia, or Germany? The Napoleonic wars and shifting allegiances in the Rhineland', *Central European History*, 39 (2006), pp. 611–40.
77. Jean-Lambert-Joseph Saive, born on 1 June 1790, was drafted in the 4th sapper battalion. He was reported as a deserter at the end of 1809 but was in fact at the hospital of Lintz, where he wrote the letter reproduced above.

we crossed the Rien [Rhine]. We had to march 10 to 12 leagues with the backpack; it was very tiring. Thanks to God, I kept my good health. Now, it is very quiet and nobody speaks French. I think that they [the enemies] are 20 leagues on the other side of Vienna [. . .]. God preserved me from disease. Many are ill and feverish or have other things [. . .].[78]

Nicolas-Joseph Evrard,[79] serving in the light cavalry, also described his journey. Unlike many others, he was not a conscript but a substitute paid by a wealthy family to replace a son who had been drafted. Evrard wrote to the head of the family to complain about the lack of money but also took the opportunity to describe his life in Germany:

Sir,
Having arrived in Brunsuik [Brunswick], I write to tell you that my health is good. I hope the same for you. I have no money and ask you to send one *Louis d'or* [a gold coin]. Unfortunately, someone stole two *Louis* from me and I have been without money for a long time [. . .]. I have already written two times but have received no news. I am very angry because I do not think I have caused you offence. I am doing this military duty for you and I left willingly to replace your son.

I am very happy because I am very well in this country, even better than in my own, although we passed by a quite rebellious place. The people fired at us when we were sleeping. We had to take our weapons to bed. We would not eat before someone had tried the food because we feared poison. We went by a town called Sansse [Sens], in Burgundy, which we visited. We saw very strange bells, one was 30,000 [probably the weight] and the other 28. We did not need to climb a lot to see them, only 800 feet [. . .] 11 June 1807.[80]

The War of the Fifth Coalition should not be simply understood as yet another victorious Napoleonic campaign but as a transitional phase for the Allies, one during which they learned and applied valuable strategic lessons. By 1805, the French had fully adopted the army corps system, dividing the *Grande Armée* into seven formations of all arms. This organisation proved extremely successful during the 1805–7 campaigns. Understanding that their

---

78. AEL: FFP 1045. Jean-Lambert-Joseph Saive to his mother, 28 September 1809.
79. Nicolas-Joseph Evrard was born on 29 November 1781 in Andrimont. He joined the 26th *Chasseurs à Cheval* as a substitute for Jean-Baptiste Géréon on 25 March 1807.
80. AEL: FFP 1042. Nicolas-Joseph Evrard to the family of the substituted, 11 June 1807.

armies were outdated, the Austrians introduced various reforms in 1805–9, including the adoption of the corps system. For the first time since the beginning of the Napoleonic Wars, the Austrians would be able to fight back.[81]

Just over a month after the beginning of the War of the Fifth Coalition, the French and the Austrians met at the battle of Aspern-Essling (21–22 May 1809). A bloody encounter, the battle was also the first defeat for Napoleon in over a decade. The outcome came as a shock for the Emperor and his men. This commotion was visible in their letters, now filled with stories of dying friends or lucky escapes – but not of glorious moments. Antoine Philippet,[82] of the 63rd Regiment of the Line, fought at the battles of Ebersberg and Aspern-Essling. His close friend died in his arms:

In Austria Weissa 19 December [1809], near Salmbourg

To Mr Pasqué Anthon Anthonÿ[83]
[. . .] We are now one hundred leagues from Vienna and we hope to come back to France soon. We are quartered and drink and eat the farmer's geese. I quite like being a soldier and thank God for not having been wounded during a battle, despite having fought on three occasions and three days in a row. You must know that Gilles Grisar[84] was killed on my left during the battle of Eversber [Ebelsberg]. I wanted to bring him back but he died in my arms. Guillimme Barée of Juprelle was also killed [. . .].[85]

Pierre Henrotte,[86] serving with the 4th Regiment of the Line, also lost friends at the battle of Aspern-Essling:

My very dear father,
I write this letter to enquire about your health [. . .]. My very dear father, Jan Wilemme died and Tilman Bovendalle[87] was killed on 22 May. My dear father, I was left alone but, thanks God, I have not been wounded. I have to tell you that my comrades on my left and

81. Robert Epstein, 'Patterns of change and continuity in nineteenth-century warfare', *The Journal of Military History*, 56 (1992), pp. 375–88.
82. Antoine Philippet was born on 20 March 1787 in Paifve. He was not a conscript but a substitute.
83. Probably Jean-Pascal Antoni, a member of the local council of Paifve.
84. Gilles Grisard, born in Paifve on 30 July 1786, was the son of Jean Grisart and Marie Hardy. He was killed at the battle of Ebelsberg on 3 May 1809.
85. AEL: FFP 1042. Antoine Philippet to Jean-Pascal Antoni, 19 December 1809.
86. Pierre Henrotte, a farmer born on 20 December 1788 in Glons, was sent to the 4th Regiment of the Line in 1808. He was captured in Russia on 16 November 1812.
87. Tilman Bovendael, born in Glons on 22 January 1789, was conscripted into the 4th Regiment of the Line on 9 December 1808.

on my right were both killed. My very dear father, Jan Willeme[88] died at the hospital; he was ill [. . .].[89]

Guillaume-Joseph Jeunechamps,[90] who also fought at the battle of Aspern-Essling, was extremely lucky to survive both a wound and a close encounter with a cannonball:

Vienna, August 1809

My very dear father and mother
I did all the battle and I only had one little wound at the thigh. I went for three weeks to the hospital and I could not write because it was too far away from the city. I am now one league from the city. I need to tell you that my backpack was hit by a cannonball. I have lost all my belongings. I have nothing else to add except that it is a great misery to be a soldier.
    My very dear father, I do not have money and I need to buy new personal belongings. During the battle of 22 May, there were only 19 men alive in our company [. . .].[91]

Jean Spirlet,[92] who also lost his backpack in battle, tried in his own clumsy words to describe the chaos of war. He was killed in action[93] six weeks after writing the following letter:

Vienna Austria 19 May 1809

My very dear father and mother,
I write to enquire about your health. Mine is very good, thank God, and you should know that we are at the present in Austria. Concerning my brother's certificate, it was not possible to send one so early. Please tell my brother that I did everything possible to have him reformed. My very dear father, we are so tired. Many of my comrades were wounded. My very dear father and mother, the one who wrote my previous letter was killed. My backpack was

---

88. Jean Willem, born on 8 October 1788, was in the 63rd Regiment of the Line. He died of his wounds on 22 August 1809 in Znaïm, Moravia.
89. AEL: FFP 1042. Pierre Henrotte to his father, 26 October 1809.
90. Guillaume-Joseph Jeunechamps was born in Aywaille on 26 April 1785. A farmer, he was conscripted in year X (1801–2) but tried to hide. He was arrested in 1809 and sent to the 63rd Regiment of the Line. He was killed at Fuentes de Onoro (Spain) on 5 May 1811.
91. AEL: FFP 1042. Guillaume-Joseph Jeunechamps to his parents, August 1809.
92. Jean Spirlet was born in Jupille on 17 January 1790. He worked as a gunsmith before being conscripted into the 18th Regiment of the Line on 8 March 1809. He was killed in action in Austria on 6 July 1809.
93. His family was not informed of his death for a long time. An 1811 report shows that Spirlet's parents thought he was still fighting with the 18th Regiment of the Line. AEL: FFP 1051. Individual report, 1811.

destroyed but despite this unfortunate moment I was lucky enough
to find another one on the battlefield [. . .].[94]

Napoleon regained the initiative by winning the battle of Wagram (5–6
July 1809), but not without losing 18 per cent of his army. The Austrians
also suffered mass casualties, probably about 27 per cent of their men.
Pierre-Léonard Thomas,[95] an artilleryman, fought at Wagram. The few
words that he wrote about the events on 6 July were enough to allow us to
imagine the chaos:

16 January year 1810 Baiefor [Belfort]

[. . .] I crossed the Rien [Rhine] on 10 May 1808 and again on 4
January 1810. We saw some cruel battles, such as the ones on 3 and
6 July. We could not see anything else but fire and smoke and
cannonballs were falling like snow. But thanks God, nothing
happened to me [. . .].[96]

The fact that Thomas was impressed by the intensity of the fire is not
surprising. As Epstein reminded us, 'the French and Austrian armies were
subjected to a volume of artillery fire never before experienced'.[97] Henri-
Joseph Pasteger[98] was also at Wagram. A cavalryman, he was in the heart
of the action and was almost killed twice:

Vienna 1 August 1809

My very dear father and mother and all the family. [. . .].
My very dear father, I am very well, thanks to God. God kept me
alive during all these battles. I need to tell you, my dear father, that
during the last battle that happened on 6 July, I was extremely lucky to
survive. Two horses were killed under me. The last one was killed by a
cannonball, entering through its shoulder and exiting from its side.
When the cannonball went out, it took a piece of my boot and my
stirrup. A little piece of my skin was ripped but it is nothing, thanks to
God for not being wounded. My very dear father, we are based in a
village around Vienna. I do not know if we will stay long because we
do not know if there will be peace with the Austrians [. . .].[99]

---

94. AEL: FFP 1043. Jean Spirlet to his parents, 19 May 1809.
95. Pierre-Léonard Thomas was born in Boncelles on 11 November 1789. He was conscripted into
the 1st *bataillon principal du train d'artillerie* in 1808.
96. AEL: FFP 1042. Pierre-Léonard Thomas to his father, 16 January 1810.
97. Epstein, 'Patterns of change and continuity in nineteenth-century warfare'.
98. Henri-Joseph Pasteger was born in Fléron on 29 December 1789. He was sent to the 1st
Carabineers on 6 May 1808.
99. AEL: FFP 1044. Henri-Joseph Pasteger to his parents, 1 August 1809.

Joseph Schumacher[100] served as a cuirassier during the War of the Fifth Coalition. In his native German, he tried to describe the intensity of the battlefield to his brothers:

Fulde 27 March 1801 [in fact 1810]

My very dear brothers!
[. . .] I was in many battles and I have many things to tell you. My first horse was killed and the other was taken by the Austrians. I fled. A cannonball broke two legs of my third horse and I fled again. I cannot tell you everything because I would need a whole day. I really would like to know why you do not write. I think that you have forgotten me. I beg you to write so I can know how you are.

I would like to get entertained and it would be kind if you could send money [. . .]. I do not know where we are going but it might be Spain or Holland. I cannot tell because we are in Frankfurt am Main [. . .].[101]

The war ended with the signing of the Treaty of Schönbrunn on 14 October 1809. Austria once again paid a heavy price for her opposition to the French Emperor. A considerable part of her territory went to France and her allies. Napoleon even married Marie-Louise, the daughter of the Austrian Emperor, in a bid to secure an alliance, or at least eliminate Austria as a threat. However, there was no rest for the French, who still had to deal with the chaos in Spain and Portugal.

In this chapter, we have looked at the letters describing the wars against the Third, Fourth and Fifth Coalitions. It is clear that military violence was a highlight in the career of a soldier. On the surface, it seems that many men enthusiastically wrote about combat on the battlefield and boasted about the apparent invincibility of the French army. They did not hesitate to overstate enemy casualties and prisoners to embellish their victories. However, recreating a description of the battle was far from easy without a proper education. Many soldiers found it difficult to give an accurate account and struggled to express the horrific nature of violence. The letters sometimes hint at psychological trauma, especially after having narrowly escaped death, but never go into too much detail.

Soldiers were more vocal about the effects that years of service had on

---

100. Joseph Schumacher was born in Udenbreth (now Germany) on 6 September 1787. He volunteered to replace Joseph Jenniges in 1808 and served in the 1st Cuirassiers.
101. AEL: FFP 1044. Joseph Schumacher to his brothers, 27 March 1810.

their morale. Many men believed that the battle of Austerlitz would bring them home, but the formation of the Fourth Coalition in 1806 destroyed their hopes. Lassitude steadily climbed during the next years as soldiers struggled to understand why they were still fighting. The professionalisation of the Allies also troubled French soldiers. Many men lost a friend on the battlefield, an event common enough to be mentioned on several occasions from 1809 onward.

Chapter 4

The Peninsular War

The Conquest of Portugal and the Spanish Uprising

Although a major world power for hundreds of years, Spain was in a difficult position at the end of the eighteenth century. The country had a historical rivalry with France in continental Europe while her trade routes to the American colonies were threatened by the British. To ease her situation, Spain had signed the 1761 Family Pact with France in order to create a maritime bloc against Great Britain. The French Revolution brought this bloc to an end and encouraged the Spanish to join an anti-revolutionary coalition with the British. The subsequent conflict against France, known as the Pyrenees War, proved disastrous. After a few initial successes in 1793, Spain began to lose ground and was eventually forced to sue for peace in 1795. By May 1796, Spain was an ally of France and was at war with Britain.[1] This new alliance lasted until 1808 and saw, among other things, the Spanish fight alongside the French at the battle of Trafalgar.

French soldiers served in Spain from 1802. The following letter was written by a merchant who was arrested by the French army:

From Valladolid to the army of Gironde in Spain 10 *vendémiaire* year 10 [2 October 1801]

To the mayor of the borough
I left Liège for Saint-Jacques [Santiago] in Galicia with the passport that you gave me and that you sealed. I was unfortunate enough to be robbed by Spanish bandits. Spanish soldiers brought me to the French army's headquarter but since my money and my papers have been stolen, I cannot prove anything. I have been arrested as a deserter and I am imprisoned as such.

---

1. Charles Esdaile, 'War and politics in Spain, 1808-1814', *The Historical Journal*, 31 (1988), pp. 295–317.

As a result, I beg you, mayor, to ask for me to the chief of the army in Spain. They might send me to the navy if I do not provide the right papers [. . .].[2]

In 1806, Napoleon instituted the Continental System to prevent the British from exporting goods to continental Europe. Neutral Portugal was less than keen to comply as she had signed a treaty sealing an alliance with the British. On 2 August 1807, Napoleon ordered the creation of the I Corps of the Army of Observation of the Gironde, headed by Marshal Junot, to invade Portugal. Jean-Joseph Renier[3] was one among many soldiers waiting to move from his camp in the Pyrenees:

Castelnau 16 October 1807
Department of the *Hautes-Pyrénées*

My very dear father and mother
We left Versailles for Normandy on 30 August and then left again to fight in Portugal. We went through several beautiful cities in France and are now in Castelnau. I am now three hundred leagues of my country. Give my regards to my brothers, my nephews and nieces and to my uncle and aunt [. . .].[4]

François-Joseph Gilles[5] was also ready to leave France for Portugal and was obviously dreading the march:

Mannaien [probably Hendaye, near the Spanish border] 21 September 1807

My dear mother and father
[. . .] We left Lavandez [Vendée] for Balionne [Bayonne] and we are now staying with farmers. They tell us that we will leave for Portugal and we are close to Spain. If we leave for Portugal, we will have to march two hundred leagues and we are already three hundred leagues from home [. . .]. My very dear father and mother, I ask you to send money. It would make me very happy because I need it badly [. . .].[6]

---

2. AEL: Fonds Jarbinet. Vincent Destria to the mayor of Liège, 2 October 1801.
3. Jean-Joseph Renier was born in Beyne-Heusay on 12 December 1786. He was drafted into the 9th Dragoons on 19 April 1807 and died of smallpox at La Rochelle (France) on 22 October 1808.
4. AEL: FFP 1045. Jean-Joseph Renier to his parents, 16 October 1807.
5. François-Joseph Gilles was born in Petit-Hallet on 12 October 1786. He was conscripted in 1806 but fled while travelling to his regiment. He was eventually arrested and sent to the 26th Regiment of the Line in January 1807. He died in Bourbon-Vendée (France) in 1809.
6. AEL: FFP 1042. François-Joseph Gilles to his parents, 21 September 1807.

On 15 October 1807, Junot's corps crossed the border into Spain after having secured the permission of the Spanish government. Supported by 20,000 Spanish troops commanded by General Solano, the French army entered Portugal on 20 November. Portugal quickly collapsed; the royal family fled to Brazil with the help of the Royal Navy while the authorities offered no resistance to the invasion. Junot took Lisbon on 29 November without firing a shot. By December, the entire of Portugal was conquered but the population was angry. The first insurrection began on 13 December when Junot raised the French flag in Lisbon. The mob was easily dispersed by the cavalry but their anger only grew. A levy of 100 million francs and the seizure of 15,000 properties caused bitter resentment among the population. There are several letters mentioning the events in Portugal. Nicolas-Joseph Dujardin[7] was part of the initial invasion force:

Peniche Portigale [Portugal] 18 April 1808

My very dear father
[. . .] I am far away from you and the road leading to this country has been hard. We went through Spain and entered Portigais [Portugal]. All the peasants' houses were empty. They all fled and left behind their houses and possessions. We did not have any supply and had to cross many rivers. We camped in the countryside and in the woods and grouped to search for food near the camp. Because of the labours and the misery, many died on the road. We received supplies in Lisbon but did not stay there long. We only had half of our ration. For the moment, we can stay for days without receiving bread and it is already as hot here as it is at home in August. At Christmas and at the end of the year, we were swimming in the sea. As for the fruits, you can find here many oranges and figs, and laurel is as common as thorn bushes at home. Olive trees and vines are very common. My dear father, tell me what happened with the certificate for my brother Henri in your next letter.[8] I wish you a good Easter. An English ship showed just in front of our cannons and we fired at her [. . .].[9]

Jean-Joseph Renier,[10] already encountered in this chapter, similarly complained about the journey from France to Portugal:

---

7. Nicolas-Joseph Dujardin was born in Jupille on 2 February 1787. He fled after the draft but was later caught and sent to the 58th Regiment of the Line. He deserted on 30 April 1814.
8. The brother, Henri Dujardin, was born on 30 November 1783. A conscript of year XIII (1804–5), he fled before being drafted, was arrested, but fled again. He tried to be amnestied in 1810.
9. AEL: FFP 1042. Nicolas-Joseph Dujardin to his father, 18 April 1808.
10. See his 1807 letter for more details.

Lisbon, 3 May 1808

My dear father and mother
[. . .] I really suffered on the road but, thanks to God, I am now in Lisbon and I am well. I would like to know if my brother Leonard has been drafted. If it is the case, I will send a certificate to exempt him [. . .].[11]

The British army arrived in Portugal on 1 August 1808. The Royal Navy had already blockaded various Portuguese and Spanish rivers and ports since 1807 but the landing was a sign that the British were ready to intensify their pressure on the French in the Peninsula. François-Joseph Bourguignon[12] was one of the first French soldiers to mention British ships:

Faros 14 May 1808

My very dear father and mother
[. . .] It was pure misery and I had fever. I stayed in a hospital in Toulouse for six weeks but, thanks to God, I am now better. We went through Spain and Portugal. By the end of the campaign, we were really miserable and we had to sleep outside. We sometimes marched for ten days without finding a house. This is a country of mountains and forests and everything is really expensive except for fish, which is common. Bread is expensive and we have a bottle of wine per day. Otherwise, nothing important except that we are close to the sea. We can see the English every day. I ask you to answer as soon as you can and to give news of the little one [. . .].[13]

Meanwhile, Spain was in turmoil. Prime Minister Godoy faced an alliance formed around the heir to the throne and supported by several notables who wanted to reduce the power of the King. Godoy was even accused of wanting to seize the throne in the event of the death of Charles IV and later arrested for high treason. By the beginning of 1808, Napoleon had lost confidence in Spain as an ally and saw in the country's crisis the perfect opportunity to take direct action. In February, French troops were ordered to seize Madrid and the frontier fortresses. The Spanish army, confused and scattered, found itself entirely powerless. In this situation, the

11. AEL: FFP 1045. Jean-Joseph Renier to his parents, 3 May 1808.
12. There is another letter by Bourguignon and his biography in Chapter 2.
13. AEL: FFP 1042. François-Joseph Bourguignon to his parents, 14 May 1808.

royal family appealed to Napoleon to settle the dispute between Charles IV and his son Ferdinand. Meeting in Bayonne in April 1808, Napoleon forced both sides to step down and gave the crown of Spain to his brother Joseph Bonaparte. As a result, a series of revolts exploded all over the country and entire armies sprang up. Spain was a divided country with no other social or political agenda than resistance against the French.[14] In fact, the population turned against the occupier for various reasons. Some were just angered by Napoleon's treachery during the meeting at Bayonne, others were loyal to Ferdinand. The powerful Catholic Church also played a significant role in denouncing the French as atheists. The first rebellions were brutally crushed. Joachim Murat had hundreds of citizens of Madrid executed on 3 May 1808 in retaliation for the massacre of 150 French soldiers the day before. Far from intimidating the Spanish, these reprisals strengthened resistance all over the country. The situation in Spain was different from anything else encountered before; regular forces and irregular fighters prevented French soldiers from controlling the country. The deterioration of the situation forced Napoleon to rush thousands of soldiers to control the crisis. What began as a popular uprising would only end when the British, the Spanish and the Portuguese entered France at the end of 1813.

The 57th Regiment of the Line was in Madrid a month before the *Dos de Mayo* uprising. Four soldiers of the regiment, all from the same region and all conscripted on 24 July 1807, used one single sheet of paper to contact their families on 29 March 1808. These letters, written by the same hand, were obviously dictated. Jean-Joseph Jeunehomme[15] gave the longest account, primarily describing his journey from France to Spain. There was no mention of unrest or danger but an actual sense of relief of being in Madrid:

Madri [Madrid] 29 March 1808
Capital of Spain

My very dear father
[. . .] I am now in garrison in Spain. We were really miserable. We had to sleep in the snow for fifteen days and had to share a loaf of three pounds between 119 men. Now that we are in the city, the capital of Spain, we are a bit better.

---

14. Esdaile, 'War and politics in Spain'.
15. Jean-Joseph Jeunehomme was born in Latinnes on 17 February 1788. He was conscripted into the 57th Regiment of the Line on 24 July 1807. He was killed in action during the siege of Tortosa in Spain on 31 December 1810.

My very dear father, I cannot tell you where we are headed. Some say that we are going to Portugal but others tell us that we are going to sail back to France. Therefore, I cannot tell you where we will be [. . .]. We do not know if we are going to leave Spain. They say that nothing happens here [. . .].

Martin-Joseph Hela[16] focussed on his health problems:

My very dear father,
[. . .] You ask if my legs hurt. I have to tell you that I was really in pain. I could not walk for days [. . .].

Hubert-Joseph Dantinne,[17] already encountered in Chapter 2, was the cousin of Jean-Joseph Jeunehomme. He sent a very banal message to his family:

My very dear father
[. . .] I received your money. I have nothing else to say except that I am well. I kiss my father, my mother, my brother and my sister and all the members of the family and my friends.

Jean-Joseph Englebert[18] was equally brief:

Madrid Capital of Spain M 1808

My very dear father
[. . .] I have nothing else to say except that I am well. I kiss you with all my heart. I kiss my father, my sister and all the members of the family and my friends. Give my regards to those who ask about me.[19]

Four months later, Jean-Joseph Jeunehomme wrote again to tell his family about the deterioration of the situation. By then, Napoleon had dispatched columns to different parts of Spain to restore order. Marshal Bon-Adrian Jeannot de Moncey headed with 29,000 men, including Jeunehomme, toward Valencia. Despite failing to take the city in June, the worst was yet to come. Another French army, commanded by General Pierre Dupont, was crushed at the battle of Baylen in July 1808. This defeat forced the French to abandon Madrid and much of Spain to take cover behind the

---

16. Martin-Joseph Hela was born in Latinne, perhaps in 1783. He tried to avoid conscription but was arrested in 1807 and sent to the 57th Regiment of the Line.
17. See Chapter 2 for a biography and another letter.
18. Jean-Joseph Englebert was born in Vielsalm on 21 July 1788. He was conscripted into the 57th Regiment of the Line in 1807 but was later transferred to the 115th. He was badly wounded and discharged on 23 May 1809.
19. AEL: FFP 1042. Letter from Jean-Joseph Jeunehomme, Martin-Joseph Hela, Hubert-Joseph Dantinne and Jean-Joseph Englebert to their parents, 29 March 1808.

river Ebro, leaving Junot behind in Portugal. In only a few months, the invader had already lost 40,000 men. Jeunhehomme told his parents about these events but was much more concerned about a personal matter: his cousin Dantinne had disappeared.

Miranda 29 August 1808

My very dear father and mother,
I received the postal order included with the letter sent to my cousin Dantinne but I have not received the money yet. I hope to receive it soon. About my cousin Dantinne, I have to tell you that he is ill and had to go to the hospital in Madrid. I do not know where he is as many ill soldiers stayed in Madrid. I fear that he stayed there. We had to retreat from the city because, as you know, all the peasants of Spain have rebelled and fight against us. We chased them up to Valencia but we had to retreat and ended twenty leagues from the French border. We are there for the moment but do not know if we are going back to France or are headed toward Madrid. I have nothing else to tell you at the present. Tell me if the conscripts are leaving our country and if there are friends among them [. . .].[20]

Jacques Willems,[21] who wrote in Flemish, fought at the battle of Baylen and witnessed the initial rebellion in the Spanish capital:

Madrid 1 June 1808

I am 550 leagues from home, in Madrid Spain. The journey was hard. We marched day and night, carrying heavy loads like horses, sleeping on the ground. We fought against 10,000 men, infantry and horsemen, and our general in chief stayed behind.[22] I am intact. The Spanish burned the barracks in Madrid on 1 June 1808[23] and the fire lasted for six days. We eat donkey meat. The bread is still good and in the afternoon, around four, we receive a good soup with rice and, every day, half a bottle of Spanish wine. We hope to get out of Spain because we cannot understand the Spanish. But we do not have cause to complain. Ask God and the holy virgin to keep me away from danger.[24]

---

20. AEL: FFP 1043. Jean-Joseph Jeunehomme to his parents, 29 August 1808.
21. Jacques Willems was born in Aubel on 21 October 1786. He was drafted in 1806 but tried to flee. He surrendered in 1807 and was sent to the 2nd Reserve Legion. Willems later disappeared. He was first thought to be a deserter but might in fact have been killed in Spain.
22. He is talking about the battle of Baylen. General Pierre Dupont was indeed captured.
23. Jacques Willems is probably talking about the *Dos de Mayo* on 2 May 1808. Obviously he could not have written on 1 June about events which took place from 1 to 7 June.
24. This letter was stolen from AEL: FFP. Fortunately, this extract had been reproduced in Fairon and Heuse, *Lettres de Grognards*, p. 168.

Laurent-Joseph Stembert[25] was part of the column headed toward Valencia. He wrote the letter in the Spanish capital a month before Madrid was abandoned by Joseph Bonaparte.

Madrid 2 July 1808

Since we arrived in Spain, we have not slept in a bed. What is more difficult is to see that comrades have their throat slit every day. Those who are unfortunate enough to stay behind the regiment are sure to be slain. It is really painful to be in such a country. Instead of going back to France, we go forward. We were near Valencia but had to retreat in Madrid, where we are at the present. We were only five thousand men against more than forty thousand who were waiting for us. We marched day and night, doing up to fourteen leagues a day. During this journey lasting eight days, we lost four hundred men. We are waiting for reinforcements to go back to Valencia. I think we will have more than one hundred thousand men. We are waiting for the order. I have to tell you that the city of Segovia[26] [central Spain] tried to rebel. We burned all of it. They had fifteen thousand Spanish gunners. They fled against our five thousand men. We took forty cannons. We killed all the people of the city, including women and children.[27]

The Spanish gained a brief respite with the French retreat to the river Ebro but failed to organise their army. The French were also in a difficult position in Portugal. Indeed, Junot's army was defeated by the British and the Portuguese at the battle of Vimeiro on 21 August 1808. All sides came to an agreement to evacuate the French from Portugal rather than to carry on the fight. The Convention of Cintra was signed to that effect on 30 August 1808. More than 20,000 French troops were evacuated from Portugal and conveyed to Rochefort by the Royal Navy, where they arrived in October 1808. Despite the loss of Junot's army, there was still a French presence in Portugal. London soon denounced the Convention as a clumsy act returning an entire army to Napoleon. Lambert Berlandeux[28] was among the French soldiers travelling with the British Navy. He told his parents that he was going back to Portugal:

---

25. Laurent-Joseph Stembert was born in Verviers on 22 December 1788. He was conscripted into the 2nd Reserve Legion on 15 June 1807. He died in Pamplona (Spain) on 11 February 1809.
26. The city of Segovia was indeed sacked in 1808.
27. This letter was also stolen from AEL: FFP. This extract came from Fairon and Heuse, *Lettres de Grognards*, pp. 168–9.
28. 28. Lambert Berlandeux was born in Liège in March 1787. He was conscripted into the 9th Dragoons on 7 March 1807. He came home in 1814.

Niort 17 December 1808

My very dear father and mother
[. . .] When I disembarked, I was covered with vermin. I had to borrow fifteen francs from my friends to buy new shirts and trousers. I ask you to send twenty-four francs to repay my debt. The rest will be useful for the campaign of Portugal. Answer as quickly as you can as we are going to leave soon. As for Regnier,[29] I do not know where he is. He was at the hospital in Lisbon when we left and I think that he was captured.[30]

François-Joseph Bourguignon,[31] who would later die in Spain, described the Portuguese campaign of 1808 to his family:

Bourdeau [Bordeaux] 4 December 1808

My very dear father and mother
[. . .] I am well at the present. I was a bit sick when I was on a boat at sea. It is really sad that I was not able to give news or to receive your letters. We went through Spain and entered Portugal quite easily. Soon after, Spain attacked us and the whole Portugal rebelled against us. We were very miserable in this country. The English sent more than sixty thousand men to attack us. There were massive battles where more than fifteen thousand French men died. Many others died at the hospital and we were so tired and had to sleep on the ground. We had to fight day and night. It is a good thing that the English came to attack us in this country. The bandits were everywhere and would have killed us all. We had to surrender to the English and they brought the whole French army on their ships. It was pure misery on these ships. We only have two or three ounces of biscuit and we often thought we would die because of the tempests on the sea. We stayed [at sea] for more than a month before reaching France but, thank God, we came back to France with great joy. I pray God for granting me the strength and the courage to endure tiredness and difficulty. I still have to tell you, my dear father, that Spain was in an important revolution but the French entered the country. Many men died but we hope that the situation will be better. We think that

---

29. Jean-Joseph Renier, born in Beyne-Heusay on 12 December 1786, was conscripted into the 9th Dragoons on 7 March 1807. He died of smallpox in La Rochelle on 22 October 1808.
30. AEL: FFP 1045. Lambert Berlandeux to his parents, 17 December 1808.
31. The biography and another letter by Bourguignon can be found in Chapter 2.

they are more than two million men headed to the country. We are marching to Spain and then to Portugal.

My address is the 26th Regiment of the Line 4th battalion 4th company, stationed in Baionne [Bayonne] [. . .]. Tell me who left for the army in our borough. I end this letter by giving you my regards, dear father and mother and brother and family and friends. I am your loving son François Joseph Bourguignon and I ask you to pray for me.[32]

Napoleon was determined to strike back to regain the upper hand in Spain and Portugal. The Emperor knew that the defeat of the French armies was the first of its kind since 1801. The evacuation of Junot, the battle of Baylen and the retreat of King Joseph were more than humiliating moments; they were inspiring symbols for the enemies of Napoleon in Europe.

Guerrilla Warfare

By September 1808, the French were building up their strength in Navarre and Catalonia while the Spanish were struggling with the complete collapse of any central government. Among the chaos emerged provincial governments called juntas. Jealousy and the desire for regional independence made it difficult to unite Spain. A *Junta Suprema Central* was finally established in Aranjuez in September 1808 but this attempt to recentralise national power was met with scepticism and in some cases hostility. Spain was not prepared for the storm to come.[33] Napoleon came to Spain personally in November 1808. He brought with him three corps from Germany as well as a detachment of the Imperial Guard and accelerated the recruiting of the class of 1810.[34] Four weeks later, Madrid was again in French hands. The defeat of the Spanish armies was not surprising since these regional troops had no coordination and were poorly led, badly disciplined and ill-equipped. The British, commanded by General Sir John Moore, tried to assist their ally but failed to turn the course of the campaign. Moore was killed at the battle of Corunna on 16 January 1809 and the British army escaped by sea to England two days later.

Laurent-Joseph Stembert, already encountered in the previous section, took part in the November offensive. Stembert, like most other French soldiers, was haunted by guerrilla warfare. These organised groups had become a problem for the French as early as April 1808. According to the historiography, more

32. AEL: FFP 1042. François-Joseph Bourguignon to his parents, 4 December 1808.
33. Esdaile, 'War and politics in Spain'.
34. Don Alexander, 'French replacement methods during the Peninsular war, 1808-1814', *Military Affairs*, 44 (1980), pp. 192–7.

than 50,000 Spaniards joined irregular units to fight the French during the Peninsular War.[35] This was partly the consequence of the occupier's violence toward the civilian population. Requisitions, looting, but also rapes and murders, did much to alienate them. Stembert's letters clearly highlight how the French and the Spanish engaged in an endless cycle of brutality:

> Sesma, 15 November 1808
> Spain
>
> My very dear father and mother
> [. . .] You say that you want to share my pain but I do not want you to worry. My misery will soon be over. Laurent Delvaux[36] received his letter and the postal order and he is well. The other friends are also well. As for Beaujean, I have not heard of him in four months. I have no idea of what happened to Bonivert.[37] We lost many friends and soldiers.
> Do not send money until I say otherwise because as soon as we take a city we eat all its food. Then, we use either bayonets or cannons to take another one. We care about nothing. It is true that we sometimes receive food but we are the masters everywhere. We fight bad soldiers. The priests lead the armies. The greatest evil comes from the monasteries and the churches. They fire [*foutre* in French, a vulgar word] with their muskets from the windows. They have cannons in the bell towers. We cannot fight them in the field as we would. They are only capable of hiding. Despite this misery, I hope that God will save me [. . .].[38]

The British had been driven from Spain but the war was far from over. Napoleon drafted a strategy before leaving the Peninsula for Germany at the end of 1808. The Emperor's plan was to pacify the last resisting Spanish provinces and let Marshal Soult retake Portugal, where 16,000 British troops remained to defend Lisbon, by the end of summer 1809. The campaign, beginning in March 1809, was initially a success. The Portuguese were defeated at the battles of Braga and Porto, after which the second city of the country was captured. In Spain, the situation was also favourable to the French. Jean-Hubert Wégria[39] was fighting with the cavalry in Spain when he wrote this optimistic letter:

---

35. Vittorio Douglas, 'La guerrilla espagnole dans la guerre contre l'armée napoléonienne', *Annales de la Révolution française*, 336 (2004), pp. 91–105.
36. Laurent-Joseph Delvaux, born in Verviers on 12 March 1788, was conscripted into the 2nd Reserve Legion on 19 June 1807.
37. Nicolas-Joseph Bonniver was born in Sart on 13 August 1788. He also served in the 2nd Reserve Legion.
38. AEL: FFP 1043. Laurent-Joseph Stembert to his parents, 15 November 1808.
39. Jean-Hubert Wégria was born in Oteppe on 15 February 1784. He volunteered to replace Gilles-Joseph-Lambert Longrée in the 9th Dragoons on 19 April 1808.

The first of March year 1809

My very dear father and mother and sister
[. . .] I need to let you know that I am now in Spain, fifteen leagues
from Portugal. I fought in several battles but have not been
wounded. I only received your first letter. I need nothing and still
have money. There is a lot of wine, bread and meat. We will beat
Spain soon. It is bloody warm here. There is no ice or snow in
January.[40]

Pierre-Mathieu Halet[41] was recovering from wounds sustained in Spain
in a hospital near the French border. He thought that his unit would soon
leave Spain to fight in the War of the Fifth Coalition:

Tudella 18 March 1809

My very dear father and mother
I write this letter to tell you that I am in good health. I was
wounded but I am now better. I was hit in the right shoulder but
the wound was not deep. I had not seen Fanniel[42] for five months
but now we are together again. I have not received the two crowns
that you sent. They say that we will go back to France in order to
leave for Germany. I hope that if we go back, I will be able to see
you [. . .].[43]

Any optimism was in fact premature. General Sir Arthur Wellesley, the
future Duke of Wellington, returned to Portugal to command the Anglo-
Portuguese armies in April 1809. He had a clear strategy in mind. He would
defend Portugal with 20,000 men while relying on the Royal Navy to
control the sea. The ferocity of the Spanish guerrillas would stretch French
forces and make it impossible to control the whole country. The British
general promptly moved to catch the French forces off-guard. Beating Soult
at the battle of Oporto on 12 May 1809, Wellesley made a surprising turn
the next day to attack the French at their weakest point. This tactic
temporally brought the presence of the French in Portugal to an end. The
situation was also worsening in Spain. With Portugal as a base, the British
entered Spain to unite with General Cuesta's army. The Spanish commander
was a difficult character and an unreliable ally. Wellesley, who had no

---

40. AEL: FFP 1044. Jean-Hubert Wégria to his parents, 1 March 1809.
41. Pierre-Mathieu Halet was born in Goé on 12 April 1788. He was conscripted into the 2nd
Reserve Legion on 14 June 1807 and captured by the Spanish on 17 May 1809.
42. Albert-Joseph Fanielle, born in Limbourg on 17 April 1787, was also in the 2nd Reserve Legion.
43. AEL: FFP 1043. Pierre-Mathieu Halet to his parents, 18 March 1809.

control over the fiercely independent Spanish generals, felt deeply frustrated by the lack of cooperation. In June, Marshal Ney was defeated at the battle of Puente Sanpayo by Colonel Morillo. Ney joined with Soult before leaving Galicia for good in July 1809. Jean-Joseph Ledent,[44] who fought the British in Portugal and passed through Galicia, was far from enthusiastic about the situation:

> Salamanca 26 July 1809
>
> My dear father
> Do not believe that the absence of news is the result of negligence or forgetfulness. . . Be sure that I thought a lot about you when travelling through Spain without stopping, even for one day. We started the conquest of Portugal, a country covered with sharp mountains. After having fought a few battles, which we won, we took possession of this kingdom. Yet we had to retreat soon, chased by the English who had landed. After three months through Galicia, we arrived in Salamanca. I cannot describe the misery that we have experienced. It must be witnessed to be understood.
>
> Now we have to move again. We are going to besiege Rodrigo[45] and we will move in two days. May God grant me forever good health [. . .].[46]

Despite this promising start, the campaign of July–August 1809 would soon turn into a fiasco for the British and Spanish. After Soult's retreat from Portugal, Wellesley and Cuesta tried to push for the Tagus Valley, 120 kilometres from Madrid. The British and Spanish forces met Marshal Victor and the King of Spain, Joseph Bonaparte, just outside the town of Talavera de la Reina on 27 July. The battle began in the afternoon and would only end in the evening of the next day. Wellesley was victorious, for which he was made Viscount Wellington, but at the cost of 5,300 men. The French

---

44. Jean-Joseph Ledent was born in Liège in April 1784. He was drafted during the year XIII (1804–5) of the Republic and sent to the 26th Regiment of the Line. He reached the rank of sergeant, probably because he could read and write, and was discharged as a foreign citizen when Belgium was dissociated from France in 1814. See also AEL: FFP 414, 4, where there is an annexe to this letter, given to the prefect of the Ourthe Department, by Nicolas Ledent, brother of Jean-Joseph, who was conscripted in the year VII (1798–9) and was called to serve with the national garde (*garde nationale*) on 29 August 1809. The request to avoid military service reads: 'Nicolas Ledent, day labourer, aged thirty-five and living south of the city . . . points at the fact that he has two conscripted brothers in the French armies since years 9 and 13. This fact is supported by a certificate of activity and by letters. He also highlights that he is the only support for the family, living alone with a poor 74-year-old father who is almost blind, mutilated, suffering from hernia and disabled. He gives him a piece of dried bread for his hard work'. The other brother mentioned in this request is Léonard Ledent, soldier of the *Compagnie de Reserve* of the Ourthe department.
45. Ciudad Rodrigo is a small fortified town in the province of Salamanca. It was captured by the French on 9 July 1810 after a lengthy siege. Wellington recaptured the town in January 1812. Smith, *The Greenhill Napoleonic Data Book*, pp. 343–4.
46. AEL: FFP 1042. Jean-Joseph Ledent to his father, 26 July 1809.

lost more men but had also much more manpower in Spain. To make things worse for Wellesley, the Spanish failed to protect the strategic position of his army. They also refused to provide supplies, leading Wellesley to believe his position compromised and he decided to retreat to Portugal. Jean Closset[47] fought at the battle of Talavera. He later wrote about this experience to his parents:

Talavera 20 January 1810

My very dear father and mother
[. . .] I am surprised that you have not answered the last three letters. I think that the reason for this is that many of the men carrying mail are murdered. I hope to receive an answer to this letter. Time seems to pass slowly and I ask you to answer as soon as you receive this letter.
    Since we arrived in Spain, we have faced misery every day. We have been uncomfortable for two months because it is really cold and we are very tired. We fought a terrifying battle against the English and the Spanish in July. There were considerable losses and the fight lasted three days [. . .]. I saw a friend in Saint-Jacques in Galicia, the place where you can do a pilgrimage. Michel Demoulin[48] died at the hospital of Talavera on 19 December [1809]. [. . .] My dear sister, you ask me if the letters are opened [he is talking about censorship]. If you have anything to say, you can write it.[49]

Michel Demoulin[50] also fought in July and August 1809. His mother asked him if he had taken part in a battle. The young man was almost illiterate but did his best to answer:

From Perares 26 October 1809

My very dear mother
[. . .] You previously asked if I was in a battle. I fought in two but, thanks to God, I am well. Bullets were flying around my ears like flies. We took many cannons and pillaged cities but there is no wine in this country.[51]

The British retreat after the battle of Talavera was to have important consequences as Wellington was now disillusioned with the *Junta Central*

---

47. Jean Closset was born in Herstal on 7 April 1789. He was conscripted into the 86th Regiment of the Line on 26 May 1808 and captured on 18 June 1813.
48. There is a letter written by Michel Demoulin later in this chapter.
49. AEL: FFP 1043. Jean Closset to his parents, 20 January 1810.
50. Michel Demoulin was born in Seraing on 24 March 1788. He was conscripted into the 86th Regiment of the Line on 26 May 1808. Another letter in this chapter states that he died at the hospital in Talavera on 19 December 1809.
51. AEL: FFP 1043. Michel Demoulin to his mother, 26 October 1809.

and refused to back it. Despite the lack of British support, the Spanish went on the offensive in the second half of 1809. The army of General de Areizaga suffered a crushing blow at the battle of Oçana on 19 November 1809. The northern Spanish army of General Del Parque won minor battles against General Marchand during the autumn but was finally defeated at the battle of Alba de Tormes on 26 November 1809. These two defeats, in just a week, left behind large numbers of soldiers as well as quantities of weapons and supplies. The Spanish army was also too weak to protect Andalusia, conquered by the French in December. This string of bad news forced the *Junta Central* to abdicate in favour of a regent, General Castanos, and the *Cadiz Cortes*, a parliamentary assembly.[52] Jean-Lambert Grandjean,[53] who fought in Spain in 1808 and 1809, wrote to his parents on the eve of the battle of Ocana. He had an unconventional idea to save his brother from a violent death on the battlefield:

Caspet Spain 18 November year 1809

Dear father and mother and all the family
[. . .] I ask you to tell me how my brothers are. You never tell me if they are going to be drafted. I recommend that my brothers learn a wind instrument because if they were unlucky enough to be conscripted, they could join a military band. I hope that you will send money with your answer. I have to tell you that Hubert Pasleau[54] was killed in Saragossa.[55] There is no military band in the 115th [Regiment of the Line]. There was one band but they were all slain.
      Send my regards to the widow Fortin[56] and tell her that her son is well [. . .].[57]

Hubert-Joseph Aubot[58] was about to take part in the victorious offensive against Andalusia. His letter seems to suggest that French soldiers once again believed in victory:

---

52. Esdaile, 'War and politics in Spain'.
53. Jean-Lambert Grandjean was born in Huy on 22 October 1788. He was conscripted into the 61st Regiment of the Line in 1807 and later transferred to the 115th Regiment of the Line. He was captured by the British on 8 August 1810.
54. Hubert Pasleau, born in Huy on 8 August 1788, conscripted into the 57th Regiment of the Line on 24 July 1807. He died in Saragossa on 29 January 1809.
55. The city of Saragossa was besieged from December 1808 to February 1809. Four thousand French soldiers were killed during the action.
56. The son was Joseph Fortin, born in Huy on 13 May 1787, conscripted into the 57th Regiment of the Line on 24 July 1807. He was transferred to the Imperial Guard on 3 March 1813.
57. AEL: FFP 1043. Jean-Lambert Grandjean to his parents, 18 November 1809.
58. Hubert-Joseph Aubot was born in Stembert on 28 May 1787. He was conscripted into the 9th Dragoons on 24 February 1809 and transferred to the 26th Dragoons in 1812.

Madridejos 8 December 1809

[. . .] I am well despite having to march all the time around the country. I am also on guard duty and have to endure the miseries of a soldier at war. The English and the Spanish fought on different occasions but I have always been lucky. We are stationed a few leagues from the enemy and are waiting for the Emperor to come with reinforcements in this country to march on Andalusia. This will put the war to a stop. Other than that, there is a lot of food and the wine is abundant. It eases our pain [. . .].[59]

The Spanish armies were weak but guerrillas were still causing considerable problems. More men had to be sent to Spain to fight the Coalition and maintain order. Jean-François Boux[60] had just heard that his unit, the 11th Dragoons, was going to Spain when he wrote the following letter to his parents:

Blois 28 December 1809

My very dear father and mother
[. . .] I am with all my friends in Blois. We had a good time and drunk a lot of wine together. Wine costs four *sous* for a bottle. In our country, it costs thirty *sous*. My horse is wounded. I have to stay in Blois until my horse is healed and then I will go back to the depot of Hesdin. All the men in Bois will leave for Bordeaux, the last city of France, on the first of January. We will go for Madrite [Madrid] Spain. It is so warm that it is like in August at home. In Blois, there are fifty thousand cavalry men about to leave for Spain [. . .]. Give me news of the country although I know already a lot because I write for all my comrades.[61]

The British Outnumbered
If the fall of the *Junta* did not cause the capitulation of Spain, Napoleon's victory was still looking more and more likely. The country, already in bad shape, received an influx of French soldiers at the end of 1809 and the beginning of 1810. Veterans of the War of the Fifth Coalition were now redirected to the west to pacify the last chaotic regions of the French Empire. The British, the Portuguese and the Spanish were completely outnumbered

---

59. This letter was also stolen from AEL: FFP. This extract came from Fairon and Heuse, *Lettres de Grognards*, p. 179.
60. Jean-François Boux was born in Bettincourt on 4 December 1790. He was conscripted into the 11th Dragoons in 1809. He was later captured by the British.
61. AEL: FFP 1043. Jean-François Boux to his parents, 28 December 1909.

by the 325,000 French soldiers. But the entire population was hostile to King Joseph's regime and was determined to resist. Despite the size of the French army, soldiers were totally demoralised by the guerrillas. Melchior-François Pétry[62] wrote a dramatic letter to his parents:

Segovia 1 January 1810

My very dear parents
I am saddened by your negligence toward me. It is the seventh letter in a row without receiving an answer. I am sad to be abandoned by my father and mother. I thought that you loved me but it is true that I have been a cause of troubles and tears since I was a child. You have to forgive me. I was a young man then. I only understand how wrong I was now. I think I have been punished enough with conscription. I suffered a lot and I think that you are too human to refuse to forgive my past and my future. I hope to correct my mistakes. I suffer enough in this country and I do not need you to add to my sorrow [. . .]. I was unfortunate enough to be discovered by bandits. My horse saved my life for the second time but was killed. Servais[63] is with me and is well. I saw my friend Jean Dubois in Madrid. He told me that Malherbe[64] was dead. This news hurt me.[65]

As often in times of crisis, alcohol became a way to temporarily escape hardship. Jacques Lempereur[66] did not shy away from telling his mother about his wine consumption:

17 January 1810 Quaenne

[. . .] My mother, if only you knew how much I have been marching back and forth as a soldier these last two years. At least I feel better because we drink as much wine as we can. I was at Extremadura but I was not wounded, thanks to God.[67]

In April 1810, Napoleon sent one of his most talented Marshals, André

---

62. Melchior-François Pétry was born in Theux on 5 June 1784. He enlisted in the light cavalry on 17 February 1807. He survived the Napoleonic Wars and came home in 1814.
63. Antoine-Joseph Servais, born in Theux on 7 July 1790, enlisted in the same regiment as Pétry and later served in the 27th Chasseurs à Cheval. He was captured by the enemy on 11 August 1811.
64. Jacques-Joseph Malherbe, born in Olne on 25 July 1790, was conscripted in 1810. Pétry was wrong as Malherbe was in fact wounded and discharged.
65. AEL: FFP 1044. Melchior-Joseph Pétry to his parents, 1 January 1810.
66. Jacques Lempereur was born in Jupille on 24 December 1796. He was conscripted into the 55th Regiment of the Line on 19 August 1808 and discharged on 2 June 1814.
67. AEL: FFP 1043. Jacques Lempereur to his mother, 17 January 1810.

Pre-printed letterhead showing a soldier of the *Jeune Garde* of the Imperial Guard.

Pre-printed letterhead showing an elite gendarme of the Imperial Guard.

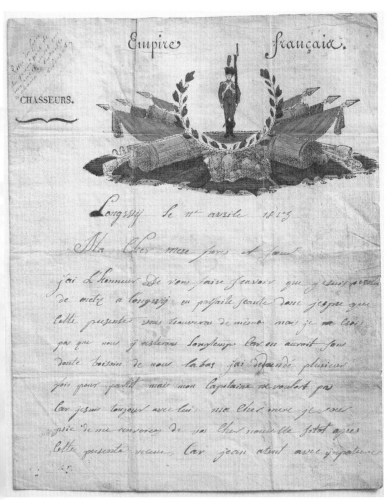

Letter by Jean-François Renier, killed in action in 1813. It was found in his backpack and sent to his family.

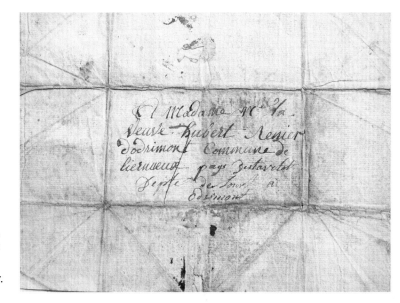

The same letter, folded, with the address of Renier's mother.

Officer of the grenadiers of the Imperial Guard.

Napoleon and his staff at the battle of Austerlitz on 2 December 1805.

General Vandamme leading his men at Austerlitz.

General Hautpoul mortally wounded at the battle of Eylau on 8 February 1807.

Emperor Alexander of Russia and Napoleon meeting at Tilsit on 7 July 1807.

Portrait of Joseph Bonaparte, King of Naples and Sicily (1806–8), and later King of Spain (1808–13).

The burning of Moscow on 14 September 1812.

A dying soldier of the Imperial Guard during the retreat from Moscow in 1812.

The retreat of the *Grande Armée* in Russia in 1812.

Masséna, to the Peninsula in order to lead the conquest of Portugal. Soldiers, like Jean Bourdouxhe,[68] had expected the French army to make this move:

Burgos 23 February 1810

My very dear father and mother
[. . .] We are tired of marching. My dear father, you know what it is to be a soldier. Ever since we entered Spain, we have not received any money. You would help me a lot if you could send money. You would save me from misery. However, life is quite good. Bread is not very expensive. Send my regards to my uncle, aunt, family and friends. We have no idea where we are headed next. We have been in a camp for quite a while. We believe that we will go to Portugal [. . .].[69]

Léonard-Antoine Pierry[70] was also on his way to attack Portugal:

Safra an Extramador 16 March 1810

My very dear father and mother
[. . .] Dear father, this is the second letter without an answer. I am sad. I have an answer about the death certificate of Gilot[71] of Francorchan [Francorchamps].
I asked and they said that his death certificate was on its way home. This is all I know my dear father and mother. We are marching all around Spain. We are at the border with Portugal. I would like to be as far as I can from Spain because I am unwell in this unfortunate country. It is not that the country is bad but the people are really mean, unhelpful and treacherous. When they have the opportunity, they do not hesitate to slit the throats of our soldiers [. . .].[72]

Martin Lecomte[73] was counting on the new offensive to neutralise the guerrillas:

68. Jean Bourdouxhe was born in Montegnée on 3 December 1785. He was conscripted in 1809 in the 32nd Regiment of the Line. He was registered as a deserter but the family provided this letter to prove that he was serving in the army. He deserted for good on 22 January 1813, giving himself up to the opposing army.
69. AEL: FFP 1044. Jean Bourdouxhe to his parents, 23 February 1810.
70. Léonard-Antoine Pierry was born in Malmedy on 10 February 1782. He was conscripted into the 100th Regiment of the Line on 20 March 1804. He died of his wounds at the hospital of Olidença (Spain) on 19 March 1811.
71. Jean-Léonart Gilot, born in Waimes on 15 November 1781, also served in the 100th Regiment of the Line. He was killed in action during the second siege of Saragossa on 21 December 1808.
72. AEL: FFP 1042. Léonard-Antoine Pierry to his parents, 16 March 1810.
73. Martin Lecomte was born in Soumagne on 22 May 1789. He was conscripted into the 86th Regiment of the Line on 12 May 1809 but, after a long stay in the hospital, was removed from the regiment's register on 31 March 1810.

Merida, 14 March 1810

[. . .] We progressed since my last letter but for now we are waiting for reinforcements from France because there is a very strong city called Badagosse, nine leagues from here. Our task is to take it. Then, we will go to Portugal. This time, I hope we will win against those bandits. They say that we will fight them without mercy. It is very warm, as warm as it is at home in August.[74]

The French attacked Portugal with an army of 65,000 men in May 1810. This new campaign began with the siege of Ciudad Rodrigo, an important place controlling the road between Spain and Portugal. Pierre-Louis Dubois[75] was part of the initial offensive:

Ledesma 27 April 1810

My dear mother
[. . .] I am well despite the pain and the tiredness experienced every day. We sleep poorly and we sometimes do not have the time to eat because when we sit at the table, bullets hit the plate.

My very dear mother I am not anymore at the Isle Dieu [Ile d'Yeu, off the Vendée coast] or at the Croisis [Le Croisic, western France]. I miss these places. I have been in Spain for five months. We walk on the mountains, we fight every day; the bullets whistle past our ears but, thanks God, I have not been wounded. I will be a happy man if I have an answer to this letter as we are about to besiege Lodrigo [in fact Ciudad Rodrigo, Salamanca] to open the road to Portigalle [Portugal]. I have been made a scout and it means that I will be the first to fight. We are miserable. Soldiers drop like flies [. . .].[76]

The fortress of Ciudad Rodrigo, held by 5,000 Spanish troops, was not in a position to resist their overwhelming forces. Wellington had been asked by his Spanish allies to come to help but was convinced that the situation was desperate. Ciudad Rodrigo was captured by the French army on 10 July. Nicolas Boumal[77] was among the victors:

---

74. This letter was also stolen from AEL: FFP. This extract came from Fairon and Heuse, *Lettres de Grognards*, p. 174.
75. Pierre-Louis Dubois was born in Bergilers on 8 May 1784. He was conscripted into the 26th Regiment of the Line on 1 May 1805.
76. AEL: FFP 1044. Pierre-Louis Dubois to his mother, 27 April 1810.
77. Nicolas Boumal was born in Grivegnée on 19 May 1789. He was conscripted into the 86th Regiment of the Line on 21 May 1808 and killed in action in Pamplona on 30 July 1813.

Alcantara 20 August 1810

My very dear father and mother
[. . .] The heat is great in this country and I can assure you that many
soldiers dropped dead during the journey. My very dear father, you
can never understand the misery that is ours. The enemy force us to
stay close to our weapons, day and night, and do not give us a
moment of rest. Lately, we besieged Rodrigot [Rodrigo], a very rich
city with very strong fortifications. We stayed there long and made
the enemy pay. I cannot tell you the number of Spanish, Portuguese,
and English, who, seeing that they were beaten by the French army,
fled as soon as our cannons destroyed their walls. At the moment, we
are at the rear until they give us the order to join with the army of
Portugal. Nothing else to tell you at the present, except that the
postman brought me my money. He told me that it was not surprising
that my money arrived late. The couriers are stopped by the brigands
on the road and are even sometimes murdered and robbed [. . .].[78]

The capture of Ciudad Rodrigo left the northern road to Portugal open and
allowed Massena and his men moved to besiege the Portuguese fortress of
Almeida. Corneil Legros,[79] a dragoon, came back to France after three
months in Portugal:

Sainte 2 July [1810]

My very dear father and mother
I am separated from my regiment. We are now in the 17th Dragoon
regiment. I am out of Spain because my horse was killed. I ask you
to write as soon as possible and send as much money as you can.
When I joined the regiment, there were 20 people from Lieges
[Liège]. Now, all the others are dead.[80]
    I have no injury. We were in Portugal for three months and had
no bread. We had to eat horsemeat and chestnuts. It was while
leaving Portugal that I lost my second horse [. . .].[81]

While Massena was fighting in Portugal, the rest of the French army
tried to deal with the remaining opposition in Spain. By the beginning of

---

78. AEL: FFP 1043. Nicolas Boumal to his parents, 20 August 1810.
79. Corneil Legros was born in Battice on 11 February 1790. He was conscripted into the 10th
Dragoons on 30 March 1809.
80. Legros is not telling the truth. Forty soldiers from the Ourthe department served in the 10th
Dragoons. Twenty were conscripted with Legros on 30 March 1809 but in fact only four died while
serving.
81. AEL: FFP 1044. Corneille Legros to his parents, 2 July 1810.

1810, numerous regions and fortresses were still in the hands of the Spanish. The city of Cadiz was an important naval base and the seat of the new central power after the fall of the *Junta*. On 5 February 1810, 70,000 French troops began the siege of the city. Gilles Collard[82] wrote to his mother during this action:

Portre a Realle [Puerto Real, Spain]

21 March 1810

My very dear mother
[. . .] Our current situation is not so good. We are at the siege of Cadix and are very unfortunate. We have to build artillery batteries to fire at our enemies. We cannot go further because the sea stops us and we have no boat. For the moment, we cannot go further and are based two leagues from Cadiz, in a little town where there are no people. They all fled us like our enemy. We hope that, once the batteries are finished, we will bomb the city. We will try to take the island of Leon, where they keep their water supplies. It is only way to force them to surrender. From the 8 to the 10 February, there was a tempest. Several ships sunk. I was curious so I went to see that disaster. I took the opportunity to take some velvet clothes. My bedfellow and I are now very well dressed. Nothing else to tell you.[83]

Jacques Désiron[84] was also at the siege of Cadiz:

Medina Sidonia, near Cadix 1810 8 May

My very dear father and mother
[. . .] When I received your letter, I was on my way to take part in the siege of Seville. It is a very strong city. We only stayed for twenty-four hours in front of the walls because the residents were despicably weak. They surrendered and the enemy garrison fled for Cadiz, where they are at the present. We are in front of them. There is only a stretch of water between us and six hundred cannons fire every day. Sometimes, we come close to Gibraltar, near the coast of Africa where the barbarians[85] live.[86]

---

82. Gilles Collard was born in Fléron on 16 December 1781. He was conscripted into the 96th Regiment of the Line on 22 February 1804. He was sent to the *Compagnie de Vétérans*, a non-combatant unit, on 8 June 1813.
83. AEL: FFP 1043. Gilles Collard to his mother, 21 March 1810.
84. Jacques Désiron was born in Bergilers on 10 January 1787. He was conscripted into the 63rd Regiment of the Line on 1 March 1807. Désiron died of his wounds in Bayonne on 10 September 1813.
85. The French commonly referred to North Africans as 'barbarians'.
86. AEL: FFP 1044. Jacques Désiron to his parents, 8 May 1810.

Cadiz would soon turn into a symbol. As the siege progressed, the garrison progressively received aid from Spanish, British and Portuguese reinforcements. The British even attempted a landing at Fuengirola but were humiliated by a much smaller Franco-Polish army on 15 October 1810. Hubert Lismonte[87] commented on the determination of the Spanish garrison a few days after the battle of Fuengirola:

Chiclana 22 October 1810

My very dear father
[. . .] It is true that I do not have a moment to write. Since we arrived in Spain, we have not stopped for a moment. We are always chasing the enemy. I use a moment of quiet to write that we are besieging Cadiz. It is the most beautiful seaport of Spain but there is no sign that they want to surrender [. . .].[88]

Jean-Hubert-Joseph Graitson[89] was on the other side of the country, with III Corps under General Suchet. This army arrived in front of the city of Lérida on 15 April and formally began its siege on 29 April. Suchet's artillery caused serious damage to the fortifications of the city. Having breached the wall, the French fought without interruption on 12 and 13 May and finally captured the city. Seven thousand Spanish troops took refuge inside the citadel but had to surrender on 14 May 1810, in part to protect the civilian population of the city. Graitson, who explained the siege to his parents, also revealed that he was headed for the city of Tortosa, another successful siege commanded by Suchet:

Herta 21 October 1810

My very dear father and mother
[. . .] We suffered a lot. We besieged Leridat [Lérida] during the month of May. It was a lot of work and, after a month of siege, had to assault the city for twenty-four hours. We captured twelve thousand men, one hundred cannons and a large amount of ammunition. Since then, we have been camping near Tortosa as we want to besiege the city. We are always on the road without a moment of peace and we always sleep on the ground [. . .].[90]

87. Hubert Lismonte was born in Waremme on 7 September 1787. He was conscripted into the 63rd Regiment of the Line on 1 March 1807.
88. AEL: FFP 1042. Hubert Lismonte to his father, 22 October 1810.
89. Jean-Hubert-Joseph Graitson was born in Bilstain on 24 November 1782. He was conscripted into the 95th Regiment of the Line in year XIV (1805) and transferred to the 117th Regiment of the Line on 27 September 1807. He was discharged on 29 May 1811.
90. AEL: FFP 1043. Jean-Hubert Graitson to his parents, 21 October 1810.

The Spanish campaign of 1810 was initially welcomed by most soldiers. Remacle-Popon Adam[91] thought that peace was near:

Pau 2 March year 1810

My dear friend Catherine Cotüry[92]
We left from Commerci on 4 December and we arrived in Pau, at the border with Spain, on 24 February. I am about three hundred leagues from you. It is painful to be so far from you but this separation is only physical. I will have my memories for the rest of my life. I know well what I owe you. I owe you everything after God.
    [. . .] As for the news, they say that peace with Spain will come soon. Many cities already surrendered. Nothing else for the moment [. . .].[93]

Pierre-François Vidal[94] was confident in the valour of the French army:

Merida 20 May 1810 in Spain

My very dear father and mother
[. . .] I am very happy to hear that you are pleased with the certificate that I sent for my brother.[95] They do not say when the next draft will be done. You have to tell me if the certificate is good enough to free him from this annoying situation. If you hear that I could provide a better certificate, tell me so because I would blame myself for letting him go. But I hope that God will not let this happen as I could die of unhappiness. Being a soldier, I know how miserable it is to be far from you. Oh dear father and mother, I hope that one day we will have the joy of being together again. But when will this happiness come? I could leave any day [the meaning here is not clear]. Many people say that we will go back to Portugal soon and that the Emperor brought many soldiers to reinforce us. They say that the enemy has many troops since there are three powers: the Spanish,

---

91. Remacle-Popon Adam was born in Lierneux on 1 December 1781. The authorities forgot to include him in the draft list of year XI (1802–3) of the Republic. According to the law, Adam should have come forward. He was finally discovered in 1809, as the next footnote explains, and sent to the 3rd *bataillon du train des équipages militaires*.
92. Probably Catherine Couturier, the widow of Jean Bodeux. According to the mayor of La Gleize, Adam had Couturier pregnant while working for her as a servant. The young man asked the authorities for permission to marry her but was arrested instead for having failed to report for conscription. He wrote five letters to Couturier from 1810 to 1812 before disappearing. He might have died in Russia.
93. AEL: FFP 1044. Remacle-Popon Adam to Catherine Couturier, 2 March 1810.
94. Pierre-François Vidal was born in Oteppe on 28 February 1789. He was conscripted into the 86th Regiment of the Line on 28 May 1808 and was killed in action in Vick (Catalonia) on 8 May 1813.
95. The certificate was for his brother Jean-Hubert Vidal, born in Oteppe on 10 August 1791. Jean-Hubert Vidal was finally drafted in 1813 but fled.

the Portuguese and the English. But the French army has no fear and will never fear them because they are all cowards [. . .].[96]

Jean-Joseph Maréchal[97] served on the border of Spain and Portugal. He fought at the battle of the Côa[98] on 24 July 1810 before going back to Spain:

Alcantara 11 August year 1810 in Spain

My very dear uncle Louis Colard
[. . .] This is the fourth letter without receiving news. But I think about these words, my dear uncle, because they told me that the bandits are so common here that the mailmen, despite significant military escorts, are stopped and robbed. We fought at Zeresse on 25 July [1810]. We won against the enemy, Spanish, Portuguese and English and we captured one thousand men and killed two thousand. They counted them on the battlefield. When the enemy left, we camped near the city and most of the cavalry stayed inside the city like the commanding officers. When going through the city the next day, I met your dear brother Gorge.[99] We kissed and we rejoiced that none of us was wounded during the battle. Your dear brother had his horse killed under him. From there, we came back to the Portuguese border, where there is no inhabitant left. We had to harvest by ourselves if we want to have bread to survive. We believe that we will go to Portugal. I hope that we will drink wine there! And we will not be in such misery. The worst is the unbearable heat. Some of us dropped like flies during the journey. You asked about Momerce.[100] When he arrived in Leÿonne [Leon, Spain], he fell ill. He is now better but stayed to work as a secretary at the hospital. I have not heard from him since then.[101]

French victories had sometimes unexpected consequences. Théodore Hensen[102] was captured by the enemy during the initial campaign of 1808. The offensive of 1810 set him free but the French army soon believed that

96. AEL: FFP 1043. Pierre-François Vidal to his parents, 20 May 1810.
97. Jean-Joseph Maréchal was born in Bierset in 1789. He was conscripted into the 86th Regiment of the Line in 1808. He was discharged on 9 July 1814.
98. In his letter, Maréchal mentions the battle of Zeresse, the phonetic name of Xérès (or Jerez della Frontera) in French. He was probably mistaken as there was only one battle on 24 July 1810, the Anglo-Portuguese victory of Côa.
99. Georges Collard, born in Liège on 26 March 1774, conscripted into the 13th Dragoons during the year VII (1798–9) of the Republic.
100. Jean-Gérard-Henri Mommertz, born in Liège on 22 September 1789, was conscripted into the 86th Regiment of the Line on 21 May 1808 and captured in Spain in 1809.
101. AEL: FFP 1044. Jean-Joseph Maréchal to his uncle, 11 August 1810.
102. Théodore Hensen was born in Aubel on 10 January 1782. He replaced Pierre-Joseph Simons in the 9th Dragoons in 1807 and died in August 1814.

he was in fact a deserter. He was once again sent to jail, from where he wrote the following letter:

Montbrison 25 April 1810

My very dear father
I am writing to salute you. I have not had news in thirty months and I am worried for your health. I ask you to give news as soon as you can my dear father. I am in a very unfortunate position. I was captured in Cordo eighteen months ago. I have been taken back by the French after the battle of Vie in Spain and I am now in Monbrison, where I am also in prison. I beg for your help and pity and I ask you to send money to help me in my misery [. . .].[103]

On rare occasions, French soldiers expressed their happiness at being in Spain. Henri-Joseph Collard,[104] like many other men at the beginning of the nineteenth century, had never seen the sea in his life:

Yrun 18 August 1810

My very dear father and mother
We entered Spain today. I received your letter on the border. I am very happy to be there because we see lots of new things. I am mainly happy about the sea, nine hundred feet from us. We all hope that all of this will be over soon and they say that we are headed for a city near Madrid [. . .].[105]

But for most men the cost of living was far more important that the sights of nature. Due to the length of the conflict and the number of soldiers in the country, prices were extremely high. Henri-Joseph Darimont[106] complained to his parents:

Hernanÿ Spain 10 April 1810

My very dear parents father and mother
[. . .] I am still pretty fat and well despite the bad food that we have. Everything is extremely expensive and it would be impossible to survive with the ration. The journey was very hard and my feet hurt.

---

103. AEL: 1044. Théodore Hensen to his father, 25 April 1810.
104. Henri-Joseph Collard was born in Seny on 10 February 1787. He was conscripted into the 63rd Regiment of the Line on 10 November 1808. Collard was captured in Berlin but came home in 1815.
105. AEL: FFP 1043. Henri-Joseph Collard to his parents, 18 August 1810.
106. Henri-Joseph Darimont was born Jalhay on 3 March 1789. He was conscripted into the 32nd Regiment of the Line on 21 December 1809. He survived the Napoleonic Wars and came home in 1814.

I was in Bayonne for three days without drinking or eating and I wanted to go to the hospital but that was impossible. I also have to tell you that a pound of bread costs six *sous* and tobacco is so expensive that we do not dare to smoke. We fight the bandits every day but we do not fear them [. . .].

PS: Give my regards to Marie Joseph, my good friend, and tell her that I still have the same feelings for her as before [. . .].[107]

Jean-Noël Barré[108] was equally worried:

Figuere 13 May 1810

My very dear father
[. . .] Everything is so expensive in this country and it is not possible to live with our rations. My dear father, I am in Spain and we have besieged Gironde [. . .].[109]

French soldiers improved their supplies by stealing food from civilians. It was a dangerous task as the guerrillas were more active than ever. Barthélemi-Joseph Loncin[110] lost friends during one of these missions:

Valadolit [Valladolid]
14 May year 1810

My very dear mother
[. . .] My friend Leta was captured by the bandits. Many others were also taken while requisitioning supplies in villages. We are expecting to go to Odrigot any day now [. . .].[111]

The Spanish guerrillas were deliberately targeting couriers and food convoys to paralyse the French army. This strategy was also an effective way to demoralise the French. Jean-Gilles Lallemand[112] knew that he was lucky to have received his parents' letters:

---

107. AEL: FFP 1044. Henri-Joseph Darimont to his parents, 10 April 1810.
108. Jean-Noël Barré was born in Heure-le-Romain on 24 December 1788. He was called for conscription in 1808 but fled. He was arrested and sent to the 10th Battalion of the *train des équipages militaires* on 13 December 1808.
109. AEL: FFP 1044. Jean-Noël Barré to his father, 13 May 1810.
110. Barthélemi-Joseph Loncin was born in Aubel on 20 November 1785. He was conscripted into the 32nd Regiment of the Line on 10 November 1809. He died in Salamanca on 5 October 1810
111. AEL: FFP 1042. Barthélémi-Joseph Loncin to his mother, 14 May 1810.
112. Jean-Gilles Lallemand was born in Forêt on 18 April 1789. He replaced François-Joseph Fagard in the 86th Regiment of the Line on 21 May 1808. He survived the Napoleonic Wars and came home in 1814.

From Naueze 15 May 1810

My dear father and mother
This letter to enquire about your health. Mine is quite good despite the
tiredness and the misery that I experience every day. I left Saint-Malo
for Spain on 10 December. We entered Spain on 13 February. Since
then, we have been to several garrisons but I still receive your letters.
My dear father, this country is a bad country. The army is destroying
everything. At the beginning, it was better because we had half a bottle
of wine per day and sometimes even two or three [bottles] but the
minimum was half a bottle. But now that we are near Galicia, things
are not good. My dear father and mother, if you could send money, I
would be grateful because I really need it at the present [. . .].[113]

Guerrilla warfare was so effective that the French had to use vast
numbers of men in escort missions. Despite these attempts to protect the
roads, the country never became safe. Bandits were everywhere in Spain
and every civilian was a potential threat. It was either difficult or frankly
impossible to effectively control Spain. Hubert-Léonard Menestray,[114] like
all other French soldiers, called the guerrilla fighters 'bandits':

Victoria 14 June 1810

My very dear mother,
[. . .] We left from Angers to Spain on 2 May. We arrived in Victoria
four days ago and we might stay for a while. There are many bandits
on the main roads and the foreigners can only travel with
detachments. Even so, they are sometimes stopped [. . .].[115]

Search parties were organised to chase the guerrilla fighters from the
mountains but these missions were rarely successful. Jean-Pierre-Joseph
Bebronne[116] confirmed this:

Victoria 3 November 1810

My dear father
[. . .] We sometimes go in the mountains to chase the brigands but
it is really rare to catch them [. . .].[117]

---

113. AEL: FFP 1043. Jean-Gilles Lallemand to his parents, 15 May 1810.
114. Hubert-Léonard Menestray was born in Malmedy on 2 April 1790. He was conscripted into
the 1st *Tirailleurs-Chasseurs* of the Imperial Guard on 13 March 1809. He died while serving but
the death certificate has been lost.
115. AEL: FFP 1044. Hubert-Léonard Menestray to his mother, 14 June 1810.
116. Jean-Pierre-Joseph Bebronne was born in Battice on 9 March 1788. He was conscripted into
the Grenadiers of the Imperial Guard in 1808 but deserted. He used the amnesty of 25 March 1810
and was sent to the 45th Regiment of the Line on 30 May 1810. The authorities accused him once
again of desertion in 1812, but he probably died in hospital.
117. AEL: FFP 1042. Jean-Pierre-Joseph Bebronne to his father, 3 November 1810.

The French used brutal methods to deal with the danger of guerrilla warfare. The subsequent massacres inevitably triggered an endless cycle of violence between soldiers and civilians. Jean-François-Joseph Sauvage[118] explained to his father how the French army dealt with the rebels:

Haro 9 December 1810

My very dear father
[. . .] We had many bandits in the mountains. We went to hunt the bandits on Sunday 11 November [1810]. We killed around two thousand and we do not take any prisoner. As for my clothes, I have four trousers, three shirts, three pairs of shoes, one uniform and one coat and you always have to carry everything in a bag [. . .].[119]

Killing enemy soldiers or civilians was nothing especially shocking for French conscripts. In the following letter, Jacques-Joseph Boulanger[120] switched between his complicated love life, including a child born out of wedlock, and the war against guerrilla fighters:

Logrono 21 October 1810

My very dear father and mother
[. . .] Father, I ask you to tell me in which regiment and company my brother is so I can write to him. You told me that he was coming to help us in Spain. Father, you gave me news of my good friend [he means his girlfriend] but I do not know how she behaves. I have received four letters from her since I arrived in Spain. She told me that you do not want to be the godfather and the godmother of the child.[121] [. . .] I ask you to send money as I need it. I borrowed money from my captain to buy pants for winter. We need to bivouac at night because of the bandits. We fight every day. I am now done and kiss you [. . .].[122]

A few months later, Boulanger wrote again about his girlfriend. He also mentioned large massacres of 'bandits':

---

118. Jean-François-Joseph Sauvage was born in Hodimont on 30 June 1790. He replaced Jean-François Ziane in the *Conscrits-Tirailleurs* of the Imperial Guard on 11 November 1809.
119. AEL: FFP 1044. Jean-François-Joseph Sauvage to his father, 9 December 1810.
120. Jacques-Joseph Boulanger was born in Mélen on 9 September 1790. He replaced a conscript in the 4th Regiment of the *Grenadiers-Conscrits* of the Imperial Guard on 26 May 1809. He came home in 1814.
121. Jacques-Joseph Boulanger married in October 1814.
122. AEL: FFP 1042. Jacques-Joseph Boulanger to his parents, 21 October 1810.

Séloudilliot 14 February 1811

My very dear father and mother
[. . .] Father, I ask you to show this letter to mister Dor, the mayor
of Dertenne [in fact Retinne]. Mister Dor, I want my father to send
me two Louis as I am in love with a very nice girl who makes me
happy [. . .]. Mister Dor, there is no need to say anything about this
girl, good or bad, as I do not want to hear anything at all.[123]

We fight every day the bandits and we captured fifteen hundred
of them. The general ordered to execute most of them with bayonets
[. . .].[124]

Ferdinand-Henri-Joseph Chantreine[125] probably wrote one of the most
interesting letters about guerrilla warfare in Spain. He was obviously
shocked by the mutilations inflicted on French prisoners:

Madrid 3 November 1810

We are now in the Spanish capital, but the journey was not easy. We
were tormented by the brigands on the road, sometimes three times
a day. Three men were killed and two others were wounded, one in
Miranda, one between Vitoria and Burgos, and three killed and one
wounded between Valladolid and Segovia. From Segovia to
Madrid, we saw nine French with their throats slit; one had his
private parts cut off and stuffed in his mouth, the other had his eyes
plugged out of his head, five fingers of his left hand cut off and his
private parts in his right hand. This is how these mountain brigands
take care of our unfortunate comrades when they catch them. On the
other hand, when we catch them, we shoot them and we leave them
to hang until they are eaten by the worms. Do not believe that we
deal with small groups. Sometimes they gather more than ten
thousand men. Every day we have to chase them in the surrounding
villages of Madrid with our cannons. Alas, my dear parents, my pen
cannot tell you as much as I would like to [. . .].[126]

At the end of 1810, the tide turned against the French. In Portugal,
Masséna's artillery destroyed the powder magazine of Almeida, causing a

---

123. As we have seen in his previous letter, Boulanger had a child with his girlfriend. Extra-marital
sex was taboo and the whole affair probably scandalised his village.
124. AEL: FFP 1044. Jacques-Joseph Boulanger to his parents, 14 February 1811.
125. Ferdinand-Henri-Joseph Chantreine was born in Wasseige on 2 June 1790. He was drafted in
the 3rd Regiment of Horse Artillery on 12 June 1809.
126. Another stolen letter reproduced in Fairon and Heuse, *Lettres de Grognards*, pp. 182–3.

disastrous explosion which killed 500 people. The French army captured the fortress on 28 August. With the road now wide open, Masséna marched west toward Lisbon. But the French Marshal did not realise that Wellington had prepared a trap for him. The British general wanted the enemy to go across the ridge of Busaco, where his men and his Portuguese allies occupied the heights. Masséna fell into the trap, losing the battle and 4,500 of his men, on 27 September 1810. The next day, Wellington withdrew his troops to the fortified Lines of Torres Vedras, using the scorched-earth strategy in his path. Masséna followed, not realising the existence of the defensive line. On 14 October, he tried to probe the Lines of Torres Vedras but was quickly driven back by a British counter-attack. The French established their camp in front of the Lines while waiting for reinforcements. They hoped that Wellesley would attack but the British did nothing of the sort. The Royal Navy supplied the British and the Portuguese while the French endured starvation and disease. They decided to leave at the end of 1810, having lost another 25,000 men. The evacuation of Portugal would not be completed until spring 1811, with the exception of the fortress of Almeida. Jean-Joseph-Remacle Leloup[127] witnessed the misery of the French army:

Soro 22 May 1811

My very dear uncle

[. . .] I wanted to write earlier but it was impossible. We were in Portugal where there is no post office or courier and we had no free passage because the English and the Portuguese armies were blocking us. We were able to push them back five miles from Lisbon after having won the battle of Hoinbre, where 17 thousand men of both sides died or were wounded on the battlefield. But five miles from Lisbon, we lacked supplies. For the next three months, we only had grapes to survive. Many men of the army died of starvation. Having no resources left to survive, the prince Duslinke [André Masséna, first Prince of Essling], commander in chief of the army in Portugal, gave the order to go back to Spain. I was wounded during the retreat but I was still extremely happy to be back [. . .]. Let me know if my mother is married because I have not received any news in two years. I know this by a friend. Let her know that

---

127. Jean-Joseph-Remacle Leloup was born in Verviers on 4 July 1789. He was conscripted into the 86th Regiment of the Line on 12 May 1808 and was captured by the British in Spain on 18 June 1813.

she should not stop writing because of that. I am impatient to have news [. . .].[128]

1811

At the beginning of 1811, the conflict in the Peninsula was about to take another direction. Wellington had won the confidence of London and was promised reinforcements to launch an offensive from Portugal. The British hoped to recapture the key fortresses controlling the exit points of the country and then move to the heart of Spain. They also tried to relieve the city of Cadiz, besieged by the French since February 1810. An Anglo-Spanish army landed south of Cadiz in an attempt to attack the siege lines in the rear. At the battle of Barrosa on 5 March 1811, the British routed their enemy but did not manage to exploit their victory. The French eventually regained their positions and carried on with the siege of Cadiz until August 1812. Joseph-Bernard Nouprez[129] fought at Barrosa:

Santa-Maria 14 April 1812

My very dear father and mother
[. . .] I have to tell you that I was very lucky to survive so far. I was at the siege of Cadiz for eighteen months and we were bombarded without interruption. I was never wounded. On 5 March 1811, we fought a difficult battle against the English. Of the 113 men of my company, 18 came back. Of the 18 who came back, only four of us were not wounded. I was only lightly injured. Since I arrived in Spain, I have had enough supplies, thanks to God. But everything is very expensive. The bread costs 25 *sous* for a pound and the vegetables are also expensive. The only exception is wine. A bottle is worth six *sous*.

Starvation is everywhere in Spain and you can see people dropping dead in the streets.

My very dear parents, I wrote three letters but I have not received any answer since I arrived in Spain. I know that the road is dangerous and perhaps the couriers had their throat slit. But you might be angry because I did not stop by your home when I left Germany for Spain. I had an illness in Mainz and was evacuated to Aguenau, near Strasbourg. After that, I was not authorised to leave

---

128. AEL: FFP 1042. Jean-Joseph-Remacle Leloup to his uncle, 22 May 1811.
129. Joseph-Bernard Nouprez was born in Malmedy on 3 May 1781. He was conscripted into the 13th Dragoons in year XI (1802–3) but was later transferred to the 8th Regiment of the Line. He died on 5 October 1813.

and had to walk to Madrid without interruption. I hope you will be convinced that it is not my fault [. . .].[130]

In April, Wellington moved to besiege the city of Almeida. Masséna reformed his army and headed west to relive the French garrison. The British general and the French Marshal met at the battle of Fuentes de Onoro on 3 May. Masséna launched a frontal attack, making the same mistake as at the battle of Busaco. The fight, lasting until 5 May, was inconclusive but the British were able to continue the blockade of Almeida. This success was tempered by the escape of the French garrison. Indeed, General Brenier managed to blow up the fortifications before slipping through the British lines during the night of 10 May. Following the loss of Almeida, Masséna was recalled to France and was replaced by Marshal Auguste Marmont. Further south, Soult moved into Estremadura and Andalusia. The British, commanded by General Beresford, abandoned the siege of Badajoz to fight Soult at the battle of Albuera on 16 May 1811. Both sides suffered heavy casualties but the French were forced to retreat. Beresford continued the siege of Badajoz but was forced to leave a month later, when a reformed French army of Portugal threatened his position. Jean-Marie Poitier[131] took part in the battle of Fuentes de Onoro and saw the result of the siege of Badajoz:

Jaraiz 10 August 1811
Potié to his father

My very dear parents and friends
[. . .] I will give you a few details about our movements and misery. We had ten days of rest and we gathered some supplies to last fifteen days. We left for Almeda [Almeida] to help the garrison. They were besieged by the English, who had an army of 60,000 men against the 40,000 men of the army of Portugal. We attacked when we were three leagues from Almeda, the last city of Portugal, on 5 May. We captured two leagues of ground and we took quantities of prisoners. Many of them were French. On the sixth and seventh of this month, we did nothing. During the night of the seventh to eighth, His Excellence the Prince Massénat sent a spy, who ordered the commander of the garrison to save his men and blow up the fortress. This was a success and the city exploded.

---

130. AEL: FFP 1042. Joseph-Bernard Nouprez to his parents, 14 April 1812.
131. Jean-Marie Poitier was born in Spa on 14 October 1789. He was conscripted into the 86th Regiment of the Line on 12 May 1808. He was captured by the British at Salamanca on 22 July 1812.

There are only rocks left and they are all broken. We were without bread for four days and we were eating the dead horses from the battlefield. We went back to Spain. We thought that we would rest but we were wrong. We gathered food to last eighteen days and then we left for Badagos [Badajoz] in Estramadoure [Estramadura]. The English army was there and had besieged the fortress, just like the other. They heard about our army and evacuated without delay for Portugal. They burned all their supplies and their ammunitions when they heard that we were eight leagues from Merida. They had breached the walls on three different points but had seen all the trenches filled with their cadavers and they were scared to lose more men. We stayed to harvest the fields in the area of Badagos because the peasants had left. This is, my dear father, the results of the movements of the army of Portugal. Blutz[132] is like me. He is well now but he almost died because of the heat near Plaisanta. He stayed for two hours on the mountains, like a dead man, but he is better now [. . .].[133]

Jean-Jacques Blutz,[134] the soldier mentioned in the previous letter, wrote the exact same letter to his family. He just changed the part about his near-death experience in the mountains:

Jaraiz 15 August 1811

My very dear father and mother,
[. . .] While going to Plasencia, I almost died. I was abandoned on the mountain but soldiers carrying food saw me and took me on their horse when they realised I was not dead. These men are the reason for which I am still alive. I was like dead for two hours. I am better now, thanks to God, but the situation is miserable because the army never pays us [. . .].[135]

Mathieu Viatour[136] was in Portugal with Masséna's army:

Valencia 25 November 1811
We gathered an army corps in Salamanca to go to Portugal. We had food for twelve days but we lasted fifteen days with that. I still had

---

132. Jean-Jacques Blutz. See the next letter.
133. AEL: FFP 1042. Jean-Mathieu Poitier to his parents, 10 August 1811.
134. Jean-Jacques Blutz was born in La Reid on 24 September 1789. He was conscripted into the 86th Regiment of the Line on 12 May 1808. He was killed near Salamanca on 22 July 1812.
135. AEL: FFP 1042. Jean-Jacques Blutz to his parents, 15 August 1811.
136. Mathieu Viatour was born on 13 January 1788. He was conscripted into the 4th *Voltigeurs* of the Imperial Guard in 1808. He was captured at Salamanca.

a bit of money and I bought bread. A pound costs two francs. We were sent to the frontline to fight. But only the infantry fought. We could hear the cannonballs flying around us. But the British had to retreat but we had to leave them as we did not have enough supplies. On the twenty-third of the same month, we left at ten in the evening. We were 150 and we had to attack 300 Spanish men. We captured forty men, killed as many and took one hundred horses, without having any killed or wounded [. . .].[137]

Thomas Delrez[138] fought at the battle of Albuera:

Port Royale 25 July 1811

My very dear father and mother
[. . .] We had two or three battles against the British during the months of April and May. But I have not been wounded, thanks God. We went to unlock Badagosse and we stayed for twelve days. They surrendered and then we had orders to join our regiment at siege of Cadiz. We marched 200 leagues to join them and we went through the whole of Dalausie [Andalusia] and in very high mountains. We arrived on the eighteenth of this month without harm, except for the heat because in this country it is extremely warm [. . .].[139]

Jean-Guillaume Bastin[140] met the British on the battlefield. He was impressed by their strength:

Valadolid 26 September 1811

Dear father and mother
[. . .] Everything is extraordinarily expensive here. We only have a small ration to survive and a bit of wine [. . .]. I think that we will leave soon for Portugal. Joseph is here with his wounded horse and with two hundred men of his regiment. They are back from the mountains of Asturias and Galicia. He thinks that he will soon go back to his regiment because his horse is getting better. Dear father, yesterday we went to the church of the convent in which we are sleeping. My two friends and I put our feet on the head of a little saint to climb the statue of a bigger saint. The poor tall saint. We broke his neck and I also destroyed a bell [. . .].

---

137. This is another stolen letter, previously reproduced in Fairon and Heuse, *Lettres de Grognards*, p. 192.
138. Thomas Delrez was born in Lambermont on 20 August 1789. He was conscripted into the 63rd Regiment of the Line on 17 December 1808. He came back alive in 1814.
139. AEL: FFP 1043. Thomas Delrez to his parents, 25 July 1811.
140. Jean-Guillaume Bastin was born in Bombaye on 21 December 1790. He was conscripted into the 10th Dragoons on 9 April 1809. He came home in 1814.

I asked about Jean Joseph Ernotte.[141] His regiment is around Grenada or in the Extremadura. They are in the south but we are in the north of Spain. Our poor lancer regiment is really in bad shape. We relieved Rodrigo with our Guard division against the English and the Spanish. They were around thirty thousand men; real soldiers and not like the bandits. They hold still. I might leave soon for a new horse. Three hundred of us are leaving for Germany. If I can, I will go with them [. . .]. Many soldiers come from Italy. This winter is going to be warm. There are soldiers everywhere. Unfortunately, there is a lack of supply and we only have biscuits. They could make me die.[142]

The French found themselves unable to deal with the guerrillas, still a heavy burden on men and logistics in 1811. More French soldiers complained about these irregular fighters than about the British or the Spanish armies. Jean-Guillaume Bastin[143] told his parents of his dislike for Spain:

Hesdin 21 April 1811

My very dear father and mother
[. . .] You ask why I came back to France. My horse was killed under me. My foot is very good, thank God. As Joseph Gurtin wrote, they refused to grant a leave to see you. I ask for your forgiveness but if they had given it to me, I would have taken it with pleasure. I am still doing my job.[144] I have nothing else to do [. . .].
My very dear father, I really hope that I will never return to Spain. It is a very sad country for soldiers. In this country, it is impossible to get out of a town or a village without having your throat slit [. . .].[145]

Jacques-Joseph Collette[146] fell into a trap with his unit while patrolling in the mountains. Surrounded, the French decided to risk everything to get out of this dangerous situation:

Haro 18 June [1811]

My very dear father and mother
I write these lines to let you know that I am well and hope that you are also fine. Renier and I are very well. When we have three *sous*

---

141. Jean-Joseph Ernotte, born in Berneau on 23 September 1789, and was conscripted into the 86th Regiment of the Line on 21 May 1808. He deserted on 18 June 1814.

142. AEL: FFP 1044. Jean-Guillaume Bastin to his parents, 26 September 1811.

143. Jean-Guillaume Bastin was born in Bombaye on 21 December 1790. He was conscripted into the 10th Dragoons on 9 April 1809 and came home in 1814.

144. He was a farrier in Belgium, a useful job in a cavalry regiment.

145. AEL: FFP 1044. Jean-Guillaume Bastin to his parents, 21 April 1811.

146. Jacques-Joseph Collette was born in Petit-Rechain on 26 April 1789. He was conscripted into the 2nd Regiment of the Grenadiers of the Imperial Guard on 11 November 1809.

for the two of us, we are too afraid to keep them for the next day as we fear to be killed at night. We drink this money on the same day as we receive it. I was quite happy to receive four of your letters. I read that Jean Gile Hanquet died and that our priest and Naval died.[147] You will know that we have no straw and we only receive two *liard* per day to buy tripoli [a mineral used to polish] to clean our buttons. We are quite miserable in this nasty Spain. This is why I do not write more often. I do not have enough money to buy paper.

I would be grateful if you could send a bit of money. I really need it to whiten our shirts. You can understand that money is needed to buy soap and thread. When you keep a shirt for ten days on you, you are filled with vermin. This is a nasty country. It is filled with fleas, vermin and there are more bugs than there are hairs on a cow. We cannot sleep quietly because the bandits systematically attack us. Every night, we need one hundred men to stop the bandits and, where we are, we always need one hundred and fifty men when we go on patrol. They still attack us. We looked for the bandits in the mountains for fifteen days. When we were in the mountains far from the city, the bandits blocked our way and we stayed for four days without bread. We had to eat the horse of our captain. We realised that our fate was doomed so we said: live or die. We charged with our bayonets and made an opening and escaped. When we leave a city, the bandits take it. There are bandits everywhere in Spain. At the present, there are new bands every day. In our camp, we have to fight every day [. . .].[148]

A few months before his death, Jean Piedboeuf[149] wrote about the intensity of the war against the Spanish:

Granada 14 July 1811

My very dear father and mother
[. . .] Last May, we fought against the Spanish. They had six thousand men against our six thousand men. But I was lucky to be unharmed, thank God. We won but three of our officers were killed as well as our battalion commander. We are very close to the enemy

147. Jean-Gilles Hanquet died in Petit-Rechain on 10 February 1810. There is no trace of anyone called Naval but a man named Constant Lavalle died on 3 December 1810.
148. AEL: FFP 1044. Jacques-Joseph Collette to his parents, 18 June 1811.
149. Jean Piedboeuf was born in Bellaire on 12 June 1789. He was conscripted into the 32nd Regiment of the Line in 1809 and died of fever in Grenada on 12 October 1811.

and we see him very often. I am about to become a gunner because they do not have enough of them. Perhaps I will do that for good. I saw Jean Thone[150] but we did not have enough money to drink a bottle together. He is well and sends his regards [. . .].[151]

Fighting the guerrillas was a good opportunity to pillage. In rare cases, French soldiers even enjoyed committing atrocities against civilians. Nicolas Joseph Evrard[152] told a friend that he liked killing Spanish people:

10 October [1811]
I have a day of rest and I take the opportunity to write this little note to let you know that I am in good health but also to let you know that I am at the moment in a city called Vitoria, 40 miles of Madrid, and that we are waiting every day to go. We entered the city once but we were not enough and we had to retreat from Vitoria in Spain and I will tell you that we fought in a city called Ville bauzz.[153] We took the city and killed many people and it brought me happiness and I took almost one hundred *Louis*.[154] It is a very awful country with many mountains. The peasants are very badly dressed but the weather is good for wine. We have as much white bread as we want and we eat chicken. The country is very dangerous and peasants try to kill us all the time when we look for supplies and we risk being killed. I will tell you, we have been miserable since we have been in Spain because we have not been able to sleep once in a bed. Always outside in a bivouac. I received two postal orders on the first of August [. . .].[155]

A few soldiers found a way to avoid dangerous missions and lead a comfortable life. Jean Lhomme[156] had no taste for military service, having been arrested while trying to avoid conscription. He was more than happy to become his lieutenant's servant:

---

150. Probably Jean-Joseph Thone, born in Fléron on 13 June 1779, who served in the 32nd Regiment of the Line.
151. AEL: FFP 1043. Jean Piedboeuf to his parents, 14 July 1811.
152. See Chapter 2 for his biography and for the end of this letter.
153. Nicolas Joseph Evrard was almost illiterate and probably misidentified the place.
154. One hundred Louis would be approximately 2,000 French Francs of the time – several years' pay for a day labourer. Victor Guilloteau, *Nomenclature des monnaies françaises 1670-1942*, Versailles, 1942.
155. AEL: FFP 1042. Nicolas-Joseph Evrard to a friend, 10 October 1811.
156. Jean Lhomme was born in Wamont on 15 October 1790. He was conscripted in 1809 but became a refractory conscript. He surrendered to the authorities on 26 May 1809 and was sent to the 11th Dragoons on 26 August 1809.

Pinneranda 26 December 1810

My very dear father and brother and sister
My horse was killed under me at the battle of Odiego. As for me, I
was unhurt and I took part in another battle during which I spent a
day and a half with Albert Fise Journée.[157] I came back intact. I
thank God and the holy virgin and all the saints for saving me in
these dangerous situations. My very dear brother and sister, I
suffered a lot and was very tired but I have to tell you that I am now
better. I am the servant of my lieutenant and have nothing else to do
than to take care of my master's horses. I have never been better. I
stay in the best house in the city with my master and I am loved like
at home [. . .]. My regards to the son of Jean Petit Jean.[158] [. . .] Tell
him to join us as soon as possible. We will recruit him so he does
not have to work. It is less heavy to carry a sword than to carry your
tools on your shoulder.[159]

He wrote again to his parents the following year, confirming the comfort
of his position:

4 September 1811

My very dear mother and brother and sister
[. . .] I am back in Palancia with the officer. Dear mother, money is
not a problem here and I still have my watch in my pocket. I need
nothing. I was offered to go back to France with the others but I did
not want to do so. I like to be with the officer. I have been with him
in Spain for forty-three months. I stayed for a year in Penerandat
and I was better than at home. I left a month ago for Paloncina and
when I left, everybody cried. My dear mother, the war in Spain is
not more finished now than when it began [. . .].[160]

Mechior-Joseph Goffart[161] and Ignace-Joseph Nihotte[162] served in the
32nd Regiment of the Line. Unlike most other soldiers, these two friends
enjoyed their time in Spain. Both used the same letter to contact their

157. Lambert-Joseph Journée, born in Trognée on 7 September 1790, also served in the 11th
Dragoons.
158. There were two Jean Petitjean in Wamont in 1809. One had three children and the other four.
159. AEL: FFP 1044. Jean Lhomme to his family, 26 December 1810.
160. AEL: FFP 1044. Jean Lhomme to his family, 4 September 1811.
161. Melchior-Joseph Goffart was born in Thisnes on 8 March 1788. He was drafted in 1808 but
fled. He was arrested and sent in the 32nd Regiment of the Line on 25 May 1810. He was sent
home in 1814.
162. Ignace-Joseph Nihotte was born in Thisnes on 20 June 1787. He was called up in 1809 but
tried to flee. He was arrested and sent to the 32nd Regiment of the Line on 27 March 1810. He
deserted on 12 May 1814.

families. By chance, Goffart had met a fellow Walloon who had served in the Walloon Guard of the Spanish army. This unit, incorporated in the Royal Guard, was mainly used for public order:

> Almeria 22 October 1811
>
> My very dear father and mother
> [. . .] Nihotte and I are still in the same company, the first of the third battalion. We are still very good friends. Almeria is a city with a port looking at the Mediterranea. It is 25 leagues west of Grenada and it is warmer here than it is at home during the celebrations of Saint-Jean [a traditional Christian holiday, in June]. I have to tell you that I met a man from Tirlement [Tirlemont], a veteran of the Walloon Guards serving for the King of Spain. He told me that he knew Grégoire Hallet[163] of Wansin, who served in the same Guard unit. He died in Almeria two years ago. [. . .]
> PS: We fought against the Spanish on 10 August. They retreated for 30 leagues. We did not have many killed but we have many wounded.

Ignace Nihotte continued the letter, telling his parents that he liked the country:

> My very dear father,
> [. . .] We are quite well in this country. We are not harassed by the Spanish or by the British. Fish is quite cheap and the sea is not cold. There are no waves. We escorted a group of prisoners to Geladix. This is why I take the opportunity to write [. . .].[164]

In the following letter to his parents, Jean-François-Joseph Henroteaux[165] wrote on several occasions that he liked serving in Spain, despite two close calls:

> Spain 28 October 1811
>
> My very dear father and mother
> [. . .] I have been transferred to another regiment. I am now in the

---

163. Probably Jean-Grégoire Hallet, born on 21 September 1750.
164. AEL: FFP 1043. Melchior-Joseph Goffart to his parents, 22 October 1811; Ignace-Joseph Nihotte to his father, 22 October 1811.
165. Jean-François-Joseph Henroteaux was born in Seilles on 22 September 1790. His draft number was initially substituted but he was finally conscripted into the 8th Dragoons on 5 July 1809. He was transferred to the 15th Dragoons on 16 October 1811. Henroteaux was captured in Molsheim, then freed, and finally killed in action before Tuleda (Spain) on 18 August 1812.

15th Dragoons and I really like it there [. . .]. I really like it in Spain. Two horses died under me but I am still there [. . .].[166]

At the end of June 1811, Wellington moved in the direction of the vital city of Ciudad Rodrigo. The decision to head for this fortress near Salamanca was unexpected as the British general was not equipped to assault the place or to carry out a long siege. In fact, his position was rapidly threatened by Marshals Soult and Marmont, who united their forces and advanced on him. Wellington was once again forced to retreat to Portugal in September. By the end of 1811, the war in the Peninsula was once again a stalemate. The French had considerable forces, over 350,000 men, but more than two-thirds of them had to be used to protect the army's supply lines. Wellington was stuck in Portugal but had at least demonstrated that the British were worthy fighters and strategists. Jean-Michel Richers[167] told his mother that the British were, in his opinion, excellent soldiers:

2 February 1812

My beloved mother and brothers
[. . .] I fell ill and got into hospital and stayed there while our army was beaten in Portugal. I stayed in hospital at the borders of Portugal in the hospital of Rothrico. Everything was expensive [. . .]. I was at the hospital for three long months and I did not get anything. I joined my regiment and sleep in the fields and lie in the rain and snow and when I got back to my regiment, we embarked to travel again. I had to go to my old regiment which was one hundred hours away near Padacos. We are still there now. Our regiment has been around here for three years now, something further ahead and something backwards. We fought twice since I joined the regiment. One time on the day of Toussaint [All Saints' Day] and once during the New Year eve. I am not with the cannons anymore because our battalion was torn apart. Now I am a grenadier and saw Mathias Elsen in Salamanca eight months ago but I do not know any news of him because [words missing] and there is a comrade called Kreutz from Wirtzfeld.[168] One friend of Elsenburen and one of Niderum fell into captivity and they were the best comrades.

In the first one, there were fifteen thousand English, a Spanish

---

166. AEL: FFP 1044. Jean-François-Joseph Henroteaux to his parents, 28 October 1811.
167. Jean-Michel Richers was born in Meyrode on 7 April 1788. He was conscripted into the 40th Regiment of the Line to replace in his brother Nicolas in 1808.
168. Servais Kreutz, born in Butgenbach on 21 March 1789, was conscripted into the 40th Regiment of the Line in 1808.

division and a Portuguese division. Our army had two infantry regiments and three regiments of cavalry, in total five thousand men. We had to retreat fast and, in a fight lasting at least three hours, only 350 men of the 40th and 34th regiments came back [. . .]. There is no doubt that the war must end soon because the English are too strong.[169]

In that context, Jean-Henri Binot[170] wrote one of the most interesting letters of the Peninsular War. Mixing in his narrative private and military life, he also demonstrated the willingness of the Spanish population and the French army to believe in superstition:

Galisteo 14 November 1811

My very dear father and mother
I read with pleasure the letter from 14 May 1811 but this letter did not have good legs because it took a long time to arrive. I received it on 29 October and I cried with joy when I recognised the writing and when I heard that you were still well. I hope that you are still well. As for me, I am fine and I thank God for surviving an illness, caught in Zamora. I was away from the regiment for five months, which is why I did not write [. . .]. Lemaire was captured on 27 September 1810 [. . .]. They say that the army of Portugal will go back to France soon. If it is the case, I will visit you [. . .].
    Since I left, you suffered many miseries. My sister had the thumb of her left hand chopped and you tell me that my brother will lose a finger. I am not unhappy about my brother because he will be discharged. As for my sister, it would have been better if I had lost my thumb. It would have been easier to come home. I will tell you that you need to claim what you sent me by the post because I received nothing except for six francs in Paplume [Pamplona]. Jacob Lemaire was wounded in Coimbre. A bullet mutilated two fingers of his left hand and he has been captured by the British. It is his fault if he is not home because he did not want to listen to me. I always manage easily when I do something because I am smarter than when I was home. You tell me that Guillaume Falis[171] married on the day of Pentecost. I am very surprised because he never said anything when he was with me, but things change in two years and

---

169. AEL: FFP 1042. Jean-Michel Richers to his parents, 2 February 1812. This letter was written in German.
170. Jean-Henri Binot was born in Malmedy on 18 December 1789. He was called up in 1809 but tried to avoid conscription. He was arrested and sent to the 17th Regiment of the Line on 28 June 1809.
171. Guillaume-François Faliz, born in Malmedy on 23 January 1783, was too short to serve in the army. He married Marie-Anne Garnier on 27 June 1811.

a half. Give him my regards and wish him and his wife happiness. I hope to be in the same situation one day. You tell me that Gaspare Wanti[172] died. This is very good for the country because there is one madman less. I dreamt that my father was dead for two nights in a row. I hope that this dream is untrue. When the weather is clear, there is white smoke coming out of a star. I do not know if you can see in France that the smoke is now red.

People in this country say that it is a sign. You can easily see its beams in the sky. In Gais, we live like pigs. My dear father, I do not want you to be sad about my fate because I am quite happy. It is true that I suffer more than you but a good day is enough to forget fifteen bad days [. . .]. I will tell you that the army of Italy arrived in Spain and replaced us. We hope that our army will be relieved by fresh troops. I hope to explain my career in details in the future. Being a soldier is beautiful and respectable because you learn to live like a good boy.[173]

The Struggle of the French Army in Spain

The year 1812 began with a major success for the French army. At the end of December 1811, Suchet, the relentless siege expert, was ordered by Napoleon to capture the city of Valencia. It was obvious that the city was not prepared to withstand a siege. There was not enough food to feed the garrison and the 100,000 civilians trapped inside the walls. As a result, Valencia only held out for two weeks. The Spanish General Blake was forced to capitulate with 16,000 of his men on 9 January 1812. Thomas-Joseph Ancia,[174] who wrote a few months before his death, felt optimistic after this major victory:

Panpelune [Pamplona] 28 January 1812

My dear father
[. . .] We are in a very expensive country and we are not paid. I am happy to say that we captured Vallance [Valencia] on 9 January. The *Grande Armée* is marching forward [. . .].[175]

French troops were obviously proud of having captured so many enemy soldiers. Jean-Pierre Nizet[176] mentioned the number of prisoners taken after the siege of Valencia:

---

172. Gaspard Wattry, who died on 28 October 1811.
173. AEL: FFP 1043. Jean-Henri Binot to his parents, 14 November 1811.
174. Thomas-Joseph Ancia was born in Heure on 11 October 1791. He was conscripted into the 60th Regiment of the Line on 19 May 1811 and died of disease at the military hospital in Tarragona on 8 July 1812.
175. AEL: FFP 1043. Thomas-Joseph Ancia to his father, 28 January 1812.
176. Jean-Pierre Nizet was born in Vielsam on 4 July 1791. He was conscripted into the 60th Regiment of the Line in 1811. Nizet was discharged on 9 June 1814.

Figaire 21 June 1812

My very dear father and mother
[. . .] I just got out of the hospital. I was unwell after having been in
the mountains. We did the siege of Valencia and we slept for three
weeks outside, working day and night. We captured eighteen
thousand infantry soldiers, fifteen hundred cavalry and twelve
hundred officers [. . .].[177]

Jean-François Delforge[178] exaggerated the extent of the victory:

Figaire 7 July 1812

My very dear father
[. . .] We just did a campaign and it was very bad for us. We only
had 12 ounces of bread per day for two months. I was thinking a lot
about home. My very dear father, we did a campaign and we
besieged Vallenze [Valencia]. The siege lasted a month but after a
month they surrendered. We captured 24 thousand men [. . .].[179]

The regiment of Henri-Joseph Louis[180] was not at the siege of Valencia. The
young man still told his father that he took part in the action:

Lérida 24 April 1812

My dear father
[. . .] We besieged a large city named Valencia. We did not have to fight
because they surrendered and we only stayed for six or seven days in
the city.[181] Since that time, we have stayed in the mountains [. . .].[182]

Suchet pushed further south, capturing further cities and towns, but fell
seriously ill. Soldiers, such as Pierre-Henri Flament,[183] were mentally
exhausted by these sieges:

---

177. AEL: FFP 1042. Jean-Pierre Nizet to his parents, 21 June 1812.
178. Jean-François Delforge was born in Soumagne on 11 May 1791. He was conscripted into the
60th Regiment of the Line on 19 May 1811 and died at the hospital in Spain on 19 October 1812.
179. AEL: FFP 1042. Jean-François Delforge to his father, 7 July 1812.
180. Henri-Joseph Louis was born in Aywaille on 28 September 1791. He was conscripted into the
60th Regiment of the Line on 9 May 1811 and died of fever at the hospital of Lerida (Spain) on 17
July 1812.
181. The regiment of Henri-Joseph Louis did not take part in the action. He probably stayed in the
city after its capitulation.
182. AEL: FFP 1042. Henri-Joseph Louis to his father, 24 April 1812.
183. Pierre-Henri Flament was born in Basse-Bodeux on 31 July 1787. He was conscripted into
the 32nd Regiment of the Line on 10 November 1809. Flament was discharged in 1814.

Baja 3 February 1812

My very dear father
[. . .] I will tell you that, after marching a lot and suffering, I finally met my regiment in the city of Grenada. Since then, nothing important has happened except that we attacked the city of Caravaca. It was not useful at all and we had to go to one city and then to another and sometimes in little villages in this miserable country [. . .].[184]

The year 1812 also saw several battles against the British. The French Emperor planned to invade Russia in June, a campaign for which he withdrew 27,000 soldiers from the Peninsula. The British, still trapped in Portugal, saw this transfer as an opportunity to strike. Wellington opened the siege of the key fortress of Ciudad Rodrigo on 8 January. The British army breached the walls on 19 January, capturing the city during the night. Wellington then moved to the well-defended town of Badajoz. The French garrison was totally outnumbered but the town had strong fortifications. On the night of 6 April, the British attempted to climb the walls without being noticed but a French sentry raised the alarm and brought reinforcements within minutes. The capture of the city turned into a massacre, in which more than 5,000 British soldiers were killed. The aftermath was not pretty either as the British sacked the city. With the border now secure, the British advanced into central Spain. Wellington's path was threatened by Marshal Marmont and his army of 50,000 men. French soldiers, like Mathieu Remouchamps,[185] had been sent to counter the British offensive:

Zamora 5 April 1812

My mother
[. . .] I was at the hospital but now I am well. I hope the same for you. The bandits took four wagons carrying gunpowder from us. Unfortunately, my backpack was in one of them. They burned them and I am now without any equipment. I have nothing left except what is on my body. I have to tell you that the bandits did three thousand French in a convent during the night [the meaning is unclear. Either captured or killed].
[. . .] We are getting ready to resume the war with the English. We are waiting for the order to go to fight the enemy in Portugal. I

---

184. AEL: FFP 1042. Pierre-Henri Flament to his father, 3 February 1812.
185. Mathieu Remouchamps was born in Hollogne-aux-Pierres on 23 December 1788. He was conscripted into the 76th Regiment of the Line on 12 March 1808. He deserted at an unknown date but came back to his regiment voluntarily. He was transferred to the 6th Regiment of Foot Artillery in August 1811 and, according to the records, was at the prison of Pigneroles in October 1814.

am very happy to be in a new regiment. It is a good one and I have many responsibilities [. . .].[186]

Henri Maréchal[187] avoided the initial counter-offensive against Wellington's army:

11 April 1812

My very dear father and mother and sister
[. . .] War is still going on in Spain. As before, we fight left and right. Our regiment left for the second time for Extremadura, where the English are once again. There was a big battle there but I had to stay back at the hospital because I was unwell [. . .].[188]

Both sides attempted flanking manoeuvres for weeks before meeting at the battle of Salamanca on 22 July 1812. The wound that Marshal Marmont sustained in the first minutes of the battle brought confusion among the French. Wellington won the day, losing 5,000 men to Marmont's 14,000. This disaster had important consequences for Spain. The British captured Madrid on 12 August before moving to the castle of Burgos. Jean-Joseph Jérôme[189] was lucky to survive the battle of Salamanca:

Vitoria 18 August 1812

My dear father and mother
[. . .] I am still well but it is really miserable here. Everything is very expensive. I recently fought against the English and the Spanish. The sleeve of my uniform was pierced by a bullet and three buttons of my shirt were ripped, but without wounding me [. . .].[190]

The second half of 1812 turned into a nightmarish *déjà-vu* for Wellington. The French armies, totalling 60,000 men, converged to relieve Burgos in September 1812. This counter-offensive managed to push the Anglo-Portuguese army all the way back to Portugal. Remi-Joseph Randaxhe[191] took part in the pursuit:

---

186. AEL: FFP 1044. Mathieu Remouchamps to his mother, 5 April 1812.
187. Henri Maréchal was born in Liège on 25 June 1788. He was reformed in 1808 but replaced Gilles-François Pirenne in the 65th Regiment of the Line on 25 November 1812. He came home in 1814.
188. AEL: FFP 1043. Henri Maréchal to his parents, 11 April 1812.
189. Jean-Joseph Jérôme was born in Spa on 11 December 1790. He was conscripted into the 3rd *Voltigeurs* of the Imperial Guard in 1809. He was captured in Germany at the end of the Napoleonic Wars.
190. AEL: FFP 1044. Jean-Joseph Jérôme to his parents.
191. Remi-Joseph Randaxhe was born in Olne on 4 June 1790. He was conscripted into the 32nd Regiment of the Line on 25 November 1809 and transferred in the 3rd Regiment of Horse Artillery on 1 December 1811.

Toledo 1 January 1813

My very dear brother
[. . .] I am very well and I am now serving with the third regiment of horse artillery since 1 November 1811.

I am now the orderly of General Rotÿs.[192] There are eight of us and we are very well dressed, have good horses, and supplies are in abundance. We are not bothered but we have to take care of three different uniforms and the pay is not enough. A pair of boots costs forty-four francs. As for the war in this country, we retook Madrit [Madrid], the capital city. After, the whole army chased the English and the Portuguese and the Spanish. This battle [he is in fact talking about the pursuit of the British army] lasted for three months and we fought every day. We were in the woods and in the mountains for seven days and we ate nothing but acorns and chestnuts, even the generals. We are in a quiet city and we have nothing to do but to talk walks with the general [. . .].[193]

Antoine-Joseph Lecrenier[194] gave a similar account:

Madrid 1 January year 1813

My very dear father and mother
[. . .] I hope that I will have the pleasure of seeing you this year. We all hope to come back to France. We really want it because this country is miserable. We are entirely disgusted to be soldiers. The last letter was from Saint-Philippe in the Kingdome of Valencia. I told you everything that has happened since we left the channel. We left this country during the month of October to come back, once again, to Madrid to chase the English. They had left before we arrived but we found their army in Salamanca and we drove them back to Cuidat Rodrigo, at the border of Portugal. But this country is only covered with forests and is not very populated. We were forced to eat acorns for five to six days. This might seems strange to you but this is because there were two powerful armies and it was impossible to find food. But now we are again in Madrid. The problem is that everything is expensive and there are so many bandits that we do not dare to travel, even for half a league with ten people [. . .].[195]

192. There was no General Rotÿs in the French army. The spelling is probably wrong.
193. AEL: FFP 1042. Remi-Joseph Randaxhe to his brother, 1 January 1813.
194. Antoine-Joseph Lecrenier was born in Huy on 16 June 1782. He was conscripted into the 13th Dragoons on 9 July 1804, and discharged on 5 June 1814.
195. AEL: FFP 1042. Antoine-Joseph Lecrenier to his parents, 1 January 1813.

The men also struggled with guerrillas, still a major problem in 1812. Several letters highlight the sheer exhaustion and anger felt by the French. There was never a moment's rest, as Henri-Joseph Ravet[196] wrote, for the soldiers:

Gironne 28 January 1812

My very dear father and mother
[. . .] We need to carry our weapons day and night to protect us from the bandits [. . .].[197]

Most soldiers only briefly mentioned combats against irregular troops, preferring to use their letters for more personal matters. Jean-Dieudonné Boussar[198] was among those men:

Barcelona 8 December 1812

My very dear father and mother
[. . .] We went to Barcelona for three or four months. We are a bit tired to go in the mountains and on All Saints' Day, we had to fight hard [. . .].[199]

Others used their written communications to express their disgust. Louis-François Pirson[200] took part in several mountain missions to uncover guerrilla hideouts:

Montrette 7 April 1812

My very dear father and mother
[. . .] We are detached near Grenada and we are chasing the brigands every day. It is impossible for the moment to send a certificate but I will send it as soon as possible. You ask where my cousin Désomont died. I cannot tell you because I did not see Solhée. We are always patrolling in the mountains, chasing the brigands during the whole day. We are exposed and we lose people every day. Food is very rare and they only give bread made with Turkish wheat. We do not receive our money and we know nothing about the war or the army.

---

196. The rest of the letter and a biography of Ravet can be found in Chapter 2.
197. AEL: FFP 1042. Henri-Joseph Ravet to his parents, 28 January 1812.
198. Jean-Dieudonné Boussar was born in Liège on 2 February 1791. He was conscripted into the reserve company of the Ourthe department on 12 May 1811. He traded his position with Jean-François Dock, who was serving in the 5th Regiment of the Line, and became a substitute. He survived the wars and came home in 1814.
199. AEL: FFP 1043. Jean-Dieudonné Boussar to his parents, 8 December 1812.
200. Louis-François Pirson was born in Stavelot on 31 August 1789. He was conscripted into the 32nd Regiment of the Line on 25 November 1809.

I still hope that we will go home soon [. . .]. I will not say anything about Jasparre des Oumon because he was wounded during a battle in a city named Oubédat. I think he is on his way home. I do not ask for money because I found some by chance [. . .].[201]

Jean-Henri-Joseph Moÿse[202] lost his captain and a corporal to the guerrillas:

Chambery 18 May 1812

My very dear brother
[. . .] As for the war, they do not talk a lot about it here. They send many soldiers for Prussia and Germany. Here in Chambery, there are three battalions: the 5th, the 11th and the 79th line regiments. They tell us that we will leave for Maÿence [Mainz] and they say that it will be soon. I left Spain. Our regiment fought well and our captain was severely wounded and a corporal was killed and many others as well. And all of this because of the bandits [. . .].

You find it peculiar that I wrote that it is only three to eight days from Valence to Grenoble and you tell me that there are at least 150 leagues. There is in fact much less, probably 20 leagues, but this is because I was talking about Valence in the Dauphinet [Dauphiné] and not Valence[203] in Spain [. . .].[204]

Sometimes, irregular troops gathered in army-size formations to control important points. Jean-Joseph Lallemand[205] assaulted a city defended by Spanish civilians. He came close to being killed on several occasions:

Grenada 1 August 1812

My very dear brother
[. . .] I have to tell you, my dear brother, that the regiment has formed elite companies. I am now in the grenadiers. We fight almost every day. On the fifteenth of May, we fought a big battle at Oveda. We wanted to enter the city but we were cheated because there were many more people than expected. We were only six hundred men with cavalry and everything and they had six thousand men firing at us. Everybody was firing at us; men, women and girls. Everybody resents us. Many men were killed but, thanks God, I was

201. AEL: FFP 1042. Louis-François Pirson to his parents, 7 April 1812.
202. The rest of the letter and a biography of Moÿse are reproduced in Chapter 1.
203. In French, the Spanish city of Valencia is indeed called Valence.
204. AEL: FFP 1042. Jean-Henri-Joseph Moÿse to his brother, 18 May 1812.
205. Jean-Joseph Lallemand was born in Francorchamps on 4 February 1786. He was conscripted into the 32nd Regiment of the Line on 25 November 1809.

not wounded. The men on my both sides were killed. Three of us entered a house but I had to jump from a thirty foot high window because we saw that the Spanish were inside. One of my friends broke his arm and the other his leg but I sustained no injury except for a little knee wound [. . .].[206]

The guerrillas were confident enough to attack large formations. The regiment of Pierre-Joseph Dewiche[207] lost two entire companies to the Spanish:

Saragossa 12 October 1812

My very dear father and mother
[. . .] I am in Saragossa and we are not very well. Food is too expensive and we are not paid. I have been in Spain for ten months and have only received six francs. We are very tired because fight very often. I was almost captured by the brigands. They sent two companies of our battalion in a small garrison and they were all captured. Luckily for me, it was not our company, because it would have been the end. Dear father and mother, I have not written for a long time because we have been chasing the brigands in the mountains a lot. But now, we are a bit quieter [. . .].[208]

As in previous years, guerrilla actions affected all aspects of life. Louis-Joseph Renard[209] complained about the disruption of the post:

Alcolnetta 5 November 1812

My very dear father
I have to tell you that we are in a place where it is possible to send news. My dear father, it is impossible to send letters because they told the regiment that the enemy is blocking the passage to France [. . .].

I will tell you that we took Araquon and Valla [Valladolid] and we are in front of Iquand [Alicante] at the present. It is very miserable [. . .].[210]

---

206. AEL: FFP 1042. Jean-Joseph Lallemand to his brother, 1 August 1812.
207. Pierre-Joseph Dewiche was born in Ouffet on 23 May 1786. He was conscripted into the Imperial Guard on 1809 but deserted soon after. He was arrested, pardoned and sent to the 121st Regiment of the Line on 8 June 1810.
208. AEL: FFP 1043. Pierre-Joseph Dewiche to his parents, 12 October 1812.
209. Louis-Joseph Renard was born in Warnant on 7 January 1787. He was called up in 1807 but tried to flee conscription. He was arrested and sent to the 105th Regiment of the Line on 2 June 1807.
210. AEL: FFP 1043. Louis-Joseph Renard to his father, 5 November 1812.

The scarcity of food caused inflation. Pierre-Joseph Leclercq[211] condemned the situation:

5 February 1812

My very dear father and mother
[. . .] I have to tell you that we entered Spain twenty-five days ago. We marched for twenty days in a row. We are in a very expensive country. The bread costs twelve *sous* for a pound and the other goods are as expensive. At the present, we have not received our pay and we might not have anything for the next two or three months. The only thing we receive is a pound and a half of bread per day. Dear father and mother, soldiers are really unfortunate. If I had thirty-six brothers, I would tell them all to avoid serving. The truth is that I am in a poor state. Dear father and mother, you have to believe everything I tell you. I need to ask for help. Many friends are so unwell that they are ill but, thank God, my health has always been good. But if you have no money, you are in a difficult situation. We are now four hundred leagues from home and we believe that we might go further [. . .].[212]

Many soldiers, including Jean-François Chalseche,[213] commented on the extreme poverty of the country:

Orleans 2 April 1812

Dear father and mother
[. . .] I received your letters just when I heard that I was going back to France [. . .]. I arrived on the sixth of this month in Fontainebleau and I received the rank of corporal. I do not know in which regiment I will go. I am in such an extreme joy to be out of Spain because the misery there is so immense [. . .]. My duty in Spain was so intense that I had to go to the hospital of Dax, where there is a warm fountain. After twelve days of rest, I was well again, thank God.[214]

At the end of the year, King Joseph was once again in control of Madrid but had lost the provinces of Andalusia and Asturias. This setback would have meant little if Napoleon had not lost almost his entire army in Russia.

---

211. Pierre-Joseph Leclercq was born in Romsée on 28 June 1791. He was conscripted into the 5th Regiment of the Line on 12 May 1811. He was captured on 3 August 1813.
212. AEL: FFP 1042. Pierre-Joseph Leclercq to his parents, 28 January 1812.
213. Jean-François Chalseche was born in La Gleize on 22 March 1789. He was conscripted into the Voltigeurs of the Imperial Guard on 12 June 1808.
214. AEL: FFP 1044. Jean-François Chalseche 8 April 1812.

Morale was once again low. Jean-Michel Gilkens[215] openly expressed his anger at the situation in Spain:

Yron November 1812

My very dear father and mother
[. . .] I know nothing except that we are close to France. We are only six leagues from Baÿonne [Bayonne]. We are really fed up to serve. We are often on guard duty and we are not paid. We have not been paid once. It is really shameful [. . .].[216]

Not everyone was so depressed. Jean-Henri Lévêque[217] confirmed that the campaign of 1812 had been tough but he also declared himself ready for more:

Camougnai 24 February 1813

My very dear mother
[. . .] We suffered a lot for three months. We marched for three months and we endured everything bad that the war has to bring: famine, plague, bad weather, and very tiring forced marches. But I was always well and I have now recovered and I am ready to do more [. . .].[218]

The Collapse of the French Army
The Sixth Coalition of Russia, Prussia and Austria forced Napoleon to withdraw more troops from Spain at the beginning of 1813. The French army still had more than 200,000 men in the Peninsula, but most were scattered along the roads and in the cities. Wellington knew that the time was right to open a second front to bring the conflict to an end. The British general and his men had gained valuable experience in the previous years. Louis-Joseph Batta,[219] like many other French soldiers, regarded his British enemy with respect:

Figuer 6 February year 1813

My very dear father and mother
[. . .] I thought that they would send us to the depot but they sent us

---

215. Jean-Michel Gilkens was born in Liège in May 1792. He was conscripted into the 76th Regiment of the Line on 5 March 1812 and disappeared after being hospitalised in February 1814.
216. AEL: FFP 1043. Jean-Michel Gilkens to his parents, November 1812.
217. Jean-Henri Lévêque was born in Liège on 30 January 1788. He replaced Pierre Danz, who had initially been exempted from military duty as an ecclesiastic student, but had later been drafted after having renounced becoming a priest. Lévêque served in the 32nd Regiment of the Line from 6 February 1811.
218. AEL: FFP 1042. Jean-Henri Lévêque to his mother, 24 February 1813.
219. Louis-Joseph Batta was born in Polleur on 11 August 1791. He was conscripted into the 60th Regiment of the Line on 29 May 1811. He was discharged on 9 June 1814.

to guard a small fort called Apalamos. It is a seaport and we saw the English every day; they scared us very much every day. Our company in Apalamos was composed of old soldiers who had problems or were not well. My father, this whole company believed that they would be reformed soon but they only sent back the lame one and six others were sent to Geneva. I am in perfect health and I am bigger and fatter than I ever was at home. I saw many soldiers working hard and I asked a mason who was building a bridge if he needed another mason to help. He said yes and I said that I was a mason. I worked with the other masons and I earned forty-four *sous* per day. This money allowed me to buy bread and drink a bottle of wine once in a while. The wine is cheap and costs six *sous* per bottle. Father, you asked if your letters are opened before I receive them. No, but you have to tell me why you asked this. Do they open my letters?[220]

Batta's letter also highlights an important fact: the French army of 1813 was not the one that had won Austerlitz. This new generation of conscripts had no motivation and was unwilling to fight an endless war. Many soldiers had serious health problems and just wanted to go home. Antoine-Joseph Simon[221] described the morale situation:

Gironne 1 April 1813

Sir,

[. . .] We did not stay long in France. We came back in Catalonia to meet with our regiment three weeks ago. We went through Figaire and I met Fr Stas[222] [Jean-François Stas]. He gives his regards to his parents and he is well and we had the pleasure of drinking a bottle of wine together. I am now ten leagues from Fignire. We have to go fifteen leagues from Fignire to find straw for the horses [. . .]. My pain in the eye is still there. I cannot see well but I am still in the army because it is extremely difficult to be discharged. Even those walking with crutches have to serve. You need to have one limb missing to be discharged [. . .]. My very dear father, I was sad to hear that my brother Jean[223] left. He was the younger and was keeping you company and was helping you in the house. You need to console yourself and hope that it will end one day. You will have the pleasure of seeing all your children together again [. . .].[224]

---

220. AEL: FFP 1042. Louis-Joseph Batta to his parents, 6 February 1812.
221. Antoine-Joseph Simon was born in Merdop on 29 September 1791. He was conscripted into the 60th Regiment of the Line on 29 May 1811.
222. Jean-François Stas, born in Hannut on 20 February 1791, was conscripted into the 60th Regiment of the Line in 1811. Stas was discharged on 9 June 1814.
223. Jean-Joseph Simon, born in Merdop on 4 June 1794, was conscripted into the 61st Regiment of the Line on 22 April 1813. He died in Hamburg on 4 May 1814.
224. AEL: FFP 1042. Antoine-Joseph Simon to an unknown person, 1 April 1813.

Alexandre-Joseph Pepinster[225] showed little more enthusiasm:

Vilorial 8 June 1813

Sir Antoine Jargon,
[. . .] Spain is filled with troops, brigands and French. We fight a lot
and they have captured many of the comrades who had served with
me. We think that they are in England [. . .].[226]

In May 1813, Wellington moved from Portugal through the mountains
of northern Spain. The capture of Salamanca by General Hill on 26 May
forced King Joseph to abandon Madrid once more. Following an attempt
to outflank the French army, both sides finally met at Vitoria on 21 June.
This battle, where Wellington faced Marshal Jourdan, became the decisive
action of the Peninsular War. Not only were the French badly beaten, but
the victory invigorated the allies of Britain fighting against Napoleon in the
west. But the war was not yet over as the French, commanded by Soult,
prepared for another counter-offensive in July. The French Marshal won a
few minor battles but failed to prevent the invasion of France. Remi-Joseph
Lignon[227] fought in the final campaign against the British in Spain. He was
desperate to leave the country behind him:

Gironne 18 September 1813

My very dear mother,
[. . .] We have not received any money for 13 months. We fight
every day. The last time we lost [words missing] and only six of our
company were not killed or wounded. We would have been
captured by the Spanish if the rest of the division had not reinforced
us. We retreated for three leagues. We always run my dear mother.
I will tell you, my dear mother, that we blew up many fortifications
in Spain. There is hope that we might leave soon. My dear mother,
we are very sad in Spain because we fight against the English and
the Spanish very often [. . .].[228]

Jean-Joseph Delhalle[229] fought at the battle of the Pyrenees and was
subsequently pushed back to France:

---

225. Alexandre-Joseph Pepinster was born in Battice on 23 August 1792. He was conscripted into
the 76th Regiment of the Line on 5 March 1812. He came home in 1814.
226. AEL: FFP 1043. Alexandre-Joseph Pepinster to Antoine Jargon, 8 June 1813.
227. Remi-Joseph Lignon was born in Hingeon on 2 September 1791. He was conscripted into the
60th Regiment of the Line on 19 May 1811.
228. AEL: FFP 1042. Remi-Joseph Lignon to his mother, 18 September 1813.
229. Jean-Joseph Delhalle was born in Jehay on 26 May 1791. He was conscripted into the 47th
Regiment of the Line in 1811. He deserted on 27 July 1814.

Bayonne 22 September 1813

My very dear father and mother
[. . .] We had a bloody thing going on with the English on the last thirteenth of August. We crossed a river on foot in the morning but had to swim back while retreating in the evening. I do not know how to swim so I had to throw off my backpack and my comrade had to throw off his to help me cross the river. Without him, I would have drowned. We lost everything [. . .]. We have been in Spain for a year now and we are always unsuccessfully running after the brigands in the mountains. The only time we met them, we also met the English and the Portuguese and we fought for seven days to take a mountain.[230] They received more men every day and we had to retreat and we lost many men. We were defeated and pushed back to France. We are now six leagues from Baÿonne [Bayonne], ready to fight every day. We are at the camp, where everything is expensive. We do not have money. We have not been paid for a year [. . .].[231]

He wrote again from Bayonne a few months later as the French army prepared to repel an invasion of the country:

Bayonne 3 November 1813

My very dear father and mother
[. . .] We have been at the camp for four months and it is raining all the time. We are wet all the time and it feels like we just got out of the water. Our clothes rot all the time because we stay for fifteen days without drying. We had a fight with the English and the Portuguese and the Spanish on the seventh of the month of October.[232] We were defeated and pushed four leagues from Bayonne. We worked on fortifications and artillery batteries. We have been doing that for at least three months [. . .].[233]

In this chapter, we looked at the Peninsular War and saw that the soldiers, who had so far met the enemy mostly on the battlefield, found it hard to adapt to the nature of guerrilla warfare. Irregular Spanish troops successfully

---

230. Probably the battle of the Pyrenees, 25 July to 2 August 1813.
231. AEL: FFP 1042. Jean-Joseph Delhalle to his parents, 22 September 1813.
232. The battle of Vera, 7 October 1813.
233. AEL: FFP 1042. Jean-Joseph Delhalle to his parents, 3 November 1813.

managed to disrupt French military strategy and logistics. The use of harassment tactics and the omnipresence of violence had a considerable impact on morale. French soldiers not only detested fighting in Spain, but also hated the locals. This climate of animosity spiralled into an endless cycle of brutality. The Spanish tortured captured soldiers while the French did not hesitate to retaliate by massacring entire civilian communities. These executions were often mentioned in the correspondence, a sign that they left a mark on the soldiers, but were justified as a rational answer to the problem of irregular warfare.

The war in Spain also became a training ground for the British soldiers. The French initially looked at them as another enemy to beat. However, the talent of Wellington and the resilience of his men progressively transformed the reputation of the British army. The French, who initially believed in their own invincibility, came to fear the British soldiers on the battlefield.

Chapter 5

The Decline and Fall of the French Empire

The Russian Disaster of 1812

In 1812, the French Empire was at its height, having direct or indirect control over most of Western and Central Europe. If the *Grande Armée* had difficulty beating the Spanish and their British ally in the Peninsula, no other nation seemed willing to gamble its future against Napoleon on the battlefield. The French relied heavily on the enforcement of the Continental System to pressure the United Kingdom to sue for peace. However, Russia had no interest or taste for this policy which had negative consequences on her economy. The Tsar, Alexander I, also had another reason to be upset at Napoleon. The Treaty of Schönbrun of 1809, which ended the War of the Fifth Coalition, stated that Western Galicia would go to the Grand Duchy of Warsaw. An independent Polish nation was viewed by the Russians as a threat. It is with this official goal, the liberation of Poland, that Napoleon went to war against Russia in June 1812. In fact the French wanted to reassert their authority and ensure that the blockade was respected. Soldiers heard rumours months before the beginning of the conflict. Charles-Adrien-Joseph Chaudier[1] thought that they might fight the Russians or the Turks:

Menden [Minden, now Rheinland-Westphalen, Germany] 21 November 1811

My very dear mother,
They brought me to the depot and from there we met with the battalion in Menden. I am well but tired by the journey. In this country, the people eat only potatoes and the bread that they eat is

---

1. Charles-Adrien-Joseph Chaudez was born in Hannêche on 20 May 1791. He was conscripted into the 8th Battalion of the *train d'artillerie* on 24 August 1811.

darker than the hats we wear. Their horses, their cows and their pigs live in the same building [. . .]. Nothing else to tell you at the present. As for the great war, we hear that we will fight the Russians or the Turks.[2]

Soldiers fighting in the Peninsula did not expect to be withdrawn from the country and sent to Prussia. Quirin Jamar's[3] regiment left Spain for the west:

Toul 22 February 1812

My dear father and mother
[. . .] We stayed in Bayonne, near the Spanish border, for three months and waited for the order to go back to Spain. But it was the contrary. We are going back to the depot in Metz and we left on the first of January. We are on the road and we should arrive on the twenty-fourth of this month. This is why I write. We might only stay in Metz for eight days before going to Russia or Prussia [. . .].[4]

Gilles-Joseph Wuara[5] also heard rumours about the war against Russia. The young man did not seem to care whether he fought one nation or another:

Münster 25 February 1812

My very dear father and mother
[. . .] We marched on poorly maintained roads for a long time and we arrived with our cannons and our munitions. We heard that we will again go to war soon but we do not know who we will fight. We believe that we will fight against the Russians but, whether it is one or the other, we do not have a choice and have to go. I have accepted my fate and I do not worry anymore about the past. We travel thirty to forty leagues to escort powder every eight days. This task is hurting us because we are getting tired and we damage our shoes without a reason. But this is nothing and if we have to do it, we have to do it. We must hope that we will not see anything worst but you need to accept your fate when you are a soldier. I want to learn how to fire and how to defend myself. I want to leave sadness

---

2. AEL: FFP 1044. Charles-Adrien-Joseph Chaudier to his mother, 21 November 1811.
3. Quirin Jamar was born in Waimes on 31 January 1790. He was conscripted into the 18th Regiment of the Line on 16 March 1809 but moved to the 8th Company of the *train du genie* the same year.
4. AEL: FFP 1044. Quirin Jamar to his parents, 22 February 1812.
5. Gilles-Joseph Wuara was born in Plaineveaux on 22 February 1789. He became a substitute for Jean-Joseph Bovy at an unknown date and was sent to the 2nd Regiment of Foot Artillery.

behind and think about joy, despite the overwhelming misery. Far from you, I am sad and my memories make me nostalgic. We are here for another month. I ask you to answer to give news. Tell me if there is anything new in the country, it would make me happy. I am and I will always be your son.[6]

Pierre-Joseph Renglet[7] had served with the cuirassiers since 1808. A seasoned veteran, he was nonetheless enthusiastic about this new campaign:

Cologne 1 March 1812

My very dear father and mother
[. . .] We are leaving to cross the Rhine on the third of this month. We are going to Russia and we are going to fight but I hope, thanks to God, to be safe and to come back to you with loads of laurels [. . .].[8]

This attitude was far from usual. Thomas-Joseph Stassart,[9] another veteran who had served since 1805, voiced his resignation:

Glaugaud 20 April 1812

My very dear father and mother
[. . .] Our regiment left Bressia for Poland on 3 February. We have been marching for two months and a half and we are not yet there. We believe that we will fight the Russians. We would gladly avoid this but this is how it is and we have to accept it. At the present, the snow is still there. It is very cold but, thanks to God, we are not at the bivouac. I hope that you will answer as soon as you can because I would like to have news before fighting [. . .].[10]

Other soldiers spread incoherent rumours. Nicolas-Joseph Halleux[11] mentioned the invasion of Britain, helped by the Russians:

Lissa Poland 24 April 1812

[. . .] We do not know where we are going. They say that we are going to England. They say that the Emperor of Russia gave the

---

6. AEL: FFP 1056. Gilles-Joseph Wuara to his parents, 25 February 1812.
7. Pierre-Joseph Renglet was born in Burdinne on 14 November 1786. He tried to avoid conscription but was arrested and sent to the 1st Cuirassiers on 8 November 1808.
8. AEL: FFP 1044. Pierre-Joseph Renglet to his parents, 1 March 1812.
9. Thomas-Joseph Stassart was born in Wegnez on 17 February 1784. He was conscripted into the 95th Regiment of the Line on 7 *frimaire* year XIV (28 November 1805).
10. AEL: FFP 1042. Thomas-Joseph Stassart to his parents, 20 April 1812.
11. Nicolas-Joseph Halleux was born in Nandrin on 24 October 1789. He was first excused military duty for medical reasons but later substituted François-Joseph-Constant Bernard and was sent to the 1st Battalion of the *sapeurs* on 30 May 1811.

French Emperor a passage on land to go to England. We will have quite a march if we go. They say that if we go, we will march six hundred leagues. But I think that we will have to fire our guns quite a bit before arriving [. . .].[12]

At the end of April, French soldiers still did not know who they were going to fight. Jean-Louis-Jacques Marichal[13] was absolutely sure that the next enemy was going to be the Ottoman Empire:

Lagun 29 April 1812

[. . .] We left Brescia on 6 February. We are now in Lanquen in Prussia. I am still well but we marched for three months. The rain and the bad weather made us suffer. We march every day and we do not know when we will stop. We are going against the Turks. A very big war will happen there. All the army is marching against them and we have eight hundred and fifty thousand men, without including the Austrian army, which will come with us. I will not write until the war is over and we are at peace, if God grants me the grace of coming back alive [. . .].[14]

In 1809, Napoleon had accelerated the recruiting of the French army to compensate for the losses of the Peninsular War. As a result, many units lacked competent officers and experienced men. The new generation of conscripts had little training or motivation and suffered from a shortage of officers and NCOs.[15] Henri-Paul Froesges[16] had been in the army for a year when he wrote the following letter to his parents:

Gumbinnen 16 June 1812

[. . .] We are starting a new campaign against the Russians. It seems like it is going to be a difficult campaign for us [. . .]. My little goddaughter died and I would like to take her place. Do not forget me in your prayers, because I need it. I bid you farewell, because I might be killed . . .
      [. . .] It might be my last letter. There is no need to be sad, I am happy to die because marching is killing me.[17]

---

12. Fairon and Heuse, *Lettres de Grognards*, p. 271.
13. Jean-Louis-Jacques Marichal was born in Chevron on 22 September 1789. He was conscripted into the 8th *Chasseurs à Cheval* in August 1808.
14. AEL: FFP 1044. Jean-Louis-Jacques Marichal to his parents, 29 April 1812.
15. Alexander, 'French replacement methods during the Peninsular war'.
16. Henri-Paul Froesges was born in Butgenbach on 17 October 1785. He fled conscription but was arrested and sent to the 111th Regiment of the Line in 1811. He disappeared in Russia in 1812.
17. Fairon and Heuse, *Lettres de Grognards*, p. 274.

The Emperor did his best to reassure his men before the campaign of Russia. Guillaume-Joseph Mauxhin[18] witnessed a military parade in Saxony and even saw Napoleon:

My very dear grandfather and grandmother

[. . .] We crossed the Rhine, and then were in Germany, and then in Saxony. I am in the last city of Saxony and I will be in Berlin in three days. In 150 leagues, I will bring my cannons against the Russians. Since Frankfurt, I have not seen a single Christian. All of Saxony, they are protestants. As I cannot go to mass, I pray with those who have time to go to mass for me, so God can bless me. I have not confessed since I left. I do not know when I will be able to do it. My very dear grandfather and grandmother, I am really bothered because we will never see each other as you are too old.

We are fed by the peasants and the King of Saxony. He has to give another one thousand five hundred men to Napoleon. There will be a bloody battle. The Emperor of Austria gave him men as well. Napoleon is already in Russia. He went through Mainz when we were there. When he came, almost all houses had a candle. The next day, our soldiers held a parade; those who had horses rode them. Then he came with three of his generals. The generals were dressed in gold and the Emperor had a *chasseur* uniform and a well-worn square hat [. . .].[19]

In June 1812, the French Emperor finally launched the invasion of Russia with an army in excess of 400,000 men.[20] Outnumbering the enemy four to one, the French initially moved with ease into Russian territory. The Russian generals tried to avoid confrontation, knowing that they stood no chance in battle. François-Joseph Detiège[21] wrote to his family at the beginning of the campaign. If he did not display much enthusiasm for life in Russia, he did not find it unbearable either:

4 August [1812] Vilbac

My very dear father and mother and brother
[. . .] We are now in Russia and we are chasing the Russians. We are

18. Guillaume-Joseph Mauxhin was born in Warsage on 28 November 1792. He was conscripted into the 9th Battalion of the *train d'artillerie* in 1809.
19. AEL: FFP 1044. Guillaume-Joseph Mauxhin to his grandparents, June 1812.
20. Frederick Schneid, 'The dynamics of defeat: French army leadership, December 1812–March 1813', *The Journal of Military History*, 63 (1999), pp. 7–28.
21. François-Joseph Detiège was born in Hannut on 23 November 1787. He was conscripted into the 2nd *Fusiliers* of the Imperial Guard on 20 November 1808. He was captured during the campaign in Russia.

six hundred and fifty leagues from Paris and we are still marching forward. It is not ideal to march in this country. When the weather is bad, the ground is very bad. Our life is not so great at the present. Luckily, the peasants had food. We were very well on the road in Silesia and in Sac [Saxony]. We were fed by the peasants. But we had to leave as soon as the Emperor joined us. This is all I have to say at the present.[22]

Jean-François Chalseche[23] wrote to his parents the same day. Fighting in one of the few minor battles at the beginning of the offensive, he proudly highlighted the role that the Imperial Guard, in which he served, played in pushing back the Russians:

Vitepsk 4 August 1812

Dear father and mother
[. . .] We arrived in Russia on 30 July. We fought for three days and the first line was really damaged but the Guard did not give up and the Russians did not hold. We are still 800 leagues from Paris. We have already been at the bivouac for forty days. We are not so comfortable. The food was good in Germany and in Sacse [Saxony]. The *bourgeois* fed us and we had bread, meat and a lot of beer and many vegetables. Germany must be respected because it is one of the most beautiful and richest countries, except for wine. I think that the forest starting at the Rhine goes up to Russia. Wood is abundant. They have very nice lakes and the climate of the country is quite similar to ours [. . .]. We marched for ten to twelve hours [a day] and we could see dead horses on the road. They died of exhaustion and misery. There are five army corps, without counting the Imperial Guard, in Russia. The 1st 2. 3. 5 and 6th Corps. Pierre François Bastin[24] is no longer with me because he stayed in the 4th *voltigeur* and I am now with the *fusilier*. But I do not think that his parents are that proud [. . .].[25]

It seems that the French had a low estimation of the Russians at the beginning of the campaign. Most soldiers had nothing to say about their

---

22. AEL: 1044. François-Joseph Detiège to his parents, 4 August 1812.
23. Jean-François Chalseche was born in La Gleize on 22 March 1789. He was conscripted into the *Voltigeurs* of the Imperial Guard on 12 June 1808.
24. Pierre-François Bastin, born in La Reid on 20 March 1790, was conscripted into the Imperial Guard in 1809.
25. AEL: 1044. Jean-François Chalseche to his parents, 4 August 1812.

enemy and chose instead to complain about the lack of food or the quality of the roads. Jean-Henri Lemaye[26] was one of them:

Liozna, 4 August 1812

[. . .] We are now in Russia. We camp in Liozna for a few days. There was a lot of misery because we could not find food and had to march twenty leagues a day to chase the enemy. We left the country six months ago. We are always marching.[27]

Jean-Jacques-François-Joseph Boussart[28] did not make it to Russia. His unit stopped in Prussia to recover:

Berlin August 1812

[. . .] We have not received any straw since we crossed the Rhine. The bourgeois fed us but we slept more often on straw than in a bed. Today, we did not receive our usual supplies but three packs of bullets, so we thought that we had arrived. But they told us that the Russians were retreating. We do not know if we will go forward or if we will stay in the cities of Prussia. This kingdom is not an enemy of France but we are on the lookout, just in case. They call us with our weapons every day and we have guard duty, with the backpack and the bullets in the pouch, ready to fire. In fact, we are totally ready for war. We marched for four hundred leagues without stopping, even for two days, in a city and we marched long days, because we often did twelve leagues per day. We hope to stay in this city to recover a bit, because many men are tired and many stayed in the hospital and we have to wait for them. [. . .].[29]

Jean-Henri Rompen,[30] based in Prussia, followed the events in Russia from a distance. Propaganda, but also the impressive number of victories since 1801, led soldiers to believe that the campaign of Russia would be another swift success:

Nehrung-les-Pillau 6 August 1812

[. . .] We left Wesel for Pillau on 27 May. We arrived at the island of Pillau on 15 August. It was a march of 300 leagues. We stayed

---

26. Jean-Henri Lemaye was born in Huy on 16 September 1788. He was conscripted into the 4th Regiment of the Line in 1808.
27. Fairon and Heuse, *Lettres de Grognards*, p. 278.
28. Jean-Jacques-François-Joseph Boussart was born in Liège in September 1791. He was conscripted into the 5th Regiment of the Line on 11 November 1811 and was discharged in 1814.
29. AEL: FFP 1044. Jean-Jacques-François-Joseph Boussart to his parents, August 1812.
30. Jean-Henri Rompen was born in Teuven on 1 May 1792. He was conscripted into the 9th Regiment of Foot Artillery on 7 March 1812.

one day in Pillau and then went to the island of Nerung, where we camp. We work on the cannons every day. Our life is really bad. Our bed is made of straw and the sky is our roof. As for the supplies, we have a pound and a half of bread, half a pound of meat and a few potatoes. On this island, there is no grass, just sand and water. On one side, there is the Baltic Sea, and on the other a 300 foot wide river. You can imagine how pleasant it is to be here. It is always cold. Sometimes, the water is so difficult that navigation is not possible from Pillau. We marched for fifteen days, sometimes doing difficult stretches, and marched through the woods and the mountains. We are close to the *Grande Armée* and we will not stay much longer in Pillau. The *Grande Armée* is in Russia and everything is going well for us. Our Emperor promised to celebrate his holy day, on 15 August, in Saint-Petersburg, the capital of Russia. During the journey, the peasants gave us supplies. They always had *eau de vie* and beer on the table and good food. They had to give it all because we do not have money. The troops are really motivated and hurry to victory in Russia. Dear father and mother, we are really far from each other and we will be even more. We will not meet for New Year but I hope to see my fatherland. It is the will of God and we cannot change anything. Let us hope that God will be our guide, that he will bless our army, that he will bring this war to an end, and that he will bring us back victorious in the fatherland [. . .].[31]

This race for the Russian capital triggered several positive reactions. The letter of Jean-François Monsez,[32] who later died in Russia, illustrates its effect on morale:

Kovno 7 August 1812

[. . .] I am at the hospital of Kovno in Russia to recover. My foot is wounded because of the tiredness of the road [he marched too much]. We had a lot to carry and it was really painful but, thanks to God, my foot is better. I will tell you that the troop is marching fast. We captured many prisoners. We are only 40 leagues from Saint-Périsbourque [Saint-Petersburg], the capital city of Russia. I am very happy at the present.[33]

---

31. Fairon and Heuse, *Lettres de Grognards*, p. 291
32. Jean-François Monsez was born in Dison on 29 July 1791. He was conscripted into the 5th *Fusiliers* of the Imperial Guard on 26 June 1811. He disappeared in Russia and was removed from the regiment's books on 10 November 1812.
33. Fairon and Heuse, *Lettres de Grognards*, p. 281.

Napoleon finally caught up with the army of General Barclay de Tolly at the battle of Smolensk on 16 August 1812. The French captured the city but did not manage to prevent the destruction of the supplies there. Tons of food and weapons were burned or ended up in the river Dnieper. This scorched-earth policy had disastrous consequences for the French, who usually lived off the land to compensate for the deficiencies of their logistics. The death of his horses forced Jean-Charles Lesure[34] to stay behind in East Prussia. He soon heard about the battle of Smolensk:

Tilsix 18 September year 1812

My very dear father and mother
[. . .] I have been in this city for six weeks already and two of my horses were ill. They both died three weeks ago. I am still here and I waited for the new detachment. They passed by the city on the fourteenth of this month and I thought I would carry on with them but the Captain did not want me because I had too much to carry and they did not have a cart to transport everything. He will send me to the depot of Elbaing, in Prussia. I will leave on the twentieth of this month with a cart provided by the city [. . .]. I ask you, very dear father and mother, to talk about me to the supreme leader [he probably refers to the prefect], so I can join the gendarmerie and come closer to the country. Let me know if you need a certificate for my brother Philippes.[35] He should never be a soldier because it is much better to be in peace at home and go to bed when the day is over. We have not had more than two hours of rest ever since the campaign began. My feet hurt and it was impossible to walk. One of my comrades caught a fever and went to the hospital three days later. I went to see him but they told me that he had died [. . .].
    I have nothing else to write except that the French took the strongest city of Russia on 15 August. I hope that they [the French] will enter in Turkey. People say that the French are 200 and 80 leagues inside Russia. My Captain told me so in Tilsix [. . .].[36]

Louis-Joseph Geuget[37] also lost his horses at the beginning of the offensive. He heard good news about the campaign but equally mentioned important friendly casualties:

34. Jean-Charles Lesure was born in Mons on 5 October 1792. He was conscripted into the 7th *Chasseurs à Cheval* on 21 March 1812.
35. Philippe-Joseph Lesure, born in Amiens on 27 December 1793, was not conscripted because he had a brother on active service.
36. AEL: FFP 1044. Jean-Charles Lesure to his parents, 18 September 1812.
37. Louis-Joseph Geuget was born in Thisnes on 7 October 1789. He tried to avoid conscription but was arrested and sent to the 111th Regiment of the Line. He was later transferred to the 9th Cuirassiers.

Insterburg 14 September 1812

We left on 28 February to fight the Russians. We went through several countries, including Westphalia, Prussia, Poland and the old Prussia, and we are now at the border with Russia. I am at the depot of Insterbourg because my horse was killed. The army is 300 leagues deep in Russia and it advances every day, but many soldiers died. We are waiting for horses to join with the regiment. They [the French army] captured depots and more than six thousand Russians. They say that we will go back to France when the war is over. But we are better in this country than in France, despite the fact that it is a bad country.[38]

Meanwhile, more French soldiers reinforced the army in Russia. Jean-François Wilmart[39] faced difficult conditions during the journey through Europe:

Kainiber 30 August 1812

My very dear father and mother
[. . .] We are five hundred leagues from home and we marched all the bad roads. We went through Germany and Austria and in the desert and in Prussia and in Poland and in the old Prussia and we are about to enter Russia. We are waiting for the cannons. We have not been in a house for a month and we are still sleeping in the countryside. [. . .].[40]

After the loss of Smolensk, the Tsar appointed Mikhail Kutuzov to command the Russian army. The ageing commander had already fought against the French on several occasions, including at the battle of Austerlitz. Kutuzov had no desire to let the city of Moscow fall without a fight. The French and the Russians finally met at the battle of Borodino on 7 September 1812. Sometimes called a pyrrhic victory, the battle allowed Napoleon to head toward Moscow, where he expected to receive the capitulation of the Tsar. Jean-Noël Dehalleux,[41] who fought at Smolensk and Borodino, also believed that the Russians were about to give up:

---

38. Fairon and Heuse, *Lettres de Grognards*, p. 281.
39. Jean-François Wilmart was born in Visé on 17 July 1792. He was conscripted into the 12th Battalion of the *train des équipages militaires* in 1812. He disappeared during the campaign of Russia and was considered dead in 1813.
40. AEL: FFP 1044. Jean-François Wilmart to his parents, 30 August 1812.
41. Jean-Noël Dehalleux was born in Gomzé-Andoumont on 30 January 1785. He tried to avoid conscription but was arrested and sent to the 93rd Regiment of the Line on 10 June 1806. He disappeared in Russia and was removed from the regiment's registers on 31 December 1812.

My very dear father and mother
We had a first fight with the Russians near Smolensk, where I am now in the hospital, on 16 August. This battle lasted five days but the enemy was finally forced to retreat in the direction of the city of Moscow, fifteen leagues from there. There, they have very strong fortresses. There were small battles on 5 and 6 September. The main battle happened on the morning of 7 September. We won and the enemy was chased from his stronghold and had to flee the city. Both armies stopped marching. We believe that this stop means that peace will come or that they will give up their weapons.

One bullet went through my left arm during the last battle. This wound is not dangerous and I have almost recovered [. . .].[42]

Arnold-Joseph Riga[43] asked the authorities to be discharged from the army. He said that he had been shot three times before Moscow:

Landau 4 April 1813

To the mayor and the Baron
[. . .] I was removed from the *Grande Armée* of Russia because I received three gunshots in Mosaÿ, 18 leagues from Moskot [Moscow], the capital city of Russia. I received a bullet in the left leg, below the calf. The big toe of the same leg was crushed by a box of ammunition. I was also stabbed by a lance in the right knee. I should be discharged from the army but my parents forgot to ask for it [. . .].

Jean-François Deharaing[44] luckily survived the battle of Borodino:

Hanover 3 April 1813

My dear mother
[. . .] I lost my horse at this thing in Moucot [Moscow] on 7 September [1812]. A cannonball cut its thigh [. . .].[45]

The French took Moscow on 14 September but did not manage to prevent the city from burning down on the same night. Trapped with few

---

42. AEL: FFP 1044. Jean-Noël Dehalleux to his parents, 28 October 1812.
43. Arnold-Joseph Riga was born in Bodegnée on 24 May 1791. He was conscripted into the *Fusiliers* of the Imperial Guard on 3 May 1811, but deserted. He was arrested and sent to the 4th Regiment of the Line before deserting again. Riga was caught and transferred to the 1st Battalion of *Pontonniers*. He was discharged in 1813 and lived with his brother.
44. Jean-François Deharaing was born in Milmort on 12 February 1786. He was conscripted into the 12th Cuirassiers on 26 October 1806.
45. AEL: FFP 1043. Jean-François Deharaing to his mother, 3 April 1813.

supplies in a ruined city, Napoleon waited in vain for Alexander I's capitulation. When he finally ordered a withdrawal in October 1812, it was already too late to save the *Grande Armée*. The French were unequipped to face the Russian winter and discipline had deteriorated too much to face violent rear-guard assaults efficiently. Jean-Guillaume-Joseph Herbrand[46] survived not only the Russian winter, but also captivity:

Jülich 4 August 1813

My very dear father and mother, brothers and sister and family
[. . .] They say that our army corps will parade in front of the Emperor Napoléon on the seventh of this month. They also say that we will leave on the tenth of this month, but I cannot tell where because nobody knows. Most think that we will go in Austria, because the Emperor of Austria has occupied the border. And they say that we have peace with Russia but not with Prussia, because the Emperor Napoleon does not want peace with Prussia before the King loses the entire country. I was in Russia the last year and the cold was so cruel that there were frozen soldiers lying in the streets. But I escaped without harm. Only my arm and my big toe were frozen. Only one of ten men came back alive. I went with the French until Moscow. Then, I was captured by the Russians, who took everything. I had silver and watches, in gold and in silver, and more than two hundred gold *Louis* in my belt. They stole everything. I only kept my mess tin in my belt. [. . .] Moscow is a very big city: seven miles in circumference, and it is at least one thousand leagues from Paris. You can imagine how far it is from us. Nicolas Peiffer[47] of Nidrum died as bravely and not as a [word missing] near Moscow. He was killed by a cannonball. Buschman[48] has not been captured by the Russians [. . .].[49]

Jean-Hubert Leroy[50] followed the disaster from the rear:

Stettin 31 January 1813

My very dear father and mother
[. . .] Nothing else to tell you, except that the weather is harsh. It has

---

46. Jean-Guillaume-Joseph Herbrand was born in Butgenbach on 17 November 1792. He was conscripted into the 9th Regiment *bis* of the *train d'artillerie*.
47. Nicolas Peiffer, born in Butgenbach on 7 June 1792, was conscripted into the 9th Regiment *bis* of the *train d'artillerie*.
48. André Buschman, born in Amel on 19 May 1792, was also conscripted into the 9th Regiment *bis* of the *train d'artillerie*.
49. AEL: FFP 1045. Jean-Guillaume-Joseph Herbrand to his parents, 4 August 1813.
50. Jean-Hubert Leroy was born in La Reid on 8 February 1792. He was conscripted into the 96th Regiment of the Line on 7 March 1812. He was discharged from the army on 1 September 1814.

been freezing since the month of September [. . .]. But, thanks to God, the cold is not harming me. Here, we are staying with the *bourgeois* and they are heating well. It would have been good for our army to live like us. But, on the contrary, they had to fight and retreat all the time. The hunger, the weather and the tiredness have ruined our armies. In summer, the Russians were always beaten. But they said that two good generals were coming to help them: hunger and cold. And they were right. They went up to Kinisberg [Königsberg, Prussia] but we pushed them back. We must have captured 10,000 men [. . .].[51]

Jean-Michel Soxglet[52] wrote to the parents of Guillaume-Joseph Schoonbroodt[53] to tell them that their son was in a desperate condition. Schoonbroodt later died of fever in the hospital:

Stittin 28 January 1813

Sir
I take the liberty to write this short letter to help your son, who was admitted in the hospital in Stettin. He is back from Russia, a very bad country, and he is all frozen. I cannot talk to him as he is almost deaf. He is almost mute and he said nothing to me when I saw him. You must know that Jean Michelle Soxglet is writing. If you want to tell your son anything, you can send a letter to my address. I end this letter by giving you my regards [. . .].[54]

Jean Close[55] told his mother about the end of the Russian campaign and the beginning of the war in Germany:

Lambourd in Prussia 10 July 1813

My very dear mother
[. . .] We came back from the campaign of Russia on 25 January 1813. We stopped in Glaugot, Prussia, to defend the city. We were stuck there for three months and a half and this is why I have not written earlier. We suffered a lot during the campaign. We had 30,500 men in our regiment but only 42 came back. You can judge

51. AEL: FFP 1044. Jean-Hubert Leroy to his parents, 31 January 1813.
52. Jean-Michel Soxglet was born in Charneux on 3 March 1786. He replaced Guillaume-Joseph Delacroix in the 96th Regiment of the Line on 27 March 1812. He was discharged on 1 September 1814.
53. Guillaume-Joseph Schoonbroodt was born in Aubel on 27 May 1791. He was conscripted into the 5th Cuirassiers on 24 August 1811 and died of fever in Stettin on 18 June 1813.
54. AEL: FFP 1044. Jean-Michel Soxglet to the father of Guillaume-Joseph Schoonbroodt, 28 January 1813.
55. Jean Close was born in Butgenbach on 11 February 1781. He was conscripted into the 98th *Demi-Brigade* in year XI (1800–1).

how much we suffered. The people we lost, it was not in a battle but because of the misery and the cold. We went for three months without having bread. We only ate horse. I can swear that we killed the officers' horses in the bivouac. We killed them to eat them [. . .]. I will tell you that I was wounded twice, once in the leg and once in the hand. But, thank God, I am better now. Jacop Plaiéé[56] of Wuillevesent[57] was captured in Russia [. . .].[58]

The catastrophic campaign of Russia had immediate effects in Europe. Austria and Prussia joined Russia, the United Kingdom, Portugal and Spain in a coalition against Napoleon. The French army was in a bad shape. Soldiers were exhausted, unprepared and far less confident of victory than the years before. Nicolas Klinckhammer[59] summarised this state of mind:

Harbour 21 June 1813

Very dear father and mother, brothers, sisters, grandfather, uncles, aunts, cousins, [. . .] I hope that we will see each other one day! I hope this will happen one day but we are in a very dangerous situation. We are expecting to fight the enemy any day. I do not know anything better than the protection of God. I ask you to keep me in your prayers. If I come home one day, I will reward you for this [. . .].

They wanted to promote me to the rank of corporal. I refused because they have to do even more than a simple soldier.[60]

The German Campaign

After the catastrophic defeat of 1806, Prussia had undergone a radical process of modernisation of her army. By February 1813, this scheme resulted in an efficient citizen army based on meritocracy. In Prussia and in many other parts of Germany, popular anti-French feelings triggered mass-mobilisation, an event traditionally associated with the birth of modern German nationalism. If this view is contested, there is no doubt that the French were in difficulty in the east. The Prussians and the Russians sealed an alliance with the treaty of Kalisch on 28 February 1813. This was not good news for Napoleon and for his depleted army, as

---

56. Jacques Layes, born in Butgenbach on 3 January 1781, was conscripted into the 98th *Demi-Brigade* in year X (1801–2).
57. Weywertz, a village near Butgenbach.
58. AEL: FFP 1042. Jean Close to his mother, 10 July 1813.
59. Nicolas Klinckhammer was born in Schleyden on 19 November 1788. He was conscripted into the 21st Regiment of the Line in 1813. He later deserted.
60. AEL: FFP 1045. Nicolas Klinckhammer to his family, 21 June 1813.

most French veterans had died during the retreat from Russia. The French Emperor successfully found new conscripts to rebuild his forces and even outnumbered the Russians and the Prussians. The new soldiers, however, were not physically conditioned to endure long marches or mobile warfare. Hubert-Joseph Smal[61] had occupied a non-combatant position from 1809 to 1812. Like many others in his position, he was then promoted to the rank of corporal to fill the ranks and expected to lead a few men into battle:

From the citadel of Strasbourg 8 February 1813

Dear father and mother
[. . .] I have to tell you that I left the supply depot on 21 January and you must know that I volunteered because our regiment is almost destroyed. The major took twelve shoemakers and a few tailors. He gave us all the rank of corporal or sergeant, as we were the oldest, to complete the regiment. New conscripts have arrived today and we form the sixth battalion and we have to instruct young men of the 1814 levy [. . .].[62]

Napoleon had an audacious plan to beat his enemies. He wanted to attack in the north-east of Germany, capture Berlin and then outflank the Russians. However, this strategy was seriously flawed. The main Russian and Prussian forces were concentrated around Dresden, forcing the French Emperor to divert his forces there. Jean-Lambert Vidal[63] witnessed the initial concentration of troops. He also highlighted the hostility of the local population toward the French forces:

Hosbourg 6 April 1813

My very dear father [. . .].
I am much closer to our home. I am in Germany, fifteen days from Russia, and we have started a new campaign. We are in a strong position in this country and ready to fight. A big battle is in the making and you cannot count the number of soldiers in the *Grande Armée*. I have to tell you that Dalcourt[64] is well, except that he was hit in the hand by a gunshot fired by a peasant. He thinks that two of his fingers are paralysed [. . .].[65]

---

61. Hubert-Joseph Smal was born in Héron on 6 October 1790. He was conscripted into the 18th Regiment of the Line in 1809 and later captured in Strasbourg.
62. AEL: FFP 1042. Hubert-Joseph Smal to his parents, 8 February 1813.
63. Jean-Lambert Vidal was born in Oteppe on 4 October 1791. He was conscripted into the 60th Regiment of the Line on 30 May 1811. He was transferred to the 23rd Regiment of the Line on 8 July 1812 but disappeared in September 1813.
64. Jean-Nicolas Delcourt, born in Oteppe on 15 May 1791, was conscripted into the 60th Regiment of the Line in 1811.
65. AEL: FFP 1042. Jean-Lambert Vidal to his father, 6 April 1813.

The virtual annihilation of the French cavalry in Russia meant that the enemy had more flexibility to conduct minor raids behind the lines. Many soldiers were haunted by the Cossacks and their ability to strike suddenly. The hostility of the population, and their tendency to join hostile actions against the French, did not help. As usual, civilians paid a heavy price. Jean-Joseph Thonnard[66] fought against the Cossacks and the locals:

Lunebour 4 May year 1813

My very dear uncle
[. . .] On Easter, we fought against the Cossacks and the peasants, two leagues from Bremen. We won and we took the village. We burned 180 houses and pillaged everything but I did not take much.[67]

Denis Lambert[68] fought in similar circumstances:

Hembourg [Hamburg] 2 June 1813

[. . .] Nothing really special to tell you except that on Easter, at two in the morning, we were beaten. We fought against the Cossacks in a village near the city of Bremen. The peasants fired at us. On Wednesday, we burned the entire village at three in the morning to reward them. We captured all the bourgeois which we could find. I took the opportunity to reward myself. I found money and I still use it. We were hoping to do the same in Hembourg [Hamburg] but we entered the city without shooting even once [. . .].[69]

On 1 May, Napoleon crossed the Saale with his men to march on Leipzig and Dresden. This move left the right flank of the army exposed. Prince Wittgenstein, the Prusso-Russian commander, took the opportunity to attack III Corps under Ney on the morning of 2 May. The battle of Lützen began as a contest for the villages around the battlefield. Marshal Marmont and his VI Corps quickly came to the rescue of Ney, allowing the French to hold the line. Napoleon, who heard the battle from far away, came to the rescue at 2.30 p.m. He arrived at a critical time and decided to charge at the head of his troops. The attack of the Imperial Guard at 6 p.m. finally broke the

---

66. Jean-Joseph Thonnard was born in Liège in May 1792. He was conscripted into the 85th Regiment of the Line in 1813.
67. AEL: FFP 1043. Jean-Joseph Thonnard to his uncle, 4 May 1813.
68. Denis Lambert was born in Romsée on 4 December 1792. He was conscripted into the 85th Regiment of the Line on 19 February 1813 and later captured while in the Dresden hospital.
69. AEL: FFP 1043. Denis Lambert to his family, 2 June 1813.

Prussian and Russian lines, bringing victory to the French. However, the enemy was not routed. Napoleon still needed a decisive victory, like Austerlitz, to force a peace settlement. The French Emperor had an opportunity at the battle of Bautzen on 20–21 May. Napoleon wanted to attract the main enemy forces on the left before sending Ney and his men to deliver a crushing blow on the right flank. The French won the day once again, but the Prusso-Russian army retreated in good order. Worse, the French suffered twice as many casualties as the enemy. Laurent-Joseph Lévêque[70] had a close call at the battle of Bautzen, where his musket was destroyed by a bullet:

Spandau 24 June 1813

[. . .] I am now in a camp in a village near the city of Spranto in Prussia. We have fought hard since 2 May and, thanks to God, I have not been injured. During the battle of 20 and 21 [May 1813], our regiment fought with distinction, especially on 21 at noon. Cannonballs and grape shot were falling on our square but we held and went forward, screaming 'forward', 'forward', and a lot of us suffered but I had no bad luck. As a result, the French army marched forward to the city of Fioit [?] and we had a 48-day truce. We will soon know the good and the bad. At this battle on 21, a bullet cut my musket in two and another one it my shoulder. And then, another bullet caught my leg but, thanks to God, I was unhurt. [. . .].[71]

Joseph-Simon Piot[72] took part in the two battles:

Beuthen in Prussia 18 June 1813

My very dear father and mother
[. . .] We were ready to fight on different occasions. We saw the Russians and we saw the cannonballs coming at us. We threw ourselves to the ground when the cannonballs were falling on us. But the enemy constantly retreated because we fought them. The infantry fought all the time and we were always following it [. . .]. I forgot to tell that we made peace with the Cossacks and they say that we will go back to France [. . .].[73]

---

70. Laurent-Joseph Lévêque was born in Fraipont on 28 March 1786. He tried to escape conscription in 1806 but was arrested and sent to the 23rd Regiment of the Line on 30 November of the same year. He survived the Napoleonic Wars and came home in 1814.
71. AEL: FFP 1044. Laurent-Joseph Lévêque to his family, 24 June 1813.
72. Joseph-Simon Piot was born in Couthuin on 17 March 1790. He was conscripted into the 2nd *Fusiliers-Grenadiers* of the Imperial Guard in 1813.
73. AEL: FFP 1042. Joseph-Simon Piot to his parents, 18 June 1813.

Jean-Joseph Totelin[74] also fought at Lützen and Bautzen. He called them both 'defeats':

From the city of Liegnitz 25 June 1813

My very dear father and mother
[. . .] We fought two big battles on 2 May and 21 May. Thanks to God, I survived this defeat because our battalion lost many people. In these two defeats, we were forced to form square [. . .].[75]

Jean-Joseph Pinckers[76] lost a good friend at Bautzen. He gave graphic details of how grape shot killed his comrade:

Camp of Neudorf 15 July 1813

[. . .] We camp in a place where we receive no supplies and those who have no money, they die of hunger. As for my friend Pascal, you asked if he was killed on the battlefield or if he died in the hospital. I will tell you his adventure. At eleven in the evening, it was when we had to fight the hardest. We were side by side when came a grape shot which entered his brain and broke his whole head. And my greatest sadness was to be by his side and have no way to help him, and have to wait for the same fate at any time. I thank God for saving me from this battle. And my poor friend Pascal had to stay on the battlefield until the next day. Then, they took him to the hospital of Breslau and he died in the afternoon [. . .].[77]

Joseph Gougnard[78] wrote a long letter to explain both battles. At Bautzen, a bullet went through his shako:

Grandemberg 12 August 1813
[. . .] The truce is once again prolonged until 15 August. Today, we received the order to leave. I take the opportunity to write to let you know that I am well. War will start again on the seventeenth of this month. We must take our line of battle where we stopped. The Russian army is alongside the Oder River, where there is also the Prussian army, and we expect to have a big battle there.

---

74. Jean-Joseph Totelin was born in Herve on 12 February 1790. He was conscripted into the 18th Regiment of the Line on 8 March 1809 but was removed from the regiment's registers in the same year. It is not known how he reappeared in the 65th Regiment of the Line in 1813.
75. AEL: FFP 1042. Jean-Joseph Totelin to his parents, 25 June 1813.
76. Jean-Joseph Pinckers was born in Verviers on 11 March 1793. He replaced his brother, who was needed as a factory supervisor, in the 78th Cohort of the National Guard on 28 July 1812. Pinckers later served in the 147th Regiment of the Line and was captured in Germany in 1813.
77. AEL: FFP 1044. Jean-Joseph Pinckers to his family, 15 July 1813.
78. Joseph Gougnard was born in Hollogne-sur-Geer on 25 November 1786. He was conscripted into the 1st Regiment of Marine Artillery on 22 November 1806.

You must know that the Russians and the Prussians burned their villages and even their cities while retreating to Saxony. The inhabitants were safe. In my first letter, I told you about three big battles. The first big battle was on 2 May, a battle so honourable for the French. The enemy had one hundred and fifty thousand men more than us.[79] This battle began at nine or ten in the morning and ended at eleven and a half in the evening. There was firing in different villages and in the Russia camp and it illuminated our camp. The enemy cavalry charged our regiment three times in a row, believing that they could do better than during the day, but they failed. The victory fluctuated for a long time. This battle is named Luxenne [Lützen]. We crossed the Lippe River on 8 May. This river is as powerful as the Rhine. It was where the forces of Russia, Prussia, France and her allies, met at the battle of Bautzen, the battle on 21 [May]. We were, including both sides, more than eleven hundred thousand men together.[80] The firing lasted for two days without interruption. Twenty villages burned on the battlefield. Cannons fired constantly. The shells exploded in the air. We did not know if the men were French or Russian because there were so many of them. At the battle on the 20th, I fought, being a *tirailleur*. I played dead on the battlefield. If I had not done that, I would have been killed. A few of us did that. They spared no one. They put their swords through the wounded if they saw them moving. They wanted to take the city of Bauzen [Bautzen]. They were badly received. When they were close to the city, the horses did not want to go forward and they were jumping in the air. You must know that you cannot make an omelette without breaking eggs. If I had to explain my adventures, I would need a book and not a letter. I dare to say that in the three battles, I was always in the first line. Cannonballs, grape shot, and bullets curled my moustache on a few occasions. The shako on my head saved my life. A bullet pierced the grenade on the metal plate. It did not hurt. I also have to tell you that the countries welcoming the disease of war are to be pitied [. . .].[81]

Lambert-Gilles-Joseph Defresne,[82] a professional writer, wrote one of the most detailed letters of the Napoleonic wars.

---

79. The French and their allies had about 144,000 men, while the Prussians had 37,000 and the Russians 56,000.
80. These numbers are, as usual, far from accurate. The French army had 167,000 men and fought against 66,000 Russians and 31,000 Prussians.
81. AEL: FFP 1044. Joseph Gougnard to his parents, 12 August 1813.
82. Lambert-Gilles-Joseph Defresne was born in Liège in February 1793. He was conscripted into the Imperial Guard on 29 January 1809.

Camp of Croskobvitz 21 July 1813

Dear father and mother

I was impatient to send news and even more to hear from you. You have to excuse me for the delay; the events of the day will explain the cause. You must have heard that I fought in bloody battles. For example, the battle of Lutzenne, which happened on 2 May, was without a doubt the bloodiest battle, and I saw the moment when, being threatened, the Guard gave the most impressive lesson and showed that they wanted to win or die. I saw the first and second lines retreat up to four times, without knowing where to go. Then, the second charge was one of the most powerful and forced the enemy to evacuate the position on which they held so strongly. They lost a lot of people, up to fifty or sixty per company. We, the fusiliers, observed and did not lose many people because of the bullets. But the cannonballs and the shells rained like stones on our column, and they took a lot of us. The most precise hit, one that struck me with horror, was a cannonball fired by the enemy on our column. It knocked Marshal Mortier[83] off his horse, took off two legs in the first company, the arm of our lieutenant, who died of it, and ended its race by killing a comrade who was standing next to me. These things happened during the day. The night came and we formed the square when the cavalry charged us at full speed. We pushed them back and inflicted heavy losses. We stayed the whole night on alert. During the night, 15,000 French soldiers arrived. When the day came, the Emperor, in the middle of all these fights, led his army in multiple columns. 20,000 enemy cavalrymen entertained us with musket shots the whole morning, to give their army time to retreat. Noon came and the Emperor, seeing that the citizens [the enemy] were retreating, made us go forward and chase them. This retreat lasted until Bodzene [Bautzen], a battle on 20, 21, 22 and 23 [May]. During this chase, we lacked supplies for a few days and I had to eat rotten food, but hunger made me believe that it tasted good. I was helped by my captain on a few occasions, and he saved my life, and now I am like his child.

The battle of 20, 21, 22 and 23 was not less bloody than the one on the second, because for four days, the fighting did not stop. But

---

83. Marshal Edouard Mortier (1768–1835), Duke of Treviso, fought in the Revolutionary Wars and in most Napoleonic campaigns. He commanded the Imperial Guard in 1813.

the hottest day [the most difficult] was on 21, a costly day for us. The enemy had redoubts on the heights, where he had eight cannons pointed at us. They fired from five in the morning until five in the evening. But because our commanders gave good orders and because of our bravery, we captured their position.

And I was in the same difficult situation during this battle, in terms of supplies. The exception was that we were freer to look for food and we would sometimes find bread. Since this last battle, we stayed near Neumarck, until we stopped fighting. From there, we came back here, after staying four days in different villages where we were really well. This camp, where we worked so much, does not pay. We had to survive with our ration, which is very small: three quarters of bread, half a pound of meat. This is the daily ration which drives us to the edge.

I also have to tell you that on 27 May, the 15th line regiment and the 50th, stayed near a city, where they were looking for food. Suddenly, ten thousand Cossack cavalrymen fell on them with their sabres and lances, because they do not have many muskets. These two regiments had 25,000 men but, in five minutes, were reduced to 1,500. If the help had been delayed by 4 or 5 minutes, there would have been no one left.

The Emperor heard of this surprise and gave the order to advance. We caught them the next day, the twenty-eighth. That day, we rested and I went to the second battalion to ask a few fusiliers if they knew Hubert Michaut.[84] They said yes, they knew him well. They told me that he was behind. This did not make me happy. I asked them his company number. They said that he was with the second company of the second battalion. I immediately went to his sergeant-major. I asked for him. He told me that he was there with the company. Me, impatient to see him, I ran to find him. I found him and he was well and we chatted as old friends. But you will be surprised to know how we partied: with three quarters of potatoes that I had been carrying for three or four days in my backpack and a bit of water of my gourd. But the drum played and I had to obey and leave. My duty calls and I end this letter by kissing you with my whole heart.[85]

---

84. Jean-Joseph-Hubert Michaut, born in Herstal on 3 November 1791, was conscripted into the Imperial Guard in 1813. He was captured at the battle of Dresden on 26–27 August 1813.
85. AEL: FFP 1044. Lambert-Gilles-Joseph Defresne to his parents, 21 July 1813.

Jean-Hubert Grégoire[86] explained to his parents how his Lieutenant, who was killed in action, used to encourage him:

Golberg [Goldberg] 21 July 1813

My very dear father and mother
[. . .] You recommend that I do not forget the good Lord and the Holy Virgin. It must not be a cause of worry for you. I pray whenever I can. You also recommend that I do not mistreat people in enemy countries. I can promise that I have not taken anything from anybody since we started the campaign. I only took a piece of bread because the family made me do it. If I had done like many of our *voltigeurs*, I would have a lot of money that I do not have at the present. But I always did my duty. I have always been forward and I have never left my company. [. . .] My Lieutenant, who was shot three times, always told me: come on Grégoire, be brave, you are from Liège and the *Liégeois* will never die. I never met such a good man [. . .]. Dear father and mother, do not be sad for me. This fate comes from God and it is impossible to go against it. It is the law.

I hope to be lucky and survive this campaign and to see you and all the family together [. . .]. The truce is prolonged until the fifteenth of August and then, if peace is not agreed, we will start again [. . .]. You would not believe how awful the camp is. We only eat soup once a day.[87]

François-Richard Ceressaux[88] and André-Joseph Sohier[89] saw the battlefield of either Lützen or Bautzen. The two men felt the need to tell their parents about it:

Groutenberg 18 June 1813

My very dear father and mother, brother and sister [. . .].
We think that peace might come any day. We drink with Renkin and we sleep with Renkin. I have to tell you that we went by a battlefield. There were bodies everywhere and it was impossible to move [. . .].[90]

---

86. Jean-Hubert Grégoire was born in Malmedy on 4 February 1792. He was conscripted into the 78th Cohort of the National Guard in 1812 but later served in the 147th Regiment of the Line.
87. AEL: FFP 1044. Jean-Hubert Grégoire to his parents, 21 July 1813.
88. François-Richard Ceressaux was born in Namêche on 6 November 1793. He was conscripted into the 19th Regiment of the Line on 19 November 1812. He died in a military hospital in 1813.
89. André-Joseph Sohier was born in Namêche on 18 January 1793. He was conscripted into the 19th Regiment of the Line on 19 November 1812. He was captured in September 1813.
90. AEL: FFP 1042. François-Richard Ceressaux and André-Joseph Sohier to their families, 18 June 1813.

Following the battle of Bautzen, a truce was agreed by all sides. Napoleon knew that his men were exhausted but he also desperately wanted to rebuild his cavalry. The truce led to the signature of a six-week armistice on 5 June. The Prussians and the Russians needed the time to recover but also wanted to bring Austria onto their side. French soldiers looked at the armistice of Pleiswitz with hope. Jean-François-Arnold Wégria[91] believed that peace would come soon:

This is a village, I did not notice[92] 28 June 1813

My very dear father and mother
[. . .] You talk about the action of Lipsic. This was a bloody battle, one that we fought for a long time. We fought again for fifteen days without interruption and we went through the battlefield when we went to Prussia. I am with the Captain and I am well, because he will always take the good place to stay. We are in a castle and I am well. I am even better than at home. We went back to Saxony with the Emperor. If there is no peace, we will go back to Célésie [Silesia] but I think that peace will happen because the Emperor of Austria said that the one who did not want to make peace would have one hundred and fifty thousand cavalrymen against him [. . .].[93]

Jean-François Godin[94] hoped that the victories of Lützen and Bautzen were enough to win the peace:

From Beuten camp of Kroscovisc 4 July 1813

My very dear mother
[. . .] It has been impossible to write since I left Frankfurt. Since that day, we left and chased the enemy for 250 leagues. What a sad campaign: we march ten leagues per day, we fight all the time. Despite this misery, we are the winners and I hope that we will have a long-lasting peace.
[. . .] I make a good living, despite the fact that we do not see any money in the enemy countries. I have to let you know that I was captured by the Cossacks and I was stripped naked. I only had an old Prussian coat to wear. I had the beautiful uniform of a medical

91. Jean-François-Arnold Wégria was born in Oteppe on 3 January 1789. He was conscripted into the 2nd *Chasseurs à Cheval* in 1813.
92. This unclear sentence probably means that he does not know the name of the village he is writing from.
93. AEL: FFP 1043. Jean-François-Arnold Wégria to his parents, 28 June 1813.
94. See Chapter 2 for the biography of Jean-François Godin.

officer [*officier de santé*], but everything was stolen. And I was lucky to escape. I was locked in a city where it was impossible to get out without crossing a big river. I threw myself in the river and swam despite the cold. In this country, it is as cold in August as it is at home in March. But the climate did not damage my health, thanks to God.

[. . .] Let me know all of those who died since I left. [. . .].[95]

While the diplomats negotiated, the troops were kept busy. Nicolas Lange[96] paraded before the Emperor:

Mangnebourck 12 July 1813

My very dear father and mother
[. . .] We crossed the Rhine in Wesel on 8 July and then took the road to Bremen. When we arrived, we went to Hanbourcle [Hamburg] but we received other orders in Hantbourck [Hamburg] to go to Magnebourck [Magdeburg] and we arrived on the tenth of the same month in the city. It is a beautiful place but all the houses are in wood. We have been marching for six weeks. As for the war, I have nothing to say. All the troops are moving and our Emperor arrived on the thirteenth of this month and he inspected us in person on the sixteenth. On the thirteenth, the great general inspected us [he is still talking about Napoleon] [. . .].[97]

However, peace did not come. Austria had agreed to join the conflict on the Prusso-Russian side if the French failed to meet certain conditions. Napoleon, taking a huge risk, preferred the path of war. Servais-Joseph Lemaire[98] closely followed the events:

Bonlau Silesia 15 August 1813

My very dear father and brother and sister
[. . .] I have to tell you that we were transferred to another regiment on 25 June. We are in the first regiment of marine artillery, 5th battalion of the 6th company of the 6th army corps. We left Mainz on the first day of July and arrived in Bonslau in Silisia on the twenty-fifth. I can tell you that we were really tired and we did not

---

95. Private collection. This text has been published in Moreau, 'Le remplacement d'un conscrit amaytois de 1813'.
96. Nicolas Lange was born in Saint-Georges on 9 November 1789. He was conscripted into the 21st Regiment of the Line in 1813.
97. AEL: FFP 1042. Nicolas Lange to his parents, 12 July 1813.
98. Servais-Joseph Lemaire was born in Soumagne on 3 March 1791. He was conscripted into the 133rd Regiment of the Line on 12 May 1813 and later served in the 1st Regiment of Marine Artillery.

sleep in a city from Frankfurt to the first city of Saxony [. . .]. On 10 August, we were reviewed by the great marshal and we were at least fifty thousand men together. All the sixth army corps was there and they put an altar in the field and we sung a *te deum* with the musicians. All the bourgeois and the peasants of the surroundings came to see us, and after we were blessed. And I have to tell you that we must begin the battle on the seventeenth of this month and I am still with Mathieu Wandebert [. . .].[99]

There are no letters for the second half of 1813 or for the campaign in France in 1814. The French won an impressive victory at the battle of Dresden on 26–27 August 1813. However, the lack of cavalry prevented them from pursuing the enemy and delivering the final blow. The fate of the Napoleonic armies was decided at the battle of Leipzig, also known as 'the Battle of the Nations', on 16 to 19 October 1813. The allies inflicted a decisive defeat on Napoleon and ended his rule in Germany. The coalition invaded France at the beginning of the next year and forced the French Emperor to abdicate.

Fighting against Napoleon

The Low Countries were annexed by France during the revolutionary war of 1794. During the next twenty years, tens of thousands of Belgians were forced to serve for Napoleon. Those who had survived in the French army until 1814 found themselves in a strange situation. They suddenly became citizens of the United Kingdom of the Netherlands. As such, they were either demobilised and sent home or conscripted into the army of the Netherlands. When Napoleon returned from the island of Elba in February 1815, Belgian veterans fought with the Netherlands and its allies against France. There are only a handful of letters from that period. Jacques Goffin[100] was a medical officer who had served in the French army. Captured in 1813, he agreed to fight for the other side. He wrote the following letter a few days after the battle of Waterloo:

Louvain 30 June 1815

My very dear uncle and aunt,
Since the hostilities resumed, I have been busy day and night helping wounded soldiers. I am currently surrounded by these

---

99. AEL: FFP 1045. Servais-Joseph Lemaire to his father, 15 August 1813.
100. Jacques-Michel-Joseph Goffin was born in Saint-Séverin on 28 October 1793. He served in the French army as a medical officer before being captured in 1813. After 1814 he served in the army of the Netherlands.

unfortunates, who beg for my help. This is why I will be short in this answer. I left for Antwerp with all of those who were ill to clear some space for the wounded on the eighteenth of last month. I came back on the twenty-first. You give once more a proof that you are kind by having an interest in my fate [. . .].[101]

Guillaume Schrinder served for eleven years in the French army before deserting. He offered to enlist in the army of the Netherlands:

August 1815

To the General Commissaire of his Majesty the King of the united Netherland

Sir,
Guillaume Schrinder, deserter of the 15th regiment of *chasseurs à cheval* serving for France, aged 23 years old, from Liège, is currently in the prison of the city for deserting. He respectfully asks to be freed and says that he is a native of this city and has nothing to be blamed for. He served with honour for eleven years and he is offering to serve with the troops of his majesty as a substitute for a citizen of the city. He hopes that you will consider his request.[102]

Thousands of men were captured in Russia and in Germany. It was far from easy to come back home as identity papers and money were required to cross Europe. Gilles-Joseph Moreau[103] was one of the many men who were taken during the retreat from Moscow in 1812. Stuck in Prussia, he wrote to the authorities and to his father for help:

Village of Montag 2 June 1816

My very dear father
[. . .] It was not possible to write before. I was really sad to be unable to contact you ever since I left Spain. We marched for a long time until we reached Moscow. During the retreat, I was captured and I am now in Prussia. My very dear father, I would like to come home. I really want to see you again, my dear father. You must do your utmost to send me six Louis because I cannot do such a long

---

101. AEL: Fonds des familles Richard (FF R) 174. Jacques-Michel-Joseph Goffin to his uncle and aunt, 30 June 1815.
102. AEL: Fonds Hollandais (FH) 495. Letter to the *Commissaire general*, August 1815.
103. Gilles-Joseph Moreau was born in Burdinne on 4 January 1789. He was conscripted into the 10th Battalion of the *train des équipages* on 17 June 1808. Moreau was captured during the Russian campaign. The authorities contacted the Prussians regarding Moreau in August 1816.

journey without money. My very dear father and brother and sister and family, I ask you to do your best to send what I ask for because I have my certificate but it is valid for a limited time only. This is why I cannot come home [. . .].[104]

In this chapter, we showed that the morale of the French army was generally good at the beginning of the Russian campaign. The Peninsular War had shaken the men's confidence, but they still believed in their ability to win on the battlefield. The French did not expect the disastrous outcome triggered by the retreat from Moscow. The failure to conquer Russia had important consequences. Soldiers lost confidence in the invincibility of the French army and hoped more than ever to go home. The gravity of the defeat in Russia also struck civilian communities. Many future conscripts lost faith in the regime and refused to serve in the army. Draft-dodging and desertion became so common that the authorities were forced to take drastic actions.

The correspondence from the German campaign of 1813 confirms the steady decline of the French army. Soldiers were stunned by the strength of the Allied armies and by the level of violence on the battlefield. The triumphant tone commonly seen after the battle of Austerlitz had definitely disappeared by 1813. There are no letters from 1814, since the Belgian soldiers had been sent home, but we know that many veterans from the Ourthe department were either conscripted or volunteered to fight against the French in 1815. In the area of Liège, Napoleon's popularity had collapsed in only a few years.

---

104. AEL: FH 3691. Gilles-Joseph Moreau to his father, 2 June 1816.

Chapter 6

Wounds, Illness and Captivity

Fearing the Hospital

Created in the reign of Louis XIV, the French military medical corps was completely reformed in 1792 in order to meet the challenge posed by the war of movement. If various laws were voted between 1792 and 1801 in an attempt to improve health in the armies, they ultimately failed to address serious issues. The *Corps de Santé*, created on 18 *vendémiaire* year X (10 October 1801), was supposed to employ 843 people, including 489 surgeons. By 1806, there were only 351 surgeons and by 1812, 824. Medical units were also plagued by a shortage of supplies and the rigidity of the administration as well as the lack of training facilities and hospitals.[1] Napoleon was not overly interested in military medicine and hospitals. On several occasions he praised wounded officers who chose to stay and die on the battlefield rather than retreating to have their injuries treated.[2] Despite the risks they faced, doctors and surgeons had very little chances of gaining the Legion of Honour or a title. Unfit soldiers could find little comfort in military hospitals, usually poorly equipped places with a dreadful reputation, where most patients were badly treated.[3] Mentioning a friend from a neighbouring village in an 1812 letter to his parents, Imperial Guardsman Nicolas-Wéry Crismer[4] was under no illusion about military wards:

> [. . .] Thomas Deflandre is really ill at the hospital and he might die as all who go to the hospital never come back, especially when they are ill [. . .].[5]

Such messages were common. Replying to his parents on 27 May 1805, Henri Rousseau[6] informed them of the unfortunate fate of a friend from his native Soumagne:

1. Jacques Sandeau, 'La santé aux armées. L'organisation des services et les hôpitaux. Grandes figures et dures réalités', *Revue du Souvenir napoléonien*, 450 (2004), pp. 19–37.
2. Jean-François Lemaire, *Les blesses dans les armées napoléoniennes*, Paris, 1999, pp. 86–97.
3. Forrest, *Napoleon's Men*, pp. 156–7.
4. See Chapter 1.
5. Thomas Deflandre was born on 20 February 1793. His fate is unknown. Private collection. Letter of Nicolas-Wéry Crismer to his parents, 18 December 1812.
6. Henri Rousseau, born in Soumagne on 21 September 1782, was the father of Mathieu Rousseau and Marie Isaey. He was conscripted into the 96th Regiment of the Line in year XII (1803–4). He deserted on 28 May 1804, was caught, and deserted once again on 1 December 1812.

My dear father,
[. . .] This letter to tell you of my health. Thank God, I am well for
the moment and I wish you the same. You asked about Jean Joseph
Lemaire.[7] I have to tell that he died at the hospital in Paris [. . .].[8]

Pierre-Joseph Lannoy[9] fell ill and stayed in the hospital for a few days.
There he witnessed the death of numerous men and the collapse of morale:

Neuf Brisach 19 April 1807
[. . .] I will leave for the battalion on 24 April. I am happy to be out
of here, because the place is really bad. There has been snow since
the nineteenth of April and the mountain, a quarter of a league from
the city, is covered with snow. And this hospital is really bad too. In
eight days, 160 people died and 14 others deserted. There were so
many desertions that we cannot leave the city without authorisation
[. . .].[10]

Having a relative in the hospital was thus a cause of anxiety.
Communication was so irregular that families had sometimes no other
choice but to contact their relative's comrades-in-arms to enquire about the
fate of their loved ones. The answer was not always a happy one:

Sir,
In your last letter of 23 October 1809, you asked if it was true that
your son had died.[11] I can certify that he died in Lugos Engalise [in
fact Galicia]. He died of sickness at the hospital. He was my friend
and was writing my letters. I have nothing else important to write at
the present [. . .].[12]

Illness and infectious diseases were far more dangerous than the
battlefield. Most deaths were caused by scabies, diarrhoea, fever,
blennorrhoea, syphilis or typhus, all commonly found among Napoleonic
soldiers.[13] Wounded soldiers also faced gangrene and other related
necrosis, all of which were redoubtable killers at the time. Doctors and
surgeons often saw this 'hospital rot' as a death sentence. On 22 April

7. Jean-Joseph Lemaire, born in Soumagne on 9 February 1783, was the son of Jean-Joseph Lemaire
and Jeanne-Joseph Detrembleur. A nailer by trade, he was conscripted in the year XII (1803–4)
and sent to the 96th Regiment of the Line in the same year. He died in Paris on 10 October 1804.
8. AEL: FFP 1043. Henri Rousseau to his father, 27 May 1805.
9. Pierre-Joseph Lannoy was born on 4 March 1787. He was conscripted into the 105th Regiment
of the Line in 1807.
10. AEL: FFP 1043. Pierre-Joseph Lannoy to his family, 19 April 1807.
11. The son was Noël-Joseph Lekeu, born in Momalle on 24 December 1787. He served in the 5th
bataillon du train d'artillerie and died in Lugo (Spain) on 13 March 1809.
12. AEL: FFP 1044. Sébastien Andres to the father of Noël-Joseph Lekeu, 17 January 1810.
13. Sandeau, 'La santé aux armées'.

1810, Pierre Laschet[14] described to his siblings the ordeal of being affected by a disease:

> My greetings to my dear brother and sister,
> [. . .] I am miserable, disease has not left me and I have been at the hospital for seven months. I stayed at the hospital of Antwerp, from Antwerp I have been transferred to the hospital of Maline [Malines], from Maline I was sent to Brussels, from Brussels I came to [word deleted] and now I am in Breda with fever and scabies. My dear brother and sister, I am miserable and have no money [. . .].
> Once this letter is received, go first to my uncle Jean Schumacher and ask for money [. . .]. I need it badly because, as you can imagine, when you stay in a hospital or in several hospitals for seven months, you are guaranteed to be very miserable. And when I am once again cured of my disease at the hospital of Breda, I will have to march toward Spain as the regiment in which I have served for already so long is in Spain [. . .].[15]

Hubert Kalff,[16] a German-speaker from the same village and regiment as Pierre Laschet, suffered a similar fate. Transferred from one hospital to another, he finally disappeared. The following letter was written months before the army lost track of him:

> My very dear father and mother,
> [. . .] I have recovered my health, with the exception of my scratched [the word maimed is crossed out] feet. I hope you are in a good health. I have been at the hospital for so long, from the moment people picked potatoes until now. I stayed for three months at the hospital in Brussels where I had a daily fever. Then I was sent to Mons where I stayed five weeks and caught scabies. Once freed from scabies, I joined my company in Holland and when I reached Brittany, I had once again to go to the hospital for fever. While at the hospital, my company left Holland for Paris [. . .]. [17]

Louis-François-Ferdinand Servais[18] became ill during the Peninsular War. He wrote a dramatic letter to his family:

---

14. Pierre Laschet, born in Raeren on 4 October 1790, was the son of Corneille Laschet and Anne-Barbe Derivael. A labourer, he was conscripted into the 51st Regiment of the Line in 1809. The regiment lost track of him after his stay at the hospital.
15. AEL: FFP 1042. Pierre Laschet to his siblings, 22 April 1810.
16. Hubert Kalff, born on 22 February 1790, was the son of Jean Kalff and Marie-Joseph Cupper. He was sent to the 51st Regiment of the Line in 1809 but disappeared following his stay at the hospital.
17. AEL: FFP 1042. Hubert Kalff to his parents, 18 April 1810.
18. Louis-François-Ferdinand Servais was born in Liège in June 1812. He was conscripted into the *Tirailleurs-Chasseurs* of the Imperial Guard.

Lucrine 11 June 1813

[. . .] I was at the Val-de-Grâce but I was transferred to Lurcine, a small temporary hospital, because there were too many sick people. I was very badly treated and you can only get out of that place to go to the cemetery. People die every day. I have been here for a month and I was admitted because I was shaking and then I was cold. I caught that in Spain. I suffer of hunger and fever. The belly is painful and is getting bigger every day! I will be very lucky if I survive this time. But I do not lose hope and God helps me. Today, the eleventh of the month, in the morning, I am very unwell. Pray to Saint-Etienne and ask him to save me [. . .].[19]

Remembering that family letters were often purposely dramatised to attract pity and more importantly money, it seems that bribing hospital staff was the best way to survive. Sick men were prone to emphasise their physical condition to move their relatives. Lambert-Henri Dejosé[20] sent the following request to his wife on 7 April 1806:

My very dear wife,
I write to tell you that I was admitted to hospital in Metz with a fever on 31 March. I will have to go to Strasburg, where I will inform you of my next destination, to join my regiment. I suffered a lot on the way because of the behaviour of the gendarmerie but I hope that my sufferings will end soon. I only have another 30 leagues to walk to reach [my destination]. As soon as you have received this, I beg you, my dear wife, to send me money for food at the hospital as I am without income. It will please me greatly. I have now a good appetite but I am still weak and cannot tell you when I will be out of the hospital [. . .].[21]

On 4 July 1811, Jean-Henri Diveux[22] described his illness in detail to his father:

My very dear father,
I have received your letter of 11 June in which you explained how

---

19. This is once again a stolen letter, reproduced in Fairon and Heuse, *Lettres de Grognards*, pp. 361–2.
20. Lambert-Henri Dejosé, a nailer born in Evegnée on 8 May 1781, was the son of Nicolas Dejosé and Christine Filot. He was put in the reserve in year X (1801–2) and conscripted in year XIV (1805). He tried to flee but was arrested in 1806 and sent to the 95th Regiment of the Line. His name is not in the regiment's books, meaning that he might have died before reaching his unit. SHD: 21YC715. Register of the 95th Regiment of the Line.
21. AEL: FFP 1045. Lambert-Henri Dejosé to his wife, 7 April 1806.
22. Jean-Henri Diveux, born in Mortier on 17 June 1790, was the son of Jean-Noël Diveux and Marie-Elisabeth Dossin. A labourer, he was conscripted in 1809 but tried to flee. He was arrested and sent to the 10th Dragoons on 24 June 1809. He tried to desert soon after but was caught and sent to the 32nd Regiment of the Line.

to receive my money order. I will tell you that if the money order was delayed, it is because I was the only one of the regiment to be in Perpignant [Perpignan] and this is why the postman kept telling me that the money had not arrived. Thank God, it arrived in the end. It came on 2 July and it was very helpful as I had been so sick that now I need good food to recover. Everything is so expensive that the one who cannot scheme is quickly ruined.

As for my illness, I stayed for 22 days without any food but then was better but fell ill again with a bloody flux but now I feel a bit better. Concerning the leave you told me about, I asked the pharmacist, a German [named] Ghyot, who can speak a bit [our] local dialect. He gave me great hope about that but I need to be patient as he told me that everything cannot happen at the same time. My dear father, since I am in debt to some friends who were with me at the hospital [. . .], I ask you to send 24 [francs] so I can recover my strength or else I will drop dead like so many others. Understand that in a hospital where there are 3 thousand patients, rations are so small that people die of misery [. . .].[23]

At the hospital, French soldiers were mainly concerned for their well-being but on rare occasions thought about their reputation. Martin-Joseph Grandjean,[24] who fell ill on his way to the regiment, wrote in 1809 a letter to his mother in which he described himself as a 'victorious son'. In fact, he never saw action, and died soon after having written the following letter:

Dear Mum

I wrote about a year ago to give you news about myself. I was hoping that maternal love would encourage you to write but I have, so far, not received any answer. I have been transferred from one hospital to another without being cured. We are so unhappy in this cursed Spain and in this hospital where subsistence is hardly provided.

I know your good heart and your feelings of motherhood, which are so dear to me. Allow me to ask for help to alleviate my sad fate and ease my situation. I hope that I will be discharged for poor health. It will be a happy day when I come home; you will see a proud and victorious son and not a coward who fled his flag [. . .].

Give my regards to my brothers and to the family. Farewell good

---

23. AEL: FFP 1042. Jean-Henri Diveux to his father, 4 July 1811.
24. Martin-Joseph Grandjean, born in Blegny on 13 October 1789, was the son of Jacques-Guillaume Grandjean (deceased at the time of Martin-Joseph's conscription) and Gertrude Degref. A spinner by trade, he was conscripted into the 86th Regiment of the Line on 2 May 1808. He was reported missing in March 1809 while on his way from Bayonne to Spain. The following letter, from after his disappearance, was written from a military hospital and means that he fell ill or was wounded. Further information given in 1813 by the 86th Regiment suggests that he later died in the hospital at Vitoria.

mother. Be happy, it is my greatest wish. I kiss you and I am forever your son.[25]

Those who survived disease were well-aware that they had faced death. Arnold-Joseph Delsupexhe,[26] soldier of the 13th Regiment of the Line, wrote to his uncle and aunt in March 1812 from a hospital in Osnabrück:

> My dear uncle and dear aunt
> I send this letter to enquire about your health. I am currently quite well but I am indeed deep in misery as I was ill for a long time in Osnabrück and different hospitals and I thought that I would not see you again as I was dying. I ask you to be kind and send me money as I am really sad [. . .]. The rumour has it that we will go to Russia and Turkey for war [. . .].[27]

Not all soldiers were as negative about hospitals and sometimes even described enjoyable times. Given the conditions, it can be assumed that most positive feedback served the purpose of reassuring the family. The case of Jean-Joseph Servais,[28] from the 21st Regiment of the Line, would support that hypothesis. The nineteen-year-old had only positive things to say to his parents about the hospital where he was treated for a bullet-wound. Yet he died on 10 October 1813, a few days after having written the following letter:

> My very dear father and mother,
> I am writing to tell you how I am. My health is very good but I have been wounded in the thigh by a bullet on 25 August but thank God my wound is very good and I am waiting to be evacuated to France [. . .]. I am staying at the hospital in Dresse [Dresden] where I am very well. We are three or four from Liège in the same room and we talk about home and have fun together. There is nothing else to underline for now. I kiss you with all my heart and salute you one thousand times [. . .].[29]

The fact that Sevais did not describe the reality of battlefield hospitals to his family was hardly a surprise. There were no assigned stretcher bearers,

---

25. AEL: FFP 1043. Martin-Joseph Grandjean to his mother, 29 September 1809.
26. Arnold-Joseph Delsupexhe, born in Cerexhe-Heuseux on 10 December 1780, was the illegitimate son of Arnold Delsupexhe and Marguerite Degueldre. Delsupexhe's borough forgot to conscript him but he was arrested in 1811 and sent to the disciplinary regiment of Walcheren and then to the 13th Regiment of the Line on 10 July 1811.
27. AEL: FFP 1042. Arnold Delsupexhe to his uncle and aunt, 17 March 1812.
28. Jean-Joseph Servais, born in Theux on 24 June 1793, was the son of Marie-Joseph Servais. With an older brother in the army already, he replaced another conscript on 10 April 1813. He died at in the hospital at Dresden on 10 October 1813.
29. AEL: FFP 1044. Jean-Joseph Servais to his parents, 27 October 1813.

leaving the bandsmen of the regiment to pick the wounded soldiers. The Imperial Guard was the only unit to have a mobile ambulance. If the injured men survived transportation, they still had to face emergency treatment at the hospital. Accounts of the time mentioned pyramids of amputated limbs, spurts of blood, constant screams and an unbearable stench. Amputees sometimes kept the same bandages for days, their limbs becoming infested by maggots.[30] If being wounded or ill was not a desirable fate, working at the hospital was considered as a lucky escape. Jean-François Godin,[31] a fresh conscript in the Imperial Guard, was spotted for his medical skills by a surgeon-major but needed financial help to buy his medical instruments:

> I have been writing for the last three weeks to tell you that I need two hundred *francs*. My last two letters have been unanswered and I do not know why. I have to spend money every day. Studying surgery at the Gros Cailloux hospital, I will need to buy books and instruments. You understand, sir, that if you keep quiet for longer, I will lose my position [at the hospital] [. . .]. If you do not send me money in the next ten days, I will be sent to a fighting unit for the second time.
>
> I joined it [the hospital] by accident. Two men were fighting in the neighbourhood when one was wounded by a sword in the higher part of the ribs. I volunteered to treat the wounded. The next day, the surgeon-major asked for the person who had bandaged this man. Someone told him. He called for me and enquired about my studies. I answered and then he asked if I had the means to buy medical instruments. I said yes. The following day, we went to his place and then to the hospital, where I stayed. My fate is much better now.
>
> If you could help me stay here, it would be such a great joy for me [. . .]. I still have to tell you that the Emperor came here and reviewed us the day after I joined the hospital staff [. . .].[32]

The case of Jean-Henri Degueldre[33] was even more unusual. In a single action in 1813, he was stabbed twice in the chest and shot in the leg by Spanish guerrilla. Sent to hospital to recover, medical officers soon discovered that Degueldre was trained as a surgeon. The military was in great need for medically-trained soldiers. Only 275 of the 824 surgeons

---

30. Lemaire, *Les blesses dans les armées napoléoniennes*, p. 235.
31. See Chapter 2 for his biography.
32. Jean-François Godin to the Rome family, 26 December 1812. Found in Moreau, 'Le remplacement d'un conscrit amaytois de 1813'.
33. Jean-Henri Degueldre, born in Chênée on 22 June 1789, was the son of Olivier Degueldre and Jeanne Beaudrihaye. Trained as a surgeon, he had initially been reformed for being too short but was later drafted in the 5th Regiment of the Line. He died of fever in Perpignan on 24 November 1813.

of the French army had survived the Russian campaign. The French army had a habit of recruiting medical students and hospital workers but the medical corps was plagued by desertion. Degueldre's skills were therefore invaluable. Unfortunately, he had lost his certificates proving that he was a doctor and as a result was forced to write home to ask for duplicates:

> My dear brother,
> [. . .] My health is better now. Since I left Perpignan with the convoy for Gironne, we have been attacked by Spanish bandits. Unfortunately for me, I was at the front of the convoy, where they attacked first. I was wounded by a bullet, which entered the inner part of the right leg, and by two bayonet stabs in the chest. One stab entered between the seventh and eighth ribs and the other slid on the sixth rib on the left side. I suffered a lot but thanks to God I was at a hospital where I was known by several surgeons, among which mister Destrumon of Liège. You must know him as he knows you. He took great care of me as did mister Duplan,[34] surgeon major, who is married to a girl from Liège [. . .].
>
> My dear brother, they offered me to work in this hospital as a third class surgeon after having asked all kind of questions about anatomy, bullet wounds and how to treat diseases. They wanted to know if I was capable of working as a third class surgeon. You ask, my brother, how I lost my certificates [proving that he was a surgeon]. One day, I was walking with my medical tools and my certificate in my pocket when I had to bandage a carter who had been wounded by his horse. They probably fell on the floor while I was doing that [. . .].[35]

Degueldre, proving once and for all that military wards were unsafe, died a few months later at Perpignan's hospital. Military medicine had still a long way to go. It was not until the end of the nineteenth century and during the First World War that the French army would make significant progress.[36]

Captivity and Suffering

If wounds and illness were dreaded, soldiers equally feared the prospect of capture. Men from the ranks had little or no knowledge of what to expect

---

34. Perhaps Doctor Duplan, surgeon-major from Tarbes, who survived the Napoleonic wars. Beclard, Chomel, Cloquet, Orfila and Rostan, *Nouveau journal de médecine, chirurgie, pharmacie, etc.*, Paris, 1819, p. 171.
35. 6 May 1813.
36. Sophie Delaporte, 'Médecine et blessures de guerre', in Stéphane Audoin-Rouzeau and Jean-Jacques Becker (ed.), *Encyclopédie de la grande guerre 1914-1918*, Paris, 2004, pp. 347–56.

in case of captivity and were totally unfamiliar with enemy countries. Most surviving letters sent by prisoners of war came from Britain, where approximately 130,000 Napoleonic soldiers were held from 1803 to 1814. There, detention conditions were far from uniform; officers were either confined to a designated city called a 'parole town' or, in the best case, sent home after swearing not to fight against Britain. Soldiers and non-commission officers were in a more difficult situation. The lucky ones were under house arrest and as such enjoyed at least a bit of freedom and independence. The others were sent to prison or were held in prison hulks.[37]

Captured soldiers usually wrote home to tell their families about their unfortunate fate. Henri-Joseph Rossiny,[38] a soldier of the 26th Regiment of the Line, was captured aboard the *Infatigable* along with hundreds of other men from the Liège area in a naval battle on 25 September 1806. Brought to England soon after, he was only able to write home for the first time on 4 December 1810:

From the prison of Forton in England

My very dear mother,
I wish you a happy year to you and to my brother, sisters, parents and friends. You should know that I have been taken as a prisoner of war by the English on 25 September 1806. My health is very good, thank God, and I hope that this letter will find you in a similar state. We were sailing to Négips [wrong spelling for Egypt, but he was in fact headed for the Martinique]. We were five frigates and two brigs. The English chased us for one full day with eight three-deckers. We had to surrender as they had almost destroyed all of us. Thank God, nothing happened to me. You always told me that God would protect me in all fights and I have all faith in God. We have suffered a lot but thank God everything is good for the moment. I finish this letter by begging for your forgiveness for all my faults [. . .].[39]

The state of captivity was usually quite a shock. Brought in difficult conditions to England, French soldiers suffered from the lack of news, poor food and idleness. In these conditions, money was more essential than ever. Augustin-Alexandre Goffart[40] explained to his parents the circumstances surrounding his capture before giving instructions as how to send money:

---

37. Patrick Le Carvèse, 'Les prisonniers français en Grande-Bretagne de 1803 à 1814. Première partie', *Napoleonica*, 8 (2010), pp. 6–8.
38. Henri-Joseph Rossiny was born in Waremme on 26 December 1783. He worked as a labourer before being sent to the 26th Regiment of the Line on 3 December 1804. He was probably released in 1814.
39. AEL: FFP 1045. Henri-Joseph Rossiny to his mother, 4 December 1810.
40. Not a lot is known about him. He was probably born outside the Ourthe department and was sent to the 4th Regiment of the Line, where no other soldier from Liège served.

Porchester [Portchester] near Porsmhout [Portsmouth] 10 June
1811

[. . .] I have to tell you that I was unfortunately captured in Portugal
by the Portuguese. They brought us to the seaport of Porto where
we embarked for Lisbon, capital of Portugal. From there, we sailed
to England. We travelled for about 800 leagues. I can assure you
that I suffered a lot during this travel and I am still suffering in the
prison of Porchester [Portchester] near porsmhout [Porstmouth]. I
have help from nobody and I ask you, father and mother, to send me
money to ease my situation. I am so miserable that I had to sell
some of my rations to buy paper [. . .].

If you agree to send me something, here is how to do. Send a
letter with money to Mister Perigor,[41] banker in Paris, *Chaussée
d'antin, rue du mont blanc n. 7*. He will forward the money without
delay [. . .].[42]

English prison ships are still remembered in France today as brutal
places where captive soldiers faced inhumane conditions. Such view was
largely influenced by *Mes pontons*, a book written in the middle of the
nineteenth century by Louis Garneray.[43] François-Joseph Micha[44] was one
of these soldiers imprisoned on a ship in Plymouth. Captured in Portugal in
1809, he dictated his letters to a friend who could write and read. The young
man painted a dark picture of his captors and his life in general:

England, 28 August 1809

My dear uncle,
I take the opportunity of [meeting] a diplomat who is leaving for
France to give you news and to tell you about my misery since
leaving the country!

After having stayed for four months in St-Malo, I left for Spain
where I was captured by the English. They brought me straight to
England, where I am now. I am without money, reduced to the
limited rationing allowance that this tyrannical government gives us!

These barbarians have not only put us in irons but also stolen all
our belongings on the day they captured us. I wrote several letters

41. Alphonse Perregaux (1785–1841) was a Parisian banker. He had a monopoly over Franco-
British transactions during the Continental blockade. Alfred Fierro, André Palluel-Gaillard and
Jean Tullard, *Histoire et dictionnaire du consulat et de l'empire*, Paris, 1995, p. 1012.
42. AEL: FFP 1045. Augustin-Alexandre Goffar to his parents, 10 June 1811.
43. Louis Garneray, *Mes pontons, neuf années de captivité*, Paris, 1933.
44. François-Joseph Micha, son of Mathieu Micha and Catherine Yele, was born on 14 May 1789.
He probably survived the Napoleonic Wars.

to my father but they might unfortunately have not arrived. My uncle, I implore you, in the name of humanity and if God brings you this letter, to ask my father to do whatever he can to send me money. Tell him that this paternal duty would be remembered until the day his dear son dies! Tell him also not to worry about me as, thank God, I am in the best health possible [. . .].[45]

Receiving no news from his parents, Micha became increasingly impatient. He wrote several more letters to his family in which he tried to emphasise his mental and material distress:

England 7 January 1810

Dear father,
I have taken every opportunity to give news of myself and to let you know that I am now a prisoner of war. I wrote several letters but received none from you. In the first letters, I let you know about my need for money. My dear father, in the name of humanity, do whatever you can to send me money.

My captivity would have been very unhappy if not for the fortunate help of a sergeant of my regiment. Many of my comrades receive money from their parents, making me hope that your good heart will make you do the same and allow me to give back what I received [. . .].
P.S. This letter is written by your son's sergeant, the benefactor, who guarantees that any money sent will be used only for his education and his subsistence [. . .].[46]

Guillaume-Joseph Fransen,[47] who had volunteered for the 1st Hussars, also bitterly complained about life on a prison hulk:

My very dear aunt, my dear cousin and all my family,

I write to let you know that I am not dead, that I am still alive, but in in an embarrassing situation as I am a prisoner in England. I am so sad. We only have 18 ounces of bread per day and our drinking water smells like urine. We were at sea when the English surprised us during the night. We lost three ships and six cannonniers and now I am a prisoner. I give this letter to Rouseaux,[48] a liegeois [*liégeois*]

---

45. AEL: FFP 1045. François-Joseph Micha to his uncle, 28 August 1809.
46. AEL: FFP 1045. François-Joseph Micha to his father, 7 January 1810.
47. Guillaume-Joseph Fransen, born on 4 August 1790, was the son of Lambert-Joseph Fransen and Jeanne-Isabelle Goblet. He was probably released in 1814.
48. André-Dieudonné Rousseau, also from the 1st Hussars, was born on 25 January 1791. He was conscripted on 10 January 1810 and later captured by the British. He came home in 1811.

who is being exchanged and will return to France. I hope this letter reaches you as it will be impossible to write again. It would be fortunate if this letter arrives [. . .].[49]

As shown previously, soldiers were prone to exaggerate their misery in the hope of receiving more money from their relatives. If there is no doubt that life was hard, though one recent study suggested that mortality aboard prison hulks was in fact lower than in British prisons.[50] While Micha and Fransen complained, others were less negative about their life in captivity. Matthieu Closset,[51] from the 26th Regiment of the Line, was also detained in a ship when he wrote this letter:

[. . .] Father and mother: I have been made a prisoner of war on 27 May and brought to England. My very dear father and mother, I have been in a country far away from France called Martinique, 1800 leagues from France. Father, I am well and I hope that your health is as good as mine. As for the English, I have no reason to complain. I am looking for the day I will be given back to France and I am waiting for a happier fate [. . .].[52]

Laurent Maquet,[53] who had served in the 58th Regiment of the Line, was kept both in a ship and in a Scottish prison. Despite spending more than six years in the hands of the British, he emphasised his well-being and the importance of having close friends:

Valleÿ-feild [Valleyfield, Scotland] 28 June 1812

My dear father and mother
I will not tell you all my adventures but only that I was captured in Portugal by the English on 21 August 1808. From there, I was put on a ship sailing to England. Among the many prisoners, I recognised my unfortunate friend Michel Defflandre, captured in the same action as me, who gives his regards to his father and his uncle. We were sent to the same prison in Portsmouth England where we stayed for two years and five months. From there, we embarked for a new prison in Scotland where we are now. In this new prison, I found some of my friends from Jupille [Jupille, near

49. AEL: FFP 1045. Guillaume-Joseph Fransen to his aunt, 1 April 1811.
50. Patrick Le Carvèse, 'Les prisonniers français en Grande-Bretagne de 1803 à 1814. Seconde partie', *Napoleonica*, 9 (2010), pp. 152–88.
51. Matthieu Closset, born on 16 January 1784, was the son of Gilles Closset and Elisabeth Houge. He worked as a nailer in Jupille (near Liège, Belgium) before being sent to the 26th Regiment of the Line on 18 May 1806. He was captured aboard the *Lynx* on 25 September 1806.
52. AEL: FFP 1045. Matthieu Closset to his parents, 25 February 1809.
53. Laurent Maquet was born on 16 April 1787. A bricklayer, he was the son of Laurent Maquet and Marie-Jeanne Lejeune. He was captured in Portugal on 21 August 1808 and released in 1814.

Liège, Belgium], including André Defflandre and Germain Mathieu Clouset[54] who were captured in Martinique. They told me that Joseph Defrere[55] died fifteen days after having arrived in Martinique. It was not hard to believe as this sad island is very unhealthy. I have been a prisoner for four years but have never been ill. I am very well at the present [. . .].[56]

If social relations were important, others found unusual ways to keep themselves busy. Jean-Remi Delsupexhe,[57] of the 26th Regiment of the Line, was captured while on board the frigate *La Gloire*. His captivity made him acutely aware of the importance of having an education:

My very dear father and mother,
[. . .] I was captured on 25 September 1806. I wrote several letters but have never received any answer. I hope that if you receive this mail, you will answer as soon as possible. Father, you must leave my brothers in school as long as you can. It is the most beautiful thing that you can teach them. You must know that each day I am doing whatever is necessary to learn mathematics. Since I was put in prison, I have learned how to read.[58]

There are unfortunately no letters mentioning the long-awaited release and the return to France. Following Napoleon's abdication on 4 April 1814, the French provisional government began negotiating the release of war prisoners. To that effect, a law freeing all detained soldiers in France was voted on 13 April 1814. French ambassadors used this law to ensure that reciprocity was granted by foreign powers. Most soldiers came back to France but a few decided to stay, for one reason or another, in Great Britain. Another 13,076 men (around 10 per cent of all French prisoners) died in captivity.[59] Charles-Remi Beaujot[60] wrote a book about his captivity in

---

54. Mathieu Closset, born in Jupille on 16 January 1784, also served in the 26th Regiment of the Line. He was captured while aboard the *Lynx*.
55. All these men were indeed from the same region. André and Michel Deflandre were not related. Laurent Maquet and Michel Deflandre were both fighting in the 58th Regiment of the Line while André Deflandre and Jean-Joseph Defrère were in the 26th Regiment of the Line. Michel and André Deflandre survived captivity and returned to Belgium in 1814. Jean-Joseph Defrère indeed died of disease in the Antilles.
56. AEL: FFP 1045. Laurent Maquet to his parents, 28 June 1812.
57. Jean-Remi Delsupexhe was born on 2 February 1784. A draper by trade, he came back alive from England in 1814 after more than eight years of captivity. As soon as he arrived home, Delsupexhe was conscripted in the Prussian army but avoided military duty by hiding.
58. AEL: FFP 1045. Jean-Remi Delsupexhe to his parents, 26 December 1810.
59. Le Carvèse, 'Les prisonniers français en Grande-Bretagne de 1803 à 1814. Première partie', pp. 9–10.
60. Charles-Remi Beaujot was born in Angleur on 13 July 1784. He was conscripted into the 26th Regiment of the Line on 9 July 1805. Beaujot was hospitalised in Coimbre (Portugal) on 27 September 1810 and captured by the British on 3 October 1810. He stayed in the prison of Forton until 3 June 1814. He joined the Dutch army on 1 May 1815 and retired in 1840 from the gendarmerie in the rank of captain. He died on 1 November 1855.

England after the Napoleonic Wars. He gave interesting details about life in prison and his return:

In July 1811, we sailed for England. On board on the English ship, our compassionate hosts gave us plenty of good food. The crew, unlike the condescending Portuguese sailors, tried hard to joke and play to bring a smile on our pale and thin faces. The convoy was composed of sixty transport ships and was escorted by a few war vessels. One ship was used as a hospital and was soon filled with sick soldiers. Three of them died despite the excellent care provided by the British surgeons. I was pleased to see that the English, despite being Protestants, honoured our dead Catholic soldiers [. . .].

The convoy stopped in Plymouth, probably to drop prisoners, but was ordered to go to Portsmouth. There, the employees of the port verified the papers of the captains. They also took the usual sanitary precautions and quarantined us for a few days.

While we were in the harbour, we tried to guess our fate. What was our destination? The prisons of Scotland, where the climate is more rigorous, or England? Or were we headed for the prisons of Rochester, Norman Croce, Dartmoor or Forton? Or the horrible boat hulks of Chatham, Plymouth and Portsmouth, rightly renowned for being hell? [. . .].

[In April 1814] we arrived in Portsmouth and we were transferred to a parliamentary ship. We left in the evening. The next day in the morning, we were in the mouth of the Seine River, near Le Havre, where we landed soon after. We stayed with the locals for three days. After that, we were sent to the 155th Regiment of the Line and waited for the minister's orders. Finally, we were instructed to go to our depots and we felt very happy: we were going to see our fatherland and our friends at the regiment's depot [. . .].

They gave us two months of salary, a sum given by the government to all prisoners of war. After that, we had to serve His Majesty Louis XVIII and adopt the white cockade. But following the treaty of peace signed between the major powers, he [the Duke of Angoulême] ordered soldiers who had become foreign citizens of France to leave. I came back to Belgium.[61]

---

61. Charles-Remi Beaujot, *Relation de captivité du capitaine Beaujot, ancien sergent-major sous l'Empire français*, Liège, 1856, pp. 343–4.

In this chapter, we saw that the standards in French military hospitals were poor. Soldiers saw them as a place where the sick went to die and several letters show the desperation of those who had fallen ill. Many men were in such a bad situation that they bribed staff members or even deserted the army to escape military wards. There was only little faith in nurses and doctors, who were often powerless to help those in their care. It is true that medicine still had a long way to go. Scabies, fever and sexual diseases killed far more soldiers than the wounds sustained on the battlefield.

Prisoners of war were sometimes more fortunate. Despite being unanimously condemned in the literature of the nineteenth and twentieth centuries, there were dramatic differences between British prisons. Some, mainly prison hulks, were described as miserable places where food was scarce and discipline harsh. Others were far more welcoming for the French. Recent studies, showing that mortality was in fact lower among French prisoners than in the Napoleonic army,[62] confirm that captivity might not have been the ordeal usually described in the literature.

---

62. Le Carvèse, 'Les prisonniers français en Grande-Bretagne de 1803 à 1814. Première partie.', pp. 6-8.

Conclusions

On 22 June 1815 Napoleon abdicated in favour of his son. Soon thereafter the Allies entered Paris and restored Louis XVIII to the throne. The French Empire, which had once stretched from Spain to Moscow, was gone. Many of the young men who had fought for the Emperor had waited for peace for a long time. They had reluctantly left their civilian lives and had constantly written to their loved ones to keep those important links with home alive. What happened when they finally returned is not known as there are no letters describing these events. It is not difficult to imagine the joy of being reunited with elderly parents, a wife, a sister, a brother or a child after years of separation. Leaving behind the danger, the discipline and the discomfort must also have been a joyous feeling. However, returning soldiers likely also felt sad to leave their comrades and the unique lifestyle of the army behind. There is, at present, no study on how ex-soldiers from the Napoleonic armies coped with the experience of warfare and violence. As with other wars some probably lived with psychological problems for the rest of their lives. In retrospect many veterans felt proud to have been part of such an extraordinary adventure. In the decades following the battle of Waterloo regional associations of ex-soldiers of the First Empire were created and unofficial medals, such as the *médaille des débris de l'Armée Impériale* (remnants of the Imperial Army), were worn. In 1857, Napoleon III finally established the Saint Helena medal to recognise the surviving veterans.

The fall of Napoleon was also a relief for those who had deserted. At the end of the Empire, desperation drove large numbers of men to flee. Many heard of the crushing defeat in Russia and, despite the risk and the penalties, chose to escape rather than to serve. In 1813, 39 per cent of the conscripts of the Ourthe department became draft-dodgers. Those already mobilised were no more inclined to fight. The commander of the *Companie de Réserve* wrote to the Prefect in January 1814 to tell him that at best one out of five men was reliable in battle. Life as a draft-dodger or as a deserter was not enviable. Constantly fearing the gendarmes or denunciation, the men who had decided to flee the army were also a danger to their families. The end of the French Empire drastically improved their situation. Most of them came home or stopped hiding without having to fear any serious consequence.

There was, however, a substantial group of men who never came back. The total number of French casualties in the Napoleonic Wars will never be known. The regime did not keep official statistics and the estimates vary to a great extent: from 780,000 to 1,450,000 casualties.[1] These figures unfortunately exclude the dead from the territories lost by France in 1814, such as the Ourthe department. 25,000 men from the area of Liège volunteered or were conscripted in the French army. The death certificates in the Liège archives and the regiment's books kept at the *Service Historique de la Défense* in Vincennes show that at least 6,400 men from the Ourthe department died while serving in the French armed forces. This figure is probably far below the actual reality for the following reasons:

1. It is reached by looking only at the regiments in which more than 200 soldiers from the Ourthe department served.
2. Some registers listed the soldiers but did not keep track of their whereabouts.
3. Other books indicated that the men had deserted, disappeared in the hospital or been wounded without knowing the final outcome.
4. A few units in which many soldiers from the Ourthe department served, such as the 147th Regiment of the Line, lost their registers.

The 12th Regiment of the Line can be used to illustrate the fate of the conscripts from Liège and around. No less than 192 men from the Ourthe department served in this regiment between 1804 and 1808. Two died during the battle of Borodino, six disappeared after one battle or another, five were discharged in 1814, fifteen were transferred in another unit, twenty were never added to the register, twenty disappeared after staying in the hospital (most probably died), twenty-four died before the campaign of Russia, twenty-six were reformed, twenty-seven deserted and forty-seven were 'presumed captured' in Russia (most probably died as well). These numbers mean that out of 192 men, ninety-nine either died or were taken prisoners while fifty-eight survived. The fate of thirty-five soldiers is unaccounted for. It is estimated between 25 per cent and 40 per cent of the

---

1. Alain Pigeard, *L'armée de Napoléon*, Paris, 2000, pp. 224–5 and Tulard, *Dictionnaire Napoléon*, p. 535.

conscripts from the Ourthe department never came back. These figures are probably relevant for the whole French army as there is no reason to believe that the soldiers of the Ourthe department suffered more losses than the rest of the Empire.

Most soldiers who died during the Napoleonic Wars were quickly forgotten. Their bodies were thrown into unmarked mass graves near the battlefield or the military hospital where they had died. The practice of erecting war memorials with the names of ordinary soldiers would only emerge at the end of the nineteenth century. As a result their memory usually disappeared with the death of their immediate relatives. Their suffering and their unique war experience would have been largely forgotten without the preservation of their correspondence. As has been shown, these letters offer an uncompromising picture of life in the French army, one that is far from the romanticised version too often portrayed in the media. Rather than wearing flamboyant uniforms, most had improvised pieces of equipment, rags or civilian clothes. Discipline was harsh, life in the barracks monotonous and food generally unsatisfactory.

French soldiers kept fighting for several complex reasons. Friendship and solidarity helped many men survive the rigour of an otherwise unsavoury military existence. The cult around Napoleon also played an important part in making the French army so strong. Believing in their leader, French soldiers won an impressive streak of victories on the battlefield. These successful battles made them proud but did not protect them from psychological damage. Despite having difficulties expressing their feelings, many men were clearly disturbed by the level of violence. This does not mean that they did not commit atrocities against enemy populations, indeed they can something be seen rationalising such acts in their letters.

Ultimately, the Napoleonic armies were pushed too hard for too long. French soldiers became tired of fighting and lost faith in a positive outcome. The failure to hold on to Russia in 1812 triggered a chain-reaction. The soldiers of 1813 faced strong enemy armies who understood French strategies and had perfected their tactics in Spain and in the East. France lost the Ourthe department to the Kingdom of the Netherlands in 1814. Ironically, many Belgian veterans went on to serve in the Allied armies and would fight their former companions-in-arms at the battle of Waterloo on 18 June 1815.

Bernard and René Wilkin

Chronology

1769
15 August: birth of Napoleon Bonaparte in Ajaccio, Corsica

1779
May: Napoleon is admitted to the military academy of Brienne-le-Château

1789
14 July: storming of the Bastille

1793
22 December: Bonaparte is promoted to the rank of General

1795
27 October: Bonaparte becomes Commander of the Interior

1796
2 March: Bonaparte is given command of the Army of Italy
10 May: battle of Lodi
15 May: capture of Milan
15–17 November: battle of Arcola

1797
14 January: battle of Rivoli
17 October: Treaty of Campo Formio

1798
Campaign of Egypt

1799

23 August: General Bonaparte leaves his Army for France
10 November: Bonaparte overthrows the Directory on 18 *Brumaire* and becomes First Consul

1800

Bonaparte goes back to Italy
14 June: battle of Marengo
4 September: Malta is captured by the British

1801

9 February: the Concordat between Napoleon and Pope Pius VII establishes the Catholic Church as the main church of France
21 March: Treaty of Aranjuez between France and Spain
28 March: the treaty of Florence confirms French dominance in Italy
2 April: Copenhagen attacked by the British
31 August: the French capitulate in Egypt
1 October: a preliminary peace treaty between France and Britain is signed in London

1802

1 February: a French army led by General Leclerc lands in Saint-Domingue
27 March: Peace of Amiens between France, the Batavian Republic, Spain and the United Kingdom
8 May: Toussaint Louverture, the leader of the Haitian Revolution, is forced to resign
19 May: creation of the Legion of Honour
20 May: Bonaparte re-establishes slavery in the colonies

1803

16 May: the peace of Amiens is over. Britain declares war on France
20 May: Bonaparte occupies Hanover
12 June: The French *départements* provide boats for the invasion of Britain
12 September: the Italian Republic declares war on Britain
1 October: 200,000 French soldiers gather for the invasion of Britain

1804

18 May: Napoleon is proclaimed Emperor by the Senate

2 December: Napoleon crowns himself Emperor
13 December: Spain declares war on Britain

1805
11 April: the British and the Russians sign a treaty of alliance
9 August: Austria joins the Third Coalition
27 August: the French army leaves Boulogne for Germany
14 October: battle of Elchingen
20 October: capitulation of an Austrian army after the battle of Ulm
21 October: British victory at the battle of Trafalgar
14 November: Vienna is captured by the French
2 December: battle of Austerlitz. French victory against the Emperors of Austria and Russia
26 December: the Treaty of Pressburg is signed between France and Austria

1806
30 March: Joseph Bonaparte becomes King of Naples
5 June: Louis Bonaparte becomes King of Holland
6 October: the Fourth Coalition, including Prussia, Russia, Saxony, Sweden, Sicily and the United Kingdom, is formed against France
14 October: battles of Jena and Auerstadt
24 October: Berlin is captured by the French
21 November: the Continental System is enforced
27 November: the French take Warsaw

1807
7–8 February: battle of Eylau. The French win against Russia
26 May: Danzig capitulates
14 June: the French win the battle of Friedland against the Russians and the Prussians
7 July: the French and the Russians sign the Treaty of Tilsit
8 October: the Spanish government invites the population to welcome the French as friends
18 October: the Army of the Gironde, led by Junot, leaves Bayonne to invade Portugal
20 November: the French and the Spanish armies enter Portugal
29 November: the Portuguese royal family flees for Brazil

1 December: Junot takes Lisbon
13 December: the population of Lisbon rebels against the French

1808

2–3 May: riots in Madrid
10 May: Joseph Bonaparte becomes King of Spain and Joachim Murat King of Naples
23 May: uprisings all over Spain
6 June: the *Junta* of Cadiz declares war on France
22 July: General Dupont surrenders at the battle of Baylen
30 August: the Convention of Cintra allows the defeated French army to leave Portugal
29 October: Napoleon leaves for Spain
4 December: Napoleon arrives in Madrid

1809

3 January: Napoleon returns to France
16 January: battle of Corunna, death of General Moore
19 February: Saragossa surrenders
27 March: battle of Ciudad Real
29 March: Oporto is captured by the French
9 April: Britain, Austria, Portugal and Spain form the Fifth Coalition
11 April: the British attack the French Navy near the island of Aix
22 April: battle of Eckmühl, a French victory against the Austrians
13 May: Vienna is captured
21 May: battle of Aspern-Essling, French defeat
6 July: battle of Wagram, French victory
12 July: armistice of Znaim
28 July: battle of Talavera, British victory
29 July: the British land at Walcheren
30 September: the British evacuate Walcheren
14 December: Peace of Vienna

1810

31 January: the French capture Seville
2 April: Napoleon and the Archduchess Marie Louise are married
13 May: Lerida is captured by the French
6 June to 15 July: siege and capitulation of Ciudad Rodrigo

13 July: Holland is annexed
5 September: Marshal MacDonald wins the battle of Cervera
27–28 September: battle of Busaco
31 December: Russia abandons the Continental System

1811

2 January: the French capture Tortosa
27 January: the French besiege the city of Badajoz
5 March: battle of Barrosa, an Allied victory
11 March: Badajoz is captured by Marshal Soult

1812

8 April: Britain, Russia and Sweden form the Sixth Coalition
24 June: beginning of the French invasion of Russia
17 August: the French win the battle of Smolensk
7 September: the French win the battle of Borodino
14 September: Moscow is taken by the French
18 October: Moscow is evacuated
16 December: the French cross back over the Neiman River. The invasion of Russia is over

1813

16 March: Prussia declares war on France
2 May: battle of Lützen, Napoleon wins against the Prussians and the Russians
15 May: battle of Bautzen, a French victory
4 June: armistice of Pleischwitz
21 June: battle of Vitoria, a British victory
July–August: Congress of Prague
2 August: Austria declares war on France
26–27 August: French victory at the battle of Dresden
7 October: Wellington enters France, Bavaria declares war on France
16–19 October: battle of Leipzig, an Allied victory
11 December: treaty of Valençay, bringing back Ferdinand VII on the Spanish throne

1814

26 January: battle of Saint-Dizier, a French victory
29 January: battle of Brienne, a French victory
10 February: battle of Champaubert, a French victory
February–March: congress of Châtillon
11 February: battle of Montmirail, a French victory
7 March: battle of Craonne, a French victory
9 March: battle of Laon, an Allied victory
13 March: battle of Reims, a French victory
20–21 March: battle of Arcis-sur-Aube, an Austrian victory
31 March: capitulation of Paris
3 April: the Senate deposes Napoleon
10 April: Marshal Soult defeated at the battle of Toulouse
11 April: Napoleon abdicates in favour of his son
3 May: Napoleon is exiled to Elba. Louis XVIII arrives in Paris

1815

26 February: Napoleon escapes from the island of Elba
1 March: Napoleon lands at Golfe-Juan in France
20 March: Napoleon arrives in Paris
25 March: a Seventh Coalition is formed
16 June: battles of Ligny and Quatre-Bras
18 June: battle of Waterloo, decisive Allied victory
22 June: Napoleon abdicates for the second time
15 October: Napoleon is exiled on the island of Saint Helena

1821

5 May: death of Napoleon Bonaparte on Saint Helena

Bibliography

PRIMARY SOURCES
Archives
Archives de l'état de Liège (AEL).
    Fonds des Familles Richard (FFR) 174.
    Fonds Français Préfecture (FFP) 986, 1042, 1043, 1044, 1045.
    Fonds Hollandais (FH) 495, 3691.
    Fonds Jarbinet (FJ).

Books
Beaujot, C-R., *Relation de captivité du capitaine Beaujot, ancien sergent-major sous l'Empire français*, Liège, 1856.
Beclard, Chomel, Cloquet, Orfila and Rostan, *Nouveau journal de médecine, chirurgie, pharmacie, etc . . .* , Paris, 1819.
Bourgogne, A., *The Retreat from Moscow: the Memoirs of Sergeant Bourgogne 1812-1813*, London, 1985.
Coignet, J-R., *The Note-books of Captain Coignet: Soldier of the Empire, 1776-1850*, Tyne and Wear, 1996.
Fairon, E., and H. Heuse, *Lettres de Grognards*, Liège, 1936.
Garneray, L., *Mes pontons, neuf années de captivité*, Paris, 1933.
Gourgaud, G., *La campagne de 1815*, Paris, 1818.
Marbot, J-B., *The Memoirs of Baron de Marbot: late Lieutenant-General in the French Army*, London, 1988.
Picard, A., *Le journal de route d'un soldat de la Grande Armée*, Gilly, 1946.

SECONDARY SOURCES
Articles and book chapters
Aaslestad, K., and K. Hagemann, '1806 and its aftermath: revisiting the period of the Napoleonic wars in German central European historiography', *Central European History*, 39 (2006), pp. 547–79.
Alexander, D., 'French replacement methods during the Peninsular war, 1808-1814', *Military Affairs*, 44 (1980), pp. 192–7.
Blanton, H., 'Conscription in France during the era of Napoleon', in D. Stoker, F. Schneid and H. Blanton (eds), *Conscription in the Napoleonic era: a revolution in military affairs?*, New York, 2006, pp. 6–23.
Burrows, S., 'Culture and misperception: the law and the press in the outbreak of war in 1803', *The International History Review*, 18 (1996), pp. 793–818.
Delaporte, S., 'Médecine et blessures de guerre', in Stéphane Audoin-Rouzeau and Jean-Jacques Becker (eds), *Encyclopédie de la grande guerre 1914-1918*, Paris, 2004, pp. 347–56.
Douglas, V., 'La guérilla espagnole dans la guerre contre l'armée napoléonienne', *Annales de la Révolution française*, 336 (2004), pp. 91–105.
Dwyer, Philip, 'Napoleon and the Foundation of the Empire', *The Historical Journal*, 53 (2010), pp. 339–58.
Epstein, R., 'Patterns of change and continuity in nineteenth-century warfare', *The Journal of Military History*, 56 (1992), pp. 375–88.
Esdaile, C., 'War and politics in Spain, 1808-1814', *The Historical Journal*, 31 (1988), pp. 295–317.
Grab, A., 'Army, state, and society: conscription and desertion in Napoleonic Italy (1802-1814)', *The Journal of Modern History*, 67 (1995), pp. 25–54.
Hagemann, K., 'Occupation, mobilization, and politics: the anti-Napoleonic wars in Prussian experience, memory, and historiography', *Central European History*, 39 (2006), pp. 580–610.

Ingram, E., 'The geopolitics of the first British expedition to Egypt – I: the cabinet crisis of September 1800', *Middle Eastern Studies*, 30 (1994), pp. 435–60.

Le Carvèse, P., 'Les prisonniers français en Grande-Bretagne de 1803 à 1814. Première partie.', *Napoleonica*, 8 (2010), pp. 6–8.

Leggiere, M., 'From Berlin to Leipzig: Napoleon's gamble in north Germany, 1813', *The Journal of Military History*, 67 (2003), pp. 39–84.

Moreau, C., 'Le remplacement d'un conscrit amaytois de 1813', *Annales du Cercle Hutois des Sciences et Beaux-Arts* (1998), pp. 128–30.

Roider, K., 'The Habsburg foreign ministry and political reform, 1801-1805', *Central European History*, 22 (1989), pp. 160–82.

Rowe, M., 'France, Prussia, or Germany? The Napoleonic wars and shifting allegiances in the Rhineland', *Central European History*, 39 (2006), pp. 611–40.

Sandeau, J., 'La santé aux armées. L'organisation des services et les hôpitaux. Grandes figures et dures réalités', *Revue du souvenir napoléonien*, 450 (2004), pp. 19–37.

Wilkin, R., 'Le remplacement militaire dans le département de l'Ourthe', *Bulletin de l'Institut archéologique liégeois*, CXII (2001–2002), pp. 343–4.

Wilson, P., 'Bolstering the prestige of the Habsburgs: the end of the Holy Roman Empire in 1806', *The International History Review*, 28 (2006), pp. 709–36.

Woloch, Isser, 'Napoleonic conscription: state power and civil society', *Past and Present*, 111 (1986), pp. 101–29.

Books

Bergès, L., *Résister à la conscription, 1798-1814. Le cas des départements aquitains*, Paris, 2002.

Broers, M., *Europe under Napoleon, 1799-1815*, London, 1996.

Cabanis, A., *La presse sous le consulat et l'empire, 1799-1814*, Paris, 1975.

Crépin, A., *La conscription en débats ou le triple apprentissage de la nation, de la citoyenneté, de la république, 1798-1889*, Arras, 1998.

Crouzet, F., *L'économie britannique et le blocus continental, 1806-1813*, Paris, 1958.

Esdaile, C., *The Spanish Army in the Peninsular War: Patriots, Partisans and Land Pirates*, London and Basingstoke, 2005.

Esdaile, C., *The Peninsular War*, London, 2002.

Esdaile, C., *Fighting Napoleon: Guerrillas, Bandits and Adventurers in Spain, 1808-1814*, New Haven and London, 2004.

Fierro, A., Palluel-Gaillard, A., and J. Tullard, *Histoire et dictionnaire du consulat et de l'empire*, Paris, 1995.

Forrest, A., *Conscripts and Deserters: the Army and French Society during the Revolution and Empire*, Oxford, 1989.

Forrest, A., *Napoleon's Men: the Soldiers of the Revolution and Empire*, London, 2002.

Guilloteau, V., *Nomenclature des monnaies françaises 1670-1942*, Versailles, 1942.

Housset, G., *La garde d'honneur, 1813-1814*, Paris, 2009.

James, W., *The Naval History of Great Britain, Volume 4: 1805-1807*, London, 2002.

Leggiere, M., *Napoleon and Berlin: the Napoleonic Wars in Prussia, 1813*, Stroud, 2002.

Leggiere, M., *The Fall of Napoleon: the Allied Invasion of France, 1813-1814*, Cambridge, 2007.

Lemaire, J-F., *Les blessés dans les armées napoléoniennes*, Paris, 1999.

Martin, B., *Napoleonic Friendship: Military Intimacy and Sexuality in Nineteenth-Century France*, New Hampshire, 2011.

Muir, R., *Britain and the Defeat of Napoleon, 1807-1815*, New Haven and London, 1996.

Nafziger, G., *Napoleon at Lützen and Bautzen*, Chicago, 1992.

Pigeard, A., *L'armée de Napoléon*, Paris, 2000.

Pigeard, A., *La conscription au temps de Napoléon, 1798-1814*, Paris, 2003.

Price, M., *Napoleon: the End of Glory*, Oxford, 2014.

Smith, D., *The Greenhill Napoleonic Data Book*, London, 1998.

Tulard, J., *Dictionnaire Napoléon*, Paris, 1999.

Zamoyski, A., *1812: Napoleon's Fatal March on Moscow*, London, 2004.

Index